ECHOES FROM THE APOSTLES

World Changing Ambassadors for Christ

Dr. Allen Solheim

ECHOES FROM
THE APOSTLES
World Changing Ambassadors for Christ

Printed 2021

ACKNOWLEGEMENTS

My writing an acknowledgement to those who contributed to the writing of this book seems more like a *déjà vu* moment than a fresh expression of thanks. Or perhaps more fittingly said, a continuation of gratitude to the same individuals who were acknowledged in the writing of the book entitled *Echoes from the Gospels*.

The sudden onset of Covid-19 resulted in the sending out of the stories that were found in that previous book and the one you now hold in your hand.

I am deeply appreciative of the members of our Sunday School class that have remained loyal throughout this long year and a half of bodily separation. They found ways of sending encouragements and thanks for the material that was being sent to them via email. Even though we couldn't meet in person, our weekly stories continued to be a bonding agent that kept us emotionally and spiritually together. It is because of these loyal class members that I continue writing these weekly stories as the source of our weekly Sunday School class which is now once again meeting in person.

But the one individual that I must give the greatest thanks to is Angela Brandle, just as I did in that previous book. Each week I would send her the rough copy of the story that I had written, and she would faithfully edit that material and prepare it to be sent out to all those precious people that we had on our electronic mailing list. She has spent countless hours in this labor of love, and I believe I am only the spokesman for all the class members who so deeply appreciate all that she has done to keep our class functioning during those difficult months of separation.

I say that writing this acknowledgement is a bit of a *déjà vu* moment. The expression of thanks shared above reflects the same sentiment that I shared for her dedicated work to produce the previous book. Now having that same sentiment appear twice only underscores her faithful dedication and willingness to be so deeply involved in the lives of people. I have no doubt that the spirit expressed above about just this one little part of her ministry is undoubtedly shared by all the broader base of people that she works with in her missionary service.

For those who did not have access to that earlier expression of thanks, permit me once again to give you a little introduction to this dedicated servant of God.

Angela majored in French with German at Manchester University in England. Her graduate studies prepared her for a career as a translator and business administrator, and eventually as a missionary in Western Europe, based in France. Angela wrote for and edited Africa Evangelical Fellowship's magazine in French and served on the Editorial Committee of the Federation of Evangelicals of France, which produced a magazine covering ethical, theological, social, and church-related issues of interest to French Christians and pastors.

From 1996 – 2008, Angela and Willy served in the U.S.A., first as Ministries Directors, and following AEF's merger with SIM, as Directors for the Midwest. From 2008 to 2014, Angela was called to direct and develop a team of missionaries to and from the Province of Quebec, Canada, working mostly in French. She was managing editor of *Allons-y!* magazine for the francophone world and led the SIM International French Media Group to produce and disseminate spiritual resources in French and facilitate access to ministry for French-speakers, a role that often took her to West African countries where she continues to interpret at conferences for budding African writers and publishers offered by Magazine Training International. She is currently the Executive Director of Synergie FRANCOPHONE (formerly BLF Ministries).

Angela teaches and speaks in churches, conferences, colleges, and universities, equips church mission committees and congregations for missional involvement, provides training in communication for ministry, public speaking, and other topics related to ministry and global missions.

So, I gladly give thanks to Angela and her equally gifted husband Willy and all those wonderful members of a class that has inspired Dorthy and me and gave us a reason for the continued writing of these stories inspired by the various people that grace the pages of the Holy Bible.

PREFACE

When I began writing stories from the Gospels, it soon became evident there was ample material for two separate sets of stories, each with a different focus. I began by writing about individuals that were part of the Gospel story. Almost immediately I realized that I needed to separate these stories from those that focused on the life and ministry of the disciples of Jesus. Theirs was a story all on their own. I finished that first set of thirty-one stories that are the basis of the book entitled *Echoes from the Gospels*.

Once that book was completed, I began focusing on the lives of the disciples as seen in the Gospels. These twelve men formed a unique "band of brothers" and they deserved having their own stories told, not just as individuals, but as a group of men selected by Jesus to be his closest friends as he walked on Earth. Each story about one of the disciples can stand alone but each one is also part of a collective whole. Their lives ultimately became so interwoven that they will forever be known as "Christ's disciples". Countless people have become followers of Jesus Christ throughout the years since Jesus walked on this Earth, but forever, this group of twelve men will stand apart from all others.

When I had completed telling of the lives of these twelve unique men, I began to see that although they formed that special group we call "disciples", they were also a part of a second group of men that we often refer to as the "Apostles". When I began looking at this dual relationship, I realized that the telling of their stories needed to include two other men that are called Apostles in the Scriptures: Paul and Barnabas. So, I found myself broadening my focus and including stories about this wider group of men known as the Apostles. When I was finished, I had written thirty-three stories in the hope of having meaningfully captured the lives and impact that these men had on the world. Their stories are found in the pages to follow.

As has been true for this entire series of *Echoes from the Bible*, I have included a set of discussion questions with each story that I hope will make these stories useable for a Sunday School class or small group Bible Study. They were originally written to be shared in a class setting, each story being used as the basis of a study in the Sunday School class that I taught. It has always been my hope that by making them available in this format, it would enable others to have the same benefit and blessing that we have experienced in the class where they were originally presented.

I have never lost sight of one of my original goals when I started writing these stories. I believed that the individuals who grace the pages of Scripture were men and women just like we are. They had the same kind of emotional needs, experienced the same "ups and downs," and went through many of the same kinds of life experiences that are found in all of us who are human. So often we have either lifted these individuals into an exalted state – or demonized them – making them something different than the men and women that they were. I hope that I have not lost that focus, even expressed in Scripture itself where it says that "Elijah was a man like us." God worked through, and continues to work through, ordinary men and women, transformed by his Spirit, into usable vessels for His glory. It is my firm belief that to the degree in which we can begin to identify with these various Biblical characters as people like us, we can better begin to hope to be people like them as well.

I also hope that you, the reader, may find something of your life being told as at various times you read the story of these very "human" and "ordinary" people. Perhaps this is what was being referred to when we are admonished to "weep with those who weep" and "laugh with those who laugh." Or as Paul said, that we are to let our trials and difficulties that life brings our way enable us to be better comforters to those who share in the same kind of life's experiences. It is to whatever degree that we can emotionally and intellectually understand what others are going through that we can come alongside to offer meaningful healing in their lives as well.

TABLE OF CONTENTS

LIFE AS AN APOSTLE... 1
ANDREW The First Chosen Apostle 13
PETER A Conflicting Personality…………………………….23
PETER The Transparent One......................................33
PETER Constantly Inconsistent……………………………..45
PETER His Mountain Top Experience…………………….53
PETER AT THE PASSOVER…………………………………. 63
PETER WEEPS IN THE GARDEN………………………….73
JAMES - The Man of Ambitious Zeal……………………..81
MATTHEW - Saved from Himself……………………………91
JOHN The Aged Apostle………………………………………101
PHILIP The Pragmatist……………………………………….. 111
THOMAS The Pessimist………………………………………121
THOMAS Meeting the Risen Christ………………………131
 JAMES AND SIMON The Faithful and Zealous…………. 141
NATHANIEL AND JUDAS Those Less Honored…………. 149
JUDAS A Life that went Wrong…………………………….159
THE RESURRECTION OF CHRIST……………………….169
THE ASCENSION Receiving a New Direction…………177
PENTECOST The Empering Presence……………………185
PAUL The Man of Diverse Cultures………………………195
PAUL The Early Years of My Life…………………………203
PAUL Pursuing the Persecutor……………………………211
PAUL The Forgotten Years of Ministry…………………219
PAUL Counting the Cost…………………………………….229
PAUL Important Women in My Life………………………237
PAUL A Rookie Missionary…………………………………245
PAUL A Man with a Restless Heart………………………255
PAUL Establishing the Believers…………………………267
PAUL The Last Trip……………………………………………275
BARNABAS Reflections by Paul………………………….283
APOLLOS The Elequent Preacher……………………….. 293
INDEX

1
LIFE AS A DISCIPLE

What was it like being a disciple of Jesus? That is an interesting question to which the answer is as complex as the lives of the twelve of us who became his followers.

Ups and Downs; Joys and Challenges

I hardly know where to begin even to give just an overview of what our life was like. So many paradoxes come to mind. As we lived and walked with Jesus, we experienced the whole gamut of emotions, from paralyzing fear to inexpressible joy. Only if you have faced imminent death yourself, will you be able to imagine the fear we felt, helpless against a storm that threatened to drown us on the Sea of Galilee. Or the crushing defeat and desperation we all felt when Jesus was crucified, only to be replaced by a level of joy beyond description when we came to understand without a shadow of doubt that Jesus had indeed risen from the dead and was alive again!

The best example of what I am trying to convey to you happened on the Sunday when we were all gathered in the upper room, and Jesus suddenly appeared. At first, we were afraid at the inexplicable appearance of a person in the room who could not have entered through the securely locked door. Our initial shock and fright were swiftly supplanted by reassurance and delight when Jesus began speaking, assuring us that it was indeed him, back from the dead. That day is a microcosm of how we regularly lived. Rather than a smooth, familiar road or a predictable routine that most of us had known before we met Jesus, the three-year path we walked with Him was full of hills and valleys, twists and turns, challenges, and dangers, as well as new vistas of life and spirituality, a far cry from the "normal" life that had previously been ours.

Diverse yet United

Eleven of us were from Galilee, several from the thriving district of Capernaum and Bethsaida. We reflected the local culture and ways of our fellow citizens. The fact that some of us were fisherman tells you something of what our life was like as we plied our trade. One of us, Matthew, was a tax collector. I am sure you are aware of the hatred we Jews had for all who collected taxes. We regarded them as traitors to both our faith and our country, profiteers feathering their nests through an unholy alliance with our occupier, Rome.

When you look at the characters, affiliations, and personal views of the different types of people in our group, you can imagine the tensions that flared between us. There was Matthew who worked for Rome, and then Simon, a Zealot who wanted to overthrow Rome by violence and free our nation from the political bondage under which we lived. It took a while for those two to accept each other and begin to move onto the same page as the rest of us. But over time, the deeply seated hostilities we brought into the group faded away, being replaced by a common goal and purpose.

Being united around a common purpose does not mean, however, that we always got along. We often experienced the kind of personality conflicts that are common to any group of human beings.

I remember the time when James and John, prompted by their mother, wanted to have a prominent place in Christ's coming Kingdom and asked Jesus to promise they'd be given that promotion. It took a long time for the rest of us to get over that; our resentment toward their behavior was like a festering sore. But now, looking back and having had time to let things find their proper perspective, I can say objectively that such reactions are likely to occur when people with different personalities and temperaments spend as much concentrated time together as we did. We certainly had our moments, and I am sure we even tested the patience of Jesus himself.

Yes, with hindsight, our group dynamics resembled what occurs in any large family. While we might have had our differences and squabbles, we would nevertheless stand together as a united group if anyone from the outside opposed us.

Costs and Rewards

If we had one thing in common, it was that we had all given up everything to follow Jesus. Most of us had walked away from our business ventures and, to a large degree, we were often separated from our families. Some of us had a wife and children who saw very little of us during those years. Our three years with Jesus were an intense time for all concerned. We did come back to Capernaum often though, and that would give us some time to interact with our families but even then, ministry did not cease. Serving large and demanding crowds always brought pressure into all our lives.

Some days were long and busy, and the constant travel to and from various villages and towns was tiring. It wasn't without its rewards, however, as we were able to experience first-hand Jesus' teaching and acts. How would I even begin to tell you how it felt when we were handing out the food from a little boy's lunch that just kept multiplying itself until it fed the thousands that had gathered? It was a moment of excitement and wonder, along with awe as we began to perceive the kind of a person this Jesus really was.

Discipleship is a Process of Growth

That last statement begs further explanation. Some people probably think that we were so affected by what we heard and saw that we "immediately" became full-blown disciples who grasped and adopted all that Jesus taught and did. That is far from how it really happened. At times, Jesus could be difficult to understand. Some of his sayings just went straight over our heads. I have no doubt that our inability to comprehend spiritual truth often frustrated him. On occasions, he rebuked us for our slowness to understand what he was sharing with us. We really could be clueless about what was going on. Jesus would teach using parables, and yet we often failed to understand the moral or spiritual meaning of these stories from real life.

As I think back over his statements and predictions, I see now what we should have understood, but failed to at the times when he said them, especially about his death and resurrection. He told us he was going to be killed and would be brought back from the dead, but I don't think any one of us really got hold of that truth – until *after* events unfolded as he had said they would.

Loss and Gain

In fact, if there was ever moment when we lost all hope, it was the day they crucified him. With that, everything we had believed in and thought we were living for was brutally snatched from us. We felt utterly crushed, left without any future or direction for our lives. About all we had left during those days of loss, grief, and disappointment, as our strange and exciting chapter with Jesus had been abruptly ended by his adversaries, was each other and our memories, although at first, those memories were more a source of pain than a blessing. We huddled together out of fear for our very lives and desponded over the hopelessness of the situation we were now in. Is this what it had all come to? Our individual feelings of utter dejection, forsakenness, and desperation bonded us in a common understanding one of another.

Later, of course, the resurrection of Jesus Christ would transform all those emotions and give us back not only everything we felt had been taken from us, but more besides.

Launching into Ministry

Please don't get me wrong, I don't want to give the impression that everything was hard and confusing. We lived many wonderful high points as well. We were in awe when Jesus sent us out to minister in twos, giving us the power to heal the sick and cast out demons! We were uncertain and timid at first, but as we set about our mission, we found our groove and came back with glowing reports of everything that had happened, all of us a bit heady with an unhealthy sense of pride over what we had been able to accomplish. Jesus had to check our attitude, bringing us down to earth by reminding us that this wasn't all as important as we thought it was. What was far more important was to remember that our names were written in Heaven. It was always that way. Jesus knew how to bring us back to reality and help us refocus when our perspective was skewed.

It took all three years of being with Jesus to bring about refinement and maturation in our lives and ministry. This didn't happen overnight and was not complete at the end of that period. We were still far from the men that we needed to become if we were to be the ones to whom Jesus would entrust his teachings and ministry. It would take Pentecost and the filling of the Holy Spirit to continue the finishing process that our lives all needed, but that is a story in and of itself.

Handling Persecution

Perhaps one of the most difficult parts of being his disciple was suffering persecution from the religious leaders who hated Jesus. It didn't take long before we understood that we were on the "wrong side of the tracks" when it came to the status quo of our cultural and religious structure. As those years passed, the hatred against Jesus only intensified. By the end of those three years, I think we all knew that his life, and maybe ours too, were being lived under the shadow of likely death.

No matter how right you believe you are, it is not easy to be the object of others' hatred, especially of those who are respected and considered as leaders. As with anyone, the need to be accepted and appreciated was something we valued highly. It is never pleasant to be hated and rejected by others, yet we experienced this kind of negative social stress at an increasing level as the years passed.

At the beginning, Jesus' popularity with the crowds brought excitement to us as a group. We felt gratification and pleasure when we saw others being healed and helped in their lives. These positive emotions, however, could not mask our negative reactions to the expressed hatred of others. We were hurt and wounded as any human would be, because being a disciple of Jesus didn't make us impervious to our own humanity.

Human and Divine Dynamics in Relationships

As human beings, we brought our unique traits and quirks of personality into our group. We effortlessly formed into cliques within the larger group and had our own special friends. Even Jesus had his favorites. There were the two sets of brothers: James and John, and Peter and Andrew, who, for reasons we did not know, seemed to be the ones that Jesus was closer to. Even among them, Andrew was often left out of what would surface as the more select group. John was the youngest of all twelve of us. We all saw that Jesus had a special place for him in his heart. In fact, among ourselves we would refer to John as "the one Jesus loves."

We had a hard time to accept that some might be closer to Jesus or part of an inner circle. I am ashamed to tell you that right up to the night that Jesus was arrested, we were still squabbling over power, preoccupied with which one was the greatest among us. Maybe that shows you just how human and immature we really were. I know that we were a bit of an annoyance to Christ at times.

Sometimes, he let us know that he was disgusted or displeased with our behavior. He rebuked us for our "lack of faith" and at times indicated that he thought we should have known or understood more quickly than we did. Once, he even told Peter that he was being used by Satan! But when all is said and done, we never doubted his love for us, and our desire to serve him never wavered.

Words are Easier than Actions

We were quick to boast that we were willing to die for Jesus if need be, and in our minds and hearts, we really meant it. It is easy, however, to declare an intent when not confronted with the real possibility or necessity of following through. Our bold assertion was put to the test the night they came to arrest him. We were all in the garden with him, and we all fled and deserted him. The loyalty we had proclaimed melted like butter under a bit of heat, in only a matter of minutes. Once again, we faced our own humanity and realized how frail we really were.

Jesus, our Brother, Model, and Mentor

Here I am, trying to tell you what it was like being a disciple of Jesus. There is so much that I could say that I have had to be selective, but it seems that I have said more about our weaknesses and failures than I have about our strengths and accomplishments – maybe because life is like that. Our weaknesses and failures are more readily remembered than our strengths and accomplishments. Again, that is my humanity speaking because I would not be giving honest testimony to our life with Jesus if I did not tell you that *I never felt condemnation from him.*

To be sure, I felt as if I had disappointed Jesus at times, and I wish I could have changed some of my attitudes and actions toward others in the group, and even toward Christ himself. But with all our shortcomings as a group, Jesus never gave the impression of looking down on or rejecting us. He seemed to understand our human frailty, failures, and struggles. He empathized with our emotions. He was able to cry with us when we cried and laugh with us when we laughed. He sensed what we were feeling and responded accordingly, sometimes pulling us up with a rebuke, and sometimes lifting us up by encouraging and affirming us as persons. Just as we are so very human, in a very real way, so was he. He knew and understood what we were going through because he had become a man like us who shared all our human emotions. He too knew what it was to be hated and rejected, and the smarting pain that caused. He also knew what it was like to bring unspeakable joy to the lives of so many.

Three Years with Jesus… to Change Our Lives and the World

Jesus called each of us individually to share life and ministry with him for three years. He not only understood us, but our imperfect lives were impacted every day not only by each other, but also by his teaching, his correction, his loving goodness to those in need, and the model of his own example as we learned to live and minister as a group. We were tested by the challenges and difficulties we encountered with Him, and we ultimately came to understand the meaning of the most painful of all experiences, his crucifixion. We were surprised, delighted, and transformed by his glorious resurrection… to undertake world-changing roles in his service that we would never have imagined before he called us to be with him – as his disciples.

DISCUSSION QUESTIONS

1. We tend to think it must have been all glorious or always an exciting and positive thing to have been one of Jesus' disciples. The story above has tried to catch the range of emotions and experiences these men must have had during those three years they were with Jesus. Try to describe what you feel it might have been like being one of those twelve men during the three years they were with Jesus on earth.

2. We know there were tensions between the disciples, such as arguing over who was the greatest. Even though the Bible doesn't address the possible tensions that might have been created because of the political and cultural differences between Matthew (the tax collector) and Simon (the Zealot), share what you feel their relationship might have been like at first. Do you think they ever completely got over their differences, and if so, how do you think it happened?

3. Reflecting on question number 2, how do you think Jesus felt about these possible tensions and division among the twelve men and how do you think he might have handled that kind of situation?

4. We know that there were "cliques" among the disciples, such as the three who were especially close to Jesus – Peter, James and John. We also know that other pairs are always mentioned together whenever their names occur in Scripture, suggesting they had formed close and special friendships. Do you think this process was in any way problematic for the overall interactions between the twelve disciples?

5. Thinking about the previous question, it is obvious that Jesus was closer to the three (and at times to the four including Andrew) than he was to the other eight. How do you think the other eight felt about this closeness Jesus had with the two sets of brothers, James and John, Simon [Peter] and Andrew?

6. Thinking about question number 5, Andrew at times seemed to be included in that group that was "closer" to Christ but often was left out when Jesus took just Simon (Peter), James and John to several significant events. How do you think Andrew might have felt about this? Do you think this might have created any negative feelings between the two brothers, Simon (Peter), James and John?

7. If there was one common thing that all twelve of these men shared, it was the sacrifices they made to be followers of Jesus. They gave up much on a personal level to follow Jesus. Discuss some of the things they had to "give up" to be one of his disciples. Some may have had their own families (wife and children). We know that to be the case at least with Simon (Peter). How do you think their wives and children felt about their following Christ and being gone so much of the time?

8. The Bible tells us that the disciples often didn't understand what Jesus was telling them, sometimes not understanding the parables, for example, or not really grasping what Jesus was talking about when he told them about his impending death and resurrection. It appears that their grasp of who Jesus really was came over time and was something that had to develop and grow in their lives. What do you think it was like for them at times not to understand and to be confused over what was being said? Try to discuss what that process might have been like.

9. Thinking of the previous question, Jesus seems at times to be frustrated with the disciples and their inability or slowness in grasping what he was saying. He would rebuke them for their "lack of faith" or say, "don't you understand?" Try to describe what you feel Jesus might have felt like at times when he had to interact with the varying levels of understanding and growth in the lives of these men. Do you think they ever felt any tension either between themselves over some of these dynamics or some tension with Christ himself when they couldn't grasp what he was telling them?

10. The lowest moment in the lives of the disciples must have been the days between the crucifixion of Jesus and his resurrection. Describe what you think it might have been like, what these disciples might have felt and experienced during those days, starting with the arrest of Jesus through their being fully persuaded that he had risen from the dead.

11. Thinking about question number 10, they probably also feared for their own lives and wondered if they might be discovered and killed as well. It appears they stayed secluded and hidden during those days. Describe how you might have felt if you had been one of them.

12. Try to describe some of the feeling and thoughts the disciples might have had when Jesus sent them out and they performed miracles, healing people, casting out demons, etc.

13. Thinking about question number 12, how much do you think these experiences resulted in pride in their life and accomplishments? We know they came back to Jesus very excited about what had happened, and Jesus downplayed that to some degree by saying that this was not as important as having

their names written in Heaven. How do you think they felt about Jesus' response to their "glowing report" of success on their mission?

14. The disciples must have been encouraged and buoyant over the popularity they had among the people and the praise they received from the multitudes. Yet they also lived as objects of hate and even possible persecution and death from the religious leaders who held the real authority over what happened to them. Describe what it might have been like with both these extreme dynamics being a constant part of their life.

15. We tend to view the disciples as some special and privileged group to have spent those years so close to Jesus. In the story above, this sentence appears: "As human beings, we brought our unique traits and quirks of personality into our group." Do you think we would appreciate these men more and draw from their experiences and teachings in a more wholesome way if we remembered that they were human like us and experienced all the kinds of things that we experience? Embracing that concept, does it help you to appreciate them more or diminish your view of the disciples?

16. It was obvious that Jesus had a special interest in John, so much so that the others even referred to him once as the "one whom Jesus loved." Do you think this created any negative feelings between John and the others? How do you think James, the older brother of John felt about this unique relationship that Jesus and John had? How do you think John felt about it? Do you think the others treated John any differently because of it?

2

ANDREW

The First Chosen Apostle
John 1: 40-43; John 6: 8-9; John 12: 20-22; Mark 13: 1-4; 12: 23-24

    I am honored to be the first of the disciples to tell my story. Perhaps that is fitting because I was the first of the twelve to become a follower of Jesus. I am glad to share not just biographical facts about my life, but I will also try to be transparent about how some of my experiences have made me the man that I have become.

    Everyone seems to know about the twelve disciples after we became Jesus' followers, but sometimes people seem to forget that half our lives were lived before we ever met him. That too is a part of our story, at least a part of mine.

    I was born in Bethsaida where I spent all of my youth and young adult life before I met and followed the Master. There are some advantages to having lived in only one place for such a long time. As part of a close-knit community, you get to know your neighbors. Perhaps it would be worth telling you a little about the area where I grew up. In fact, eleven of us were raised here in Galilee, Judas Iscariot being the exception. Our cultural background will help you to understand us as a group.

    Our family was upper middle-class. My father's name was John, or Jonah, depending on which of our languages you use, giving me the full name of Andrew Bar Jonah. I wonder if you ever thought about what my first name reveals about this area where we lived. Don't be surprised. I know that people think that citizens of the nation of Israel must all be the same. What usually comes to their mind is the culture of an area like Judea with its more purely Jewish way of life. Here in Galilee, however, there is a big difference. We are situated on one of the major roadways that connect the East and the West, as well as a major road that runs from Rome to Egypt.

As I said, I grew up in Bethsaida, a city of between 2,000 and 3,000 people. The size of the population depended on what was happening with the building projects of Herod. Before the aggressive work programs of Herod, most of Galilee was rural, settled by farmers and fishermen, clustered in little hamlets like Nazareth that rarely had more than 300 or 400 inhabitants. But since Rome has been in control of this part of the world, so much has changed.

I am not sure whether all the change has always been for the better. Herod Antipas transformed sleepy Galilee by building bustling urban centers of government, commerce, and recreation. As a result of his and his father's efforts, Galilee now has some heartland cities that are far more Gentile than Jewish. Cities such as Caesarea on the shores of the Great Sea and Tiberias, located just a little way from us here on the shores of the Sea of Galilee. Many languages are spoken on the streets of our new, multicultural cities. It is true that the majority speak Aramaic, but you might just as easily hear Greek, Latin or some lesser-known languages used by the many visitors, merchants and artisans that have come here along the thoroughfares that cross Galilee.

All of Galilee has taken on a metropolitan feel, too much so in my estimation. It has become Hellenized – brought under the influence of Greek culture.

Oh, just listen to me complaining about the changes that have come to this part of our world! Before I set off down this rabbit trail, I was telling you about my name, and I said you could learn something about our family from my first name, Andrew. Andrew is a Greek name, a rather popular one I might add, among the Jews in Galilee. But it does show how much the Greek influence had bled into the fabric of our lives.

You know that I have an older brother named Simon. Now that is a good Aramaic name! So, you see that my name even reflects how this mixture of cultures has reached into our family and home. We are a microcosm of life in this part of the world.

I was just a normal child, grew into manhood, and became part of our family business. We were fishermen who had developed a good, thriving business, even shipping salted fish from the Sea of Galilee to Judea. I fully expected to live my whole life in this tranquil place and predictable way. A few years ago, however, my life was unexpectedly turned up-side down.

A real highlight in our family's life was taking our annual trip to Judea to celebrate the Feast of Tabernacles and the Passover. During one of those trips, I was exposed to the preaching of a man named John, the one they called the Baptizer. What John had to say fascinated me. I soon went into the river to be baptized by him. The time I spent with John was a wonderful chapter, as I quickly found myself spending more of my days listening to and being involved in his ministry. I guess that made me one of his "disciples."

During one of these Passover events, I had a transforming experience. You may have heard the story many times but permit me to share it with you again.

On the previous day, John had baptized a man named Jesus, someone from the little town of Nazareth. I could tell by John's reaction to Jesus and his interactions with him, that this was no ordinary baptism. I didn't fully know or understand, however, who Jesus really was.

I did not know it that day, but I would have three years to get to know and begin to unlock the full implications of Jesus' life and mission on Earth and even now, I have not fully comprehended the full significance of them. Every day that I live is a continuing experience of learning, but like everything else, it had to have a starting point.

For me, that point came the next day when Jesus returned to the bank of the Jordan River where John was preaching and baptizing. When he saw Jesus, John abruptly stopped his sermon and said, *"Look, the Lamb of God!"* I and my friend Nathaniel were captivated by this statement. Something was birthed within me that day. A feeling perhaps, an impulse, maybe just curiosity – or something more significant that is not so easily defined. Whatever my motivation, I sought Jesus out. As best as I can recall, it was Jesus who noticed the two of us following him. It was Jesus who first spoke to me, asking me a very basic question, *"What do you want?"*

I was unsure how to answer his question, for I didn't really know what it was that I wanted, maybe just to learn more about the one that John had recognized as the "Lamb of God". That description of him intrigued me. It was getting late in the day, already about four in the afternoon. Not knowing how to reply, I asked him, *"Where are you staying?"* He invited us to come along with him. We spent the rest of that day listening to so many new and wonderful teachings. So that is how it began, and while there would be some notable milestones in my experience with Jesus, this was my beginning as a follower of Christ. I didn't accompany him every day at first, as we returned to Galilee and to our life as fishermen, but in my heart and soul, I identified with Jesus from that day forward.

Immediately, I went and found my older brother, Simon, and told him about my time with Jesus and that I believed he was the Messiah, the one we had been waiting for. He gave me a *"what's-wrong-with-you?"* look. But I persisted. *"Come on,"* I said, and persuaded him despite his reluctance to go with me to meet Jesus. Before I had the opportunity to say anything or introduce Simon to Jesus, Jesus just looked at my brother and said, *"You are Simon son of John. You will be called Cephas."*

Now my older brother can be quite forceful, straightforward, and impulsive at times, but on this occasion, he just stood there, taken aback. I wondered what he was thinking, wondering perhaps how Jesus knew his name, and what he meant by giving him a new one. Could it be prophetic? I am sure you will talk to Peter, so you can ask him about his reaction. But I can tell you this: both of us left Judea that day as believers in Jesus the Messiah. And we both wanted to see a lot more of him. Little did either of us know that we would become two of the twelve men that he would choose to be his disciples. That happened sometime later.

After we returned to Galilee, we got on with our jobs in the fishing trade, and our life as it had always been. Then one day we saw him, standing on the shore near to where we were working in our boats. *"Come, follow me!"* he said, and we immediately rowed to shore and did just that! Our hearts were ready for this beginning, a whole new chapter in our lives and in the lives of two of our friends, fellow fisherman, James and John.

The changes that day brought for us stirred up some strong reactions, especially for my father who ran the family business. He looked at us in a kind of dumbfounded fog, wondering what on earth had come over his two sons. Whatever objections he voiced had no effect; we were totally focused on following Jesus who had called us.

To say that this was a time of transformation in our lives is still an understatement. That day, we left everything behind! We walked away from a lifelong career and from the security that an established family business gave to us. We walked away in many ways from our family, certainly from having the daily relationship, company, and teamwork with them that we had known for all our life up to that moment. I don't know whether my parents and the rest of my extended family ever fully understood what was happening to us, nor why we had decided to follow Christ. But for us, there was no turning back…at least not until the day they crucified him. After that terrible execution of our leader, we all returned to our former fishing trade…but only for a brief time.

Yes, that was a transforming moment. From that day on, following Jesus brought so many wonderful experiences. In fact, most of what happened during the three years we were with Jesus was nothing short of amazing. Where do I even start when describing my life as one of his disciples? I saw and witnessed so many things. I remember the day when Jesus taught a massive crowd of over five thousand men plus all the women and children. They were hungry, and Jesus told us to have them sit down, as if we were going to feed them. I found a young boy with a few fish and some pieces of bread and brought him to Jesus, saying that this was all the food we had. Little did I expect that he would multiply those few pieces of food to abundantly feed thousands!

I remember sitting with him on the Mount of Olives with my brother Simon, James, and John, and we asked him about the beautiful temple we had just visited. He gave us more than we asked: an outline of things to come. He often surprised us in such ways.

I remember the time that some Greeks were looking for Jesus. They found Philip instead, and he and I had the privilege of bringing them to meet Jesus.

However, there were also times of frustration and even fear. Toward the end of Jesus' life, when they crucified him, we too were afraid. I remember the terrifying night in the Garden of Gethsemane when they arrested him. Fearing for our own safety, we all fled for our lives. I remember the dreadful days after his crucifixion when hopelessness descended upon us.

When a loved one is gone, those left behind tend to forget the hard times and remember the good ones. Maybe that is how it is for me now. I look back and remember the best experiences I shared with Jesus as one of his disciples.

Jesus' death some years ago by no means put an end to my work for him. The last time we saw him, the day he was taken to Heaven, he told us to go and wait for the coming of the Holy Spirit, so we did. Pentecost was another new and wonderful experience with God when the Holy Spirit equipped us for the ministry we have been doing ever since. From that first day when I met Jesus, the day that changed the whole direction of my life, through the high and low experiences he used to teach and shape me, through the power of His Holy Spirit at work within me and through me in my ministry, I consider that I am one of the most blessed people in all the world and I intend to keep on serving my wonderful Lord and introducing people to him until the day I die. How could I do anything else?

DISCUSSION QUESTIONS

1. Though this was not discussed in the story above, Andrew was one of the four who most often had special times with Jesus, along with James, John and his brother Peter. Why do you think the other three are often mentioned and Andrew is left out? How do you think Andrew might have felt about not always being included with this special group of disciples?

2. Although it is not discussed in the story above, we know that Andrew's older brother, Peter, became the leader of the disciples, and was the most central figure during the ministry of Christ. Do you think Andrew was ever jealous of his brother and his success and position of authority? How much do you think some of these feelings might have potentially been in Andrew's life all through their developmental years and the years even before they became Christ's disciples? What do you think their relationship might have been like as brothers?

3. How comfortable do you think Peter, Andrew and his family might have been with the Gentile (Greek and Roman) influence they undoubtedly lived around? How much do you think it affected their family and personal lives?

4. Jesus was raised in rural Galilee. Eleven of his twelve disciples were from Galilee as well. How do you think being raised in the cultural mixture found in Galilee prepared them for the subsequent missionary activities many of them were involved with?

5. Simon (Peter) and Andrew, along with James and John, were both from families that were running a successful fishing business, probably upper-middle-class families. Do you think

their social status and position in business and society had any effect on Jesus choosing them to be his followers? Do you think this business background made them more effective disciples than they might have been without this background?

6. We don't know much about Andrew's experience with John the Baptist, other than that he was one of his disciples before following Jesus. What do you think might have attracted Andrew to John the Baptist? How do you think his family might have felt about and accepted his being one of his followers?

7. Knowing that John the Baptist preached near the Jordan river, and knowing that Simon (Peter) was there with Andrew when Jesus came to be baptized, what does that suggest about Simon (Peter) and possibly his family and their attitude toward, and interest in, the preaching of John the Baptist? Is it possible that the entire family had been baptized and were open to, or even perhaps followers of John the Baptist?

8. When Andrew heard John say that Jesus was the Lamb of God, he went and sought out Jesus and spent the evening with him. What do you think we can learn about Andrew as a person based on his response to John's statement?

9. What do you think might have gone through Andrew's mind when Jesus asked him, "What do you want?" What do you think Andrew might have been wanting from Jesus?

10. Thinking about the question above, what do you think Andrew was hoping for or thinking might happen when he said, "Where are you staying?"

11. What do you think might have been Peter's first thoughts and reaction when Jesus told him, "You are Simon son of John. You will be called Cephas"?

12. How do you think Andrew and Simon (Peter)'s father felt when both his sons left the family business so unexpectedly one day and followed Jesus? Do you think he might have tried to talk them out of going and instead remain with him working in the family business?

13. Though we do not know for sure, try to describe what kind of personality you think Andrew might have had. Remember a few glimpses we have of his person. He was a part of the main group of four disciples but was often left out of significant events that Jesus lived with the other three (Peter, James and John). Andrew is known as the person who was always bringing people to Jesus. For example, the boy with the bread and fish in the feeding of the 5,000, the Greeks who wanted to talk to Jesus, and his own brother Simon (Peter). What can we learn about Andrew as a person from these insights into his character and personality?

14. We have no indication that Andrew shared the somewhat violent personality that his older brother Simon (Peter) seemed to have. He appears to have a more balanced and steady personality. If this was true, what differences do you think there might have been in the two brothers when Jesus was crucified and later, during those days between the crucifixion and the resurrection of Jesus?

15. How do you think that growing up in a multicultural context helped them carry out Jesus' command to go and make disciples of all nations? Was it easier to take the Good News to other ethnic groups because they were not raised to be monocultural?

3

PETER

A Conflicting Personality
Various scriptural passages scattered throughout the Gospels and the Book of Acts

You don't need to apologize. It is true that I have become the person that most people look up to as the leader and spokesman of this group of twelve men who followed Jesus. I am not offended that you spoke to my younger brother Andrew first. Why should I be? I love my kid brother and there are no feelings of jealousy between us. I think Andrew is quite content to let me have the leadership role that has been thrust upon me. He deserved to tell his story first. After all, he was the first disciple that Jesus chose. I wouldn't even be one of the disciples, much less a leader in this new movement, had it not been for Andrew introducing me to Jesus so many years ago. We are two very different people in our personality styles. He is much gentler and more reserved than I, perhaps at times showing a little more refinement than I do.

You must remember that both of us, and for that matter, our business associates, James and John, were all fisherman before we met Jesus Christ, as were some of the other of the disciples as well. That statement is a fact, but I shared it for another reason. Please stop for a moment and think about the kind of life we lived and the stereotype of anyone who fished for a living. There are exceptions to what I am about to say, but with a broad stroke of the brush, I can tell you what many of us were like to a large degree, and I was no exception. In fact, I may have been among the worst of them with my outgoing and aggressive personality. I certainly cannot claim to have given any attention to godliness in those early years of my life. It is no wonder that I acted as I did after we had fished all night and caught nothing, when Jesus told us to go out and try again, resulting in a massive catch of fish. In that moment, I felt so dirty and unclean. All the filth and shame of my lifestyle became so clear to me. I fell to my knees before him and asked him to leave, confessing that I was such a sinner that I was not even worthy to be in his presence.

Calling myself a sinner was not a light or flippant statement on my part; it was a deep confession that came from hidden parts of my heart. No, we fisherman were not noted for our good lives. In general, we were known to be gruff men, often unkempt and shabbily dressed, using vile and vulgar language. We were often quick-tempered and impulsive, more than willing to tell anyone what we thought with no consideration for their feelings. We did not care what they thought about us in return. Jesus recognized these traits when he once called our business partners, James and John, "Sons of thunder" because of their uncontrolled tempers.

You don't have to look very long or hard at my life before you will find some of these imperfect or cultural attributes – a nice way of saying sinful tendencies – that lay deep in the heart of us all. I too was quick-tempered. Just remember when I pulled out my sword and cut off the ear of the servant of the High Priest. You cannot get more impulsive than that! Or the time at Casearia Philippi when I told Jesus he had it all wrong, a brash statement for which Jesus gave me the harshest rebuke.

I was proud alright! "Cocky" once described me well. Today, however, I am not the same man that I once was. No, I have mellowed a great deal between than and my old age. I trust that I don't come across as proud when I tell you that I was a natural leader who quickly became he spokesman of the twelve. I will explain more about that as my story unfolds, but I want to be sure you understand who I was before seeing the man that I have become.

I am sixty-five years old now and I don't how long it will before some uncertain fate befalls me. I just heard the shocking news that Paul was beheaded here in Rome. I know that my life is fragile given these chaotic times in which we live. I may well be next, but if so, I have much in my life for which to thank my God.

Yes, for the first half of my life, I lived the kind of life I just described to you. I don't have to tell you much about our home life because Andrew has already done that. I did meet a woman, fell in love, and married her. Andrew and I, along with our father, owned a good business, fishing and selling fish in the marketplaces around us. I was able to build a nice home almost next door to our synagogue. Despite my sinful lifestyle of which I have spoken, I was as faithful to our Jewish faith as were all the other Jews living in and around Capernaum and was part of the community that centered its existence around our local synagogue.

Then came that day when Andrew introduced me to Jesus. After that, everything changed. I went on to spend the last thirty-three years of my life faithfully serving Jesus. They have been rewarding years, though not always easy ones. I have experienced my share of hardships, imprisonments, and failures but none of that has dulled my love for and devotion to Jesus and his cause. I once boasted about my willingness to die for Jesus... then within hours denied him three times. But now, I am facing a potential death threat and I feel honestly and sincerely that I am ready to suffer for Christ if that is what is next on his agenda for me. God knows. This time I believe I will not falter in the face of death.

Let me pick up my story. I have talked about the sinfulness of the first half of my life. Some of those sinful practices began to change when I followed Jesus. It just seemed as if my vile tongue didn't fit any longer. Being in the presence of Jesus made me uncomfortable with patterns of wrong behavior that I had adopted in that period of my life. That doesn't mean that my life was totally transformed instantly and immediately, although the orientation and motivation of my behavior did. The more deeply rooted personality traits needed to be identified and worked out of my life over time. Some things in life can change instantly, but other changes come more slowly as we mature in our thinking and reactions. At least that is how it seemed to be in my life.

Even after having walked with Jesus for three years, I would still vacillate, at times unsure about what I should do. A good example of that was the time I was eating with some of the Gentile believers along with Paul. Some Jewish leaders came into the place where we were. I immediately got up and separated myself from the Gentile believers and chose to identify only with the Jewish believers. Paul openly and rightly reprimanded me in the presence of everyone. Even though it hurt and was a great embarrassment, I knew he was right.

At another time, I showed great resolve in my life, like the time I went to the home of Cornelius and later defended my actions and even defended Paul before the Jewish believers when they questioned our association with Gentiles.

There were times when I was rash and spoke without thinking, I could, and at times still can be irritable, and it is certainly not beyond me to lose my temper. Yet there are times – and at this point in my life I hope it is most of the time – when I am a gentler man, one who lives out his convictions with grace. Above all else, I hope and pray that this man who once denied Jesus is now a man with a loyal heart that is filled with the love that Jesus talked about when he said we would be known as His disciples by our love for one another.

It is true that I wasn't the most refined man. I think it is a fair and true statement to say that I was not a good scholar. I didn't care much for school, and I think I was probably a slow learner. I never had any formal training in the Mosaic Law and couldn't speak Greek even though I was exposed to many Greek-speaking people here in Galilee. I was a slow learner but when I got hold of something, it became part of me for life. Over the years, my life became refined, and I showed that I could be entrusted with responsibility, reflecting a capable man who had matured in so many ways. I am sure it fair to say that in the younger years of my life, I would probably have been voted to be the least likely of men to rise as the leader of a new movement, but God had other ideas. I can confess to you that it is my personal conviction and belief that all that I have become is only because of what God has done in my life through the power of his Holy Spirit.

Who would ever have thought that I would be the one who would preach on that amazing day when the Holy Spirit descended on us? What a joy it was to see thousands of people respond to the message I preached. I would have thought that the honor might have fallen to John, or James, or maybe Thomas. Thomas was more highly educated than I, but God chose me, a most unworthy vessel, to be the proclaimer of his grace that day.

Who would ever have thought that I would rise quickly to become the spokesman of the twelve while we walked with Jesus on Earth? I wasn't too surprised to be seen as one of the boldest of the apostles, as I was always bold and outspoken throughout my life, but I was surprised when I became the leader of the twelve so quickly.

As for my personal faith, I have already told you that I think that I am now willing to die for Jesus, and I say that while I am looking death in the face, expecting to be arrested at any time. But it wasn't always like that. Faith, like controlled personality traits and refined behavioral patterns, also had to grow and mature in my life. How can I forget my lack of faith when I walked briefly on the water and then sank in unbelief and fear, needing to be rescued by Jesus himself? Or where was my faith when they were questioning Jesus, and I was denying him in the courtyard? I think that was probably the lowest moment in my whole life. I went out and wept with tears that came from the deepest reservoirs of my soul. I didn't even believe that he was alive when I first heard the account of his resurrection from the women who had gone to the tomb early that morning. I feel my personal shame and know how deep my struggle to believe really was. But I was also the first of the twelve to confess that Jesus was the Messiah and, even though I ultimately faltered in my faith as I felt the wind and saw the waves, I was the only one who did, at least briefly, walk on water. As you can tell, I went through a real learning experience when it came to believing and trusting Jesus Christ, wavering at different times between faith and unbelief.

In fairness to myself and my story, there were strengths in my life that help compensate for the failures I have been telling you about.

I am a man who gets excited about what I do. I have always been that way. I was never satisfied to just get along but always wanted to do my best, to achieve. My success as a fisherman showed the kind of drive that motivated me in my life's endeavors.

I was a man who, once he knew what he wanted, was committed to it. I became steadfast and unmovable in my determination to achieve whatever goal I was pursuing. Looking back over the past three decades of my life, I believe you can see my commitment to Christ and to the new movement that has sprung from his teaching. I have never wavered in my commitment to Christ, at least not since the Day of Pentecost.

I believe that having a penitent heart has been another strength of my life. I sinned, more than I want to admit, but I have always been willing to repent of my sin when confronted with it or when I become aware of its grip in my life. I don't think that truth was ever more evident than it was after I denied Christ that night in the courtyard of the High Priest. But that wasn't the only time I repented. It was something that I often found myself doing. Now I have come to realize that repentance is a gift of God offered to sinners like me.

I think there was another strength in my life: my willingness to be open and honest as a person. If you had asked many people to tell you what I was like as a person, I think you would have heard many stories about my leadership, maybe how God used me in his Kingdom, how God used me to heal people and even change their theological understanding of His grace, such as when he gave me the vision of the unclean animals and showed through me that He came for the Gentiles as well as the Jews, but just about everyone would tell you that my words expressed who I was. I say what I think and reveal who I am. In that way, I have chosen to let get a glimpse of a human who struggles with his thoughts, words, and behavior. I am willing to be honest and open; I have nothing to hide.

I hope that my talking about myself honestly helps you understand that I am no different from you or anyone else. We all have our own unique quirks and personality traits. We all have our stories to tell, of defeat and victory in life. My story is not so different from so many others.

Following Jesus and being one of his disciples has been an exciting adventure about which I will tell you more. I just wanted to give you a glimpse of the real Simon (Peter), the man that I know best, the man that I was and, because of Jesus, the man that I am now.

DISCUSSION QUESTIONS

1. In this story, the unholy and sinful stereotype on the life of a fisherman was discussed to try to give us a glimpse into the type of person Simon (Peter) was and some of the factors that helped make him that kind of person. We still do this today. We hear people say, "swearing like a sailor" or "as dishonest as a lawyer (or politician)". We have our social stereotypes as well. How much do you think social status or identity with a particular group has behavioral effects on the kind of people we become? How much of this kind of behavior is "learned behavior," "social pressure to conform," or "sinful disposition"? How do you think these three factors interact with one another?

2. When looking at sinful lifestyles and the changes that come to our life after we become believers in Christ, how much of that change is quick and/or instantaneous and how much is a process of growth and maturation? What can we learn from the example of Simon (Peter)'s life and experiences about the process of change experienced by followers of Jesus?

3. When we think about Simon (Peter) falling down in front of Jesus and telling Jesus to leave him because he was too great a sinner to be in his presence, what does that tell us about Peter's attitude, personality, and character as a person?

4. How much do you think Jesus understood and accepted Peter's personality and his learned behavioral quirks and how do you think he handled them when they manifested themselves in a negative or destructive way? How patient do you think Jesus was with Peter?

5. The content of this particular story tried to capture both some of the weaknesses and strengths of Simon (Peter)'s life. Do a little brainstorming and begin listing as many strengths and weaknesses as you can about his life. Then, when you have finished that process, try to look at some of his weaknesses and discuss which are merely personality traits or learned behavior and which are more directly related to a sinful disposition, at a more moral level than just a cultural or behavioral one.

6. What were some of the personality traits in Simon (Peter)'s life that permitted him to quickly become the leader and spokesman of the group of disciples?

7. Do you find the contrasting characteristics in Simon (Peter)'s life to be an encouragement to your life or do you find it more negative? Are there ways in which you can identify with Peter and some of his struggles?

8. What kind of a husband and father do you think Simon (Peter) might have been, both before meeting and following Jesus Christ and afterwards?

9. It is probable that Simon (Peter) was always faithful to his synagogue and Jewish faith. How much do you think this constant exposure to Jewish law and the Jewish lifestyle made a personal difference in Simon (Peter)'s life?

10. Because of Simon (Peter)'s leadership role during the years he walked with Jesus, we have more information about him and his personal life and personality than about any of the other disciples. Even though we don't have their life stories, to what extent do you think Simon (Peter)'s life was the same or different from the lives of the other disciples?

11. How much do you think becoming a believer in Christ changes or alters basic personality patterns in one's life? How much do you think becoming a believer in Christ changes or alters learned behavioral patterns in life?

12. To what degree do you think personality patterns and behavior, even if they are negative, are sinful? How much do you think learned behavioral patterns in life are sinful? How much can we expect personality patterns and/or learned behavioral patterns to change after we experience Christ in life?

13. We know that the disciples in general and Simon (Peter) as an individual were not highly educated, at least in the Mosaic Law, something that a refined or educated person would be expected to know, at least among the religious leaders and Israel's elite. How much was their lack of education in this area both a strength and a weakness in their proclaiming God's message to people? How might it have both helped and hindered their efforts?

14. We can see from Simon (Peter)'s life and story that he rose quickly as an effective leader among the disciples. Why do you think this happened?

15. In this story, some of the strengths of Simon (Peter)'s personality were discussed [a man who was motivated and driven, a man who was committed to what he embraced, a man who was quick to repent when he became aware of sin in his life, a man who was honest and open about his life]. How do you think these personal strengths helped him in life and enabled him to become the spokesman and leader of the twelve disciples?

16. Simon (Peter) is usually lifted up as a special and victorious person in the church world, and to some degree that was true. He was also very human with his own struggles and needs. Having looked at this side of his life, has your image of Simon (Peter) changed at all? Is it helpful to you as a person to realize that Peter shared many of the same things that we experience?

4

PETER

The Transparent One
John 21: 15-17

A Story as Told by Andrew, his Younger Brother

Let me make sure I have this right. You are asking me to try to summarize my older brother's life, to talk about him as a person. That's a big assignment. He is such a complex individual in many ways, yet there is an aspect of him that makes it easier to try to describe the kind of man that he was. There is no one word or even overriding concept that totally encapsulates the life of this man. But if forced to try, perhaps the one phrase that I might use above all others would be that my older brother is "the transparent one."

Yes, I think I will stay with the word "transparent." No one knows him better than I do, except perhaps for his wife. But you don't have to be intimately close to him to discover what kind of person he really is.

Peter has quite the reputation among the believers and is held in high esteem by almost everyone who follows Christ. There are opponents who hate all that we stand for and, I am sure, would express plenty of negative remarks about my brother and for that matter, about all of us who are followers of Jesus.

We use the nickname "Big Fisherman" for Peter. There are several reasons why this seems to fit. Since he was young, Peter displayed leadership qualities that made him stand a little taller than the rest of us. I don't mean that in terms of physical stature, even though he is larger than many of his peers. There is something in his character that makes others look up to him and respond to his innate authority. Even in our younger years, when we would go out together with our friends to explore the caves of Galilee, Simon (Peter) would venture into the deepest, longest, and darkest caverns. When we boys took a dip in the Sea of Galilee, my brother swam out the farthest. It was always that way; he was the one out in front.

When I think about how to describe my brother, I would add other words to sketch the personality of this interesting man: words such as impulsive, impetuous, tempestuous, talented, enthusiastic, extreme, extroverted. Any of those words might depict him, and no doubt there are others. If you are looking to me, however, for one phrase or concept that reflects my view of my brother, I will still go back to the one that I shared earlier. I doubt that many men have been more transparent than Peter. Sometimes, he seems to wear a window on his heart, exposing his soul for the entire world to see. Maybe that is why he is so loved, so respected, so appreciated – because he is so transparently human.

My brother is a man who knows himself, understands what he is, and seems to be at peace with the man he has become. As I think about Peter's life, I believe that even as a young man he was in touch with himself. He never feared letting others know who he was. He was a rough man but was always real and true to himself. Whether you liked him or not, at least you knew what kind of a person he was and where you stood with him. There was nothing fake, no masks, in the way he presented himself to others. In fact, he just couldn't hide the real person inside that big body of his. When he was happy, we knew it. When he was sad, we felt it. When he failed, we watched the tears flow down his sunbaked face, and when he was angry, it was evident to us all. If ever there was a time when his knowledge of himself might have floundered, it was probably during the three years that we walked with Jesus. Those were years of change and transformation for us all, years when so much about our lives was turned upside down.

I believe it is because Peter is so honest and so transparent that his life has been used so powerfully to touch the lives of many. People can identify with the kind of person he is. They look at his life and see his failures, his repentance, his restoration, his faith, his triumphs, his struggles, and they too can relate to the same experiences in life. They see the way he reacted to real situations, and draw from his example, using him as a model of how to meet some of the challenges that life brings to us all.

Some people might see him as a big, brash, arrogant man who, they think, flaunts his position. That is not true at all. If they knew him as I do, they would perceive that he is a very humble man. Even though he has risen to be one of the two most recognized leaders in our new movement, along with Paul, he has never lost the sense of his own inadequacy, his own failures, and his own sinfulness.

If you talk with him, I have no doubt he will be honest about the kind of man he was before he met Jesus. I still remember one experience that we shared together which truly reflects the spirit of my brother. We and our partners, James and John, had been fishing all night and had caught nothing. We came to shore tired and discouraged and saw a man standing on the beach. We knew it was Jesus. He told us to go back out and resume our fishing. We were all tired, and none of us felt like doing as Jesus asked. But, true to his character, my brother was the one who did just what most people probably would have done. He objected. Physically he was exhausted, as were we all. However, there was something compelling in the command of Jesus. So, we wearily pushed our boats back out and once again, cast our nets into the water. How astonished we were when, almost immediately, our nets were full, so heavy with fish that we could hardly haul all the catch in. Yes, we were all amazed, but it was Simon (Peter), who ran to Jesus, falling on his knees and crying, *"Go, Lord, leave me, sinner that I am."*

That was how my brother had always been, for as long as I can remember, even during the younger years of our life, consciously in touch with who he really was. No pretense, just the raw expression of what he thought and felt. In that moment, he was so keenly aware of his own sin that he fell to his knees in front of everyone there and confessed it. Now compare my brother with Judas Iscariot, another disciple of Jesus. During the last days of Jesus Christ's life on earth, both men denied Christ in their own way. What was the difference between them? Both were broken, guilt-ridden men, but one was humble and the other wasn't.

Did my brother ever change? Not really. He is still as honest and open in the later years of his life as he was in the earlier ones. I have been told, for I wasn't there, about the time when he was eating in a restaurant with Gentiles, and some Jews arrived. Being afraid of offending the Jews, he got up, left the Gentiles, and moved over to the Jews. Paul just happened to be eating in the same restaurant and observed what had happened. Not too timid himself, Paul walked right over and confronted my brother for his hypocritical behavior in this situation. What did Peter do? How did he react? How would you have reacted? Knowing he was wrong, he took it like a man, never defending himself or his actions. True to the character I knew, he was humble, honest and, when called for, repentant. He might be tough and hard on the outside, but that isn't the essence of his heart.

I'd like to share with you something that he wrote in one of his letters that is circulating among Christ's followers. Some words found in that letter can be taken as autobiographical, reflecting aspects of who he is. He said, "Add to your faith virtue, knowledge, temperance, godliness, love. The man who lacks them is shortsighted and blind, he has forgotten how he was cleansed from his former sins."

I believe my brother could tell you what it is like to experience personal failures in one's life, because of his own experiences of failure. When you talk with him, he is likely to tell you about times that he fell on his face, so to speak. Why wouldn't he, for that would just reflect the transparency that I have been talking about? But let me share a couple of examples here.

I remember the night when we were caught in a storm on the Sea of Galilee, and Jesus came, walking on the water. At first, we were all terrified, thinking that we were seeing a ghost. Then Jesus identified himself, and it was my brother who said, *"Lord, if it is you, tell me to come to you over the water."* Unbelievably, Peter climbed over the side of the boat and *began walking on the water!* Looking at the angry waves that were rising and falling around him, Peter quickly lost faith and began to sink.

To be honest about Peter, he doesn't always think before he speaks, and often opens his mouth when he shouldn't, but even that is ingenuously transparent. No matter what happens, his response is always so candid, so undisguised.

Who made the first confession that Jesus was the Messiah when we were at Caesarea Philippi? My brother, of course! Who else? Explosive, spontaneous, quick to reply. *"You're the Messiah,"* he said, *"the Son of the living God."* That was commendable, but what he said next, while up front about his thoughts, completely missed the point. Jesus told us that he was going to Jerusalem to die, and my brother immediately countered that with, *"NO, Lord, this shall never happen to you."* In that moment, my brother received one of the most pointed rebukes Jesus ever gave to any of us. Jesus said, *"Get behind me Satan!"* I have no doubt that hurt my brother deeply, which was another side of him; one moment an igneous rock and the next, a dissolving lump of sandstone. He is just so human, so real, so much himself, straightforwardly letting the world know what is on the inside. One moment inspired by God, the next, a tool of the devil.

Probably nothing showed who he was more than the night when Jesus was taken to be tried. You are familiar with how Simon Peter accompanied John into the courtyard and how, during that night, he denied Jesus three times, claiming he never knew him and swearing with a curse to prove it. That too was Simon. After his denials, the rooster crowed, and they brought Jesus out into the courtyard. Jesus looked straight into Simon's eyes. Knowing Jesus, that gaze would have penetrated the innermost parts of Simon's soul. It was too much for my brother to handle. He bit his lip, and his tears started to flow. He rushed out of the courtyard square, out of the gate, his heart pounding, his emotions throbbing, the rock turning to sand, the center post of his inner strength collapsing like rotten timber.

Something happened to my brother that night that became for him a turning point, a conversion, if you will, as something died within him – his cocksure confidence, his brash bravado, his ready self-reliance, his self-sufficient strength.

Maybe Simon Peter will tell you about that night, in the same way that he readily told me how deeply he lamented what he had done. The sorrow and distress of his soul poured out in convulsive weeping and sincere cries of repentance. I don't think my brother would have cared if all the world knew how deep his grief was. He wept with a broken heart. He could do no less, for that is the kind of man he is, open, transparent, honest, and real. When that story was shared among Christ's followers, it seemed as if nothing any person had ever done could compare with this moment in the life of my brother in helping people to identify with Peter's experience as their own.

After that desperate night, Peter returned home still a broken man, wondering if he could ever be useful to Christ and his cause again. He went back to the familiar ways of life, trying hard to forget his recent failures and regrets. Again, he fished hard all night long and caught nothing. But as the sun rose into the early morning dawn, a man could be seen standing on the shore. That man was Jesus, risen from the dead! For a second time in our experience, the first being when Jesus called Simon to follow him, Jesus told us where to cast our nets and again, we caught a great school of fish. John was the first, to cry out, *"IT IS THE LORD!"* That was all my brother needed. Impetuously and true to his character, he threw himself into the water and swam eagerly ashore. Jesus had built a fire on the beach and was cooking some fish. Breakfast was ready. We ate quietly together in the early dawn. At first, even my brother did not dare to speak.

It was Jesus who reached out to my brother. With a searching look, the second time in recent days that Jesus had peered into Simon's innermost soul, Jesus called him by the new name that he had given him: PETER, THE ROCK. Simon Peter had denied Jesus three times and that morning, on three separate occasions, Jesus drilled my brother about the level of his love and commitment to him. *"Simon, son of John, do you love me?"* I looked at my brother. That question seemed to cut deeply into the denier's soul. Simon Peter was forced to search his heart deeply to be sure that he could sincerely affirm, with faltering lips, the confirmation of the love he really had for Christ. *"Yes, Lord, you know that I am your friend. You know that I love you."* Jesus again asked, *"Do you love me? Are you sure that you love me?"* I waited to hear what my brother would say. *"Yes,"* he said, *"you know that I love you."* A third time Christ asked that same heart-searching question, *"Peter, do you Love me?"* I wondered how this process was affecting my brother. I waited for his response and saw a hint of anger flash across his face, but that soon faded into a deep, repeated affirmation of his love for his Master.

Jesus was taken to Heaven, and my brother now displayed a much more subdued and humbled spirit. The personality traits that we have been talking about are still there, but they seem more controlled and focused than they had been in his earlier years. Some years have passed since we all walked with Jesus in the flesh. The Holy Spirit has used my brother to bring thousands to know Christ. Following just one sermon he preached on the day of Pentecost, over three thousand people put their faith in Christ, just some of the multitudes that he has touched with the message of his beloved Master.

Simon Peter has also borne witness to the person of Christ before religious leaders, judges, and other occupiers of high office. He has faced persecution, being arrested more than once, and put in prison. My brother who once wilted before the question of a little girl in the courtyard of the High Priest, now sometimes stood before the greatest of the great to give an unwavering testimony of his love for the Lord Jesus. The rock is no longer powdery sandstone, but has become solid granite – hard, durable... unchanging.

Knowing Peter and his honest and transparent personality as I do, I am not surprised that my brother has become a mediator between the Jewish and Gentile factions of our movement. I saw how tactfully he handled this tough situation at the first great church council in Jerusalem.

I have tried to be as honest and transparent as I can be in my sharing of my impression of my brother and how he lived his life before others. Maybe some of the people with whom you will share this story are in many ways no different than my brother. I expect you will encounter some who have sinned and faltered in their lives as well, people who have let Christ down and failed in their commitment to Him. Maybe they might have been self-confident, as my brother was at times. Others, perhaps, are rash and outspoken. I hope that my brother's example can be an encouragement to all those who struggle with the kinds of thoughts, clumsy, mistaken words, or untruthful denials that he struggled with. As Peter, they too can rush to return to their Master, tell Jesus their sorrow over their sin, repent, accept Christ's forgiveness and they too can become a Christ-honoring and witnessing "rock" among those with whom they live and work, called and transformed, as was my brother over two catches of fish, to be effective fishers of men.

DISCUSSION QUESTIONS

1. Both Andrew and his brother Simon (Peter) worked together with their father as fisherman and later both became followers and disciples of Jesus. Andrew was the first to follow Jesus and introduced his brother to Christ. Yet Simon (Peter) rose to the predominant position among the disciples and, except perhaps for Paul, among most of the early churches. How do you think Andrew felt about the rise of his brother and do you think there was any tension between them or jealousy on the part of Andrew over his brother's position?

2. Thinking about your response to the first question, it appears that the personalities and temperaments of the two brothers were different. Simon (Peter) appears to be more outgoing, forceful, and aggressive, while Andrew appears to be more introverted, quiet, and reserved. When looking at these differences, talk about how you think the two brothers interacted and related to each other, both as children and youth and then into their adult years.

3. In the story above, the word "transparent" was used as the most characteristic personality trait of Simon (Peter). To what degree does being transparent become both a strength and a weakness? When is it good to be overly transparent and when might it be better to not be so open with one's life? How much do you think Simon (Peter)'s transparency helped him in his ascent to become a leader of the twelve and, to a large degree, of the church as a whole?

4. Many people would say that being a transparent person isn't "manly," and that a "true man" hides his feelings and failures and only presents himself as a strong and in-control individual.

Simon (Peter) appears to have been "manly" in every way, a tough and perhaps, at times, crude fisherman, yet he wasn't afraid to let people know what he was thinking and feeling. What can we learn from Simon (Peter)'s example about what constitutes a "true man"?

5. When we talk about being a transparent person, we might be tempted to think that means letting everyone know everything about our life. When are there times that it is the better part of prudence not to be open? Does one's decision not to reveal some things about one's life and character mean that such an individual is not a "transparent person"?

6. In the story above, it was noted that both Simon (Peter) and Judas Iscariot denied Jesus, but each handled their denial differently. Compare and discuss the extremely different reactions of these two men and try to explain why each might have responded in the way they did.

7. We can see in the Bible how Simon (Peter) handled some of his failures. What can we learn about a person by the way he or she handles failures in life?

8. Having read the story above and with the discussion of the previous questions, just try to describe the man you visualize in your mind when you think of Simon (Peter). Has your image of this man changed at all from what it was before beginning this discussion about his life?

9. It was suggested in the writing above that Simon (Peter)'s life was always quite open and transparent from his youth to his death. Yet there were some defining moments that were referenced in the story (his failure in walking on water; his

denial of Jesus in the courtyard at the trial of Jesus). Do you think either of these two, or any other defining moments we might want to look at, made Simon (Peter) any more or less open as a person?

10. It was suggested in the story above that Simon (Peter)'s denial of Jesus in the courtyard may have endeared him to more people than any other single event of his life. Discuss how sometimes our failures can be our biggest asset in life?

11. Reflecting on that morning after the resurrection of Christ, when some of the disciples had fished all night and caught nothing, and Christ told them to cast their nets again into the water and they had a great catch of fish, how do you think Simon (Peter) might have felt when he suddenly realized it was Jesus on the seashore? How do you think you might have felt?

12. In what ways do you identify with Simon (Peter)? How much has his transparency helped you see something of yourself?

13. What characteristics of Simon (Peter) would you like to assimilate into your own life?

14. Are there any ways that Simon (Peter)'s life serves as an example in your mind of what a true believer should be like?

5

PETER

The Man who was Consistently Inconsistent

Since my husband Peter's death some years ago, people in the church have made such a legend of him that it is difficult to find in their stories the real man that I knew so well. We had a good marriage, and I accompanied my husband everywhere he went, making every effort to support and encourage him. During good times and bad, we shared life and ministry together. We knew, deep inside, that one day he would probably have to give his life for what he believed, as so many of Jesus' disciples have had to do, an incentive for us to share as much of our lives with each other as we could. The way he died was horrific, but even his death reflected the kind of life he had lived.

Not many people know that my name is Perpetua [PehR-PEY-Tuw-aa]. Those working closely with my husband and me would recognize it immediately, but most people in church circles would never know who I was, even if they had heard my name. My husband, however, is another story! Whenever anyone hears his name, all kinds of ideas and associations enter their minds. Just say Simon Peter, and they think about his denial of the Master, the time he walked on water or saw Christ transfigured on the mount. Yes, Peter, always seemed larger than life.

I have never known any other man who was as willing as Peter to reveal to others who and what he really was. It was just the way he was, not something he planned or set out to do artificially. I think it was almost impossible for Simon Peter to hide his real self. When conversing, or even giving a speech, it was as if he opened a door to his life and let you look inside. There was nothing hidden or protected about him. Maybe that is one of the keys to his greatness.

People soon learned to like Simon Peter because from the outset, they knew who he was and could identify with him in so many ways, especially after he publicly denied the Master and then wept so hard over his failure. To be sure, Christ restored him fully and publicly, and he was reestablished by the other apostles and the whole church. Since then, we were amazed to see how people came to Simon Peter and me after they too had sinned – to find understanding and solace, knowing that Peter had gone through the same experience and had found restoration and peace. Of all that my husband said, wrote and did, no other incident has touched more people, and been a comfort to so many, as this one moment in his life. At that moment he was so real, so human, so transparent, so broken, and so sorry about his failure. In that moment, everyone saw how human he really was. Because of that failure, he was able to empathize with others and point them to God's forgiveness, restoration, and transformation, so I saw how God redeemed such a bitterly painful moment in Peter's life.

I, probably more than any other, knew Peter's humanity. After all, I lived, travelled, and worked with him for years, seeing the good and the bad in his life, and there was plenty of both! In fact, when trying to summarize the Simon Peter I knew, I would say that he was a man of *consistent inconsistencies*. Let's look at his life, and you will see what I mean.

At one moment Simon Peter called Jesus the Son of God. What a day that was! The Master confirmed his statement and said that the very church itself would be built on that great confession. Yet in almost the same breath, Peter confronted Jesus about his prediction concerning his own death. Christ rebuked Peter publicly, declaring his words to be from Satan! Yes, in one breath to call him the Christ, and then to reprove Christ for what he had said! But that is how my husband was. Even the day that Christ called him to be his follower, two sides of Simon Peter responded. Amazed and impressed by the great catch of fish, and immediately understanding the nature of the miraculous power of Jesus, he fell at the Master's feet in worship and adoration. At the same time, he begged the Master to depart and leave him alone because he recognized he was too great a sinner to be in his presence.

Do you remember the day that Peter walked on the water? People still talk about it. His boldness in clambering out of the boat reflected his faith in Christ. Yet he hadn't walked too far before, looking down at the churning waves, he lost it all. He almost drowned that day and would have done so, had Christ not saved him.

Another time, Peter began by making such a fuss about Christ washing his feet and finished by begging him to wash his head and hands as well. That was my Peter! After all, wasn't it my husband who boasted that he wouldn't forsake the Master, even if everyone else did? Yet that very night, he denied him not just once, but three times! That was on the same night when, at one moment Peter brashly cut off Malchus' ear in a physical attempt to defend the Master, yet within minutes he was fleeing for his life.

Simon Peter carried great prejudice toward Gentile peoples. It took a vision to convince him that God could accept Gentiles as well as Jews, despite his knowledge of what our Jewish Scriptures say about God's desire for the nations. After his vision on the roof of Simon the Tanner, however, Peter made great strides to overcome his ingrained prejudices. I was proud of his efforts, but his consistently inconsistent patterns showed up again one day when Jews from Jerusalem, directly responsible to John, showed up at a local restaurant. Simon Peter was happily lunching with his newfound Gentile friends, until he saw the Jews enter the restaurant, at which point Simon quickly scooted out of that booth, distancing himself from his Gentile companions. I guess he deserved what happened next. Paul was there too and saw the whole episode. In front of everyone, he confronted my husband for his inconsistent actions. My husband was humiliated, but what could he say? Well, it could be said that he never tried to hide what he was, whether his commendable or notoriously reprehensible sides. Always honest and open about what was on the inside, what he said or the behavior he displayed were always authentic. The good and bad aspects of his personality and his ingenuous paradoxes were lived out with childlike candidness for the whole world to see.

Many people ask me what Peter was like, and it is a challenge to sum him up. He was everything in one man. Most people who came to know Peter after his life with Jesus would have a hard time recognizing his younger version. He was rough and crude and as hardy as any fisherman working on the Sea of Galilee. That was the man I first knew and married. During the early years of our marriage, we lived at my mother's house in Capernaum. There was no place for mother-in-law jokes at our house! Simon Peter and my mother got along well, and she was glad to have such a man around her house. After he started following the Master, Simon Peter would often bring him and his group of disciples to my mother's house. On one occasion when my mother was ill, the Master healed her, and she immediately got up and made dinner for us all!

There was another time, however, when my mother wasn't so sure about Simon Peter bringing them all home. The Master was teaching in our house, when suddenly some determined men made a hole in her roof and lowered a man into the main living room, right at the feet of Jesus. I realized later that it was a creative and ambitious attempt to get their needy friend to Jesus when they couldn't get through the packed crowd of people spilling out of our home. Jesus healed him, of course, and for most people, that's the end of the story. As you might imagine, however, my mother was greatly concerned about the hole in her roof, so it became Peter's responsibility to fix it!

I was fascinated – and happy – to see the changes that came over my husband from the moment when he first met the Master and followed him. The Master was so understanding, kind and patient in dealing with Peter's rough edges. A progression of changes occurred in my husband's life during his years of walking with Jesus, but perhaps his denial of Christ and the heart-rending repentance that followed did more to change him than anything else. That night served as a lesson in knowing himself better and after it, he was less cocksure of himself and far more understanding and gentler with the shortcomings of others.

On the first Pentecost after Jesus' resurrection, Peter was bolder but less brash, stronger but less impulsive. I could see that the Holy Spirit's presence in Peter's life was wisely controlling this otherwise impulsive talker! As his love for me deepened, I grew to love and respect that man more and more. If you have read his letters, you will see that he used our union and home as an example when likening Christ's love for us to the love between a husband and wife. He made a statement about his own home life being a good one, and it was!

What words do I use to describe this very special man? You may have heard some of them from others, but I can add aspects of Peter that were revealed in the closeness of our marital relationship. Terms such as impulsive, quick to speak and act, sometimes driven by the motives of the moment, carried away by enthusiasm, boastful at first, fearful at times, deliberate later, emotional, warm-hearted, affectionate, devoted, sincere and ingenuous. There are certainly many other terms I could have used, but you will notice that some of those words seem to be opposites. My husband knew he was a sinful human, and that he fell far short, but he knew that he was forgiven and redeemed by the grace of the Lord Jesus Christ whom he loved and followed.

There were some great, outstanding, and glorious moments in Peter's life. Even though he faltered in faith after walking on water, it was nevertheless a great moment to remember. The indescribable, heavenly appearances that he witnessed on the mount where Jesus was transfigured were hard for him to keep secret until after the resurrection, especially for a talker like Simon Peter! Yet he obeyed, saying nothing about his experience until Christ was taken back to heaven. After that, you can be sure that he did not remain quiet about it any longer! Seeing Moses and Elijah back on Earth again was some incredible experience!

That brings me back to describing my husband as the man of consistent inconsistencies. He was the one who begged Jesus to let him stay on the Mount of Transfiguration, so wonderful was that moment, and yet he objected to letting Jesus wash his feet. Only Simon Peter would do that, talking as if he knew better than the Lord. Yes, that was my husband! With one breath he boasted of his loyalty to Christ, and not long afterwards swore an oath that he never knew him.

My husband was privileged to be given a private meeting with Christ just after his resurrection. What a difference that made in Peter's life! When he heard that Jesus' tomb was empty, and that the Master was alive again, he just pushed right past John and ran boldly to the sepulcher to see for himself.

My husband often talked about the time that he was fishing on the Sea of Galilee, after Jesus had died. Discouraged and uncertain about the future, he looked up and recognized Jesus standing on the shore. Peter didn't think twice – he seldom did! He just wrapped himself in his fisherman's cloak, jumped into the water and swam to the shore. So eager was he to join his beloved Master that he couldn't be bothered to wait for the slow fishing boat to get him there. He was in such a hurry that he hurled himself into the sea, the very sea he had once walked on, and swam as fast as he could to meet the resurrected Christ. It hadn't been long since he had denied Jesus, but now he was to meet him again as a changed man – and was about to change even more.

I am not surprised that Simon Peter went on to become one of the greatest leaders in the early church. Please understand that this is a statement of what happened and not an evaluation based on a loving wife's partiality towards her husband. Once submitted to Christ, Peter's inconsistencies increasingly appeared to me as sides of the same coin. Aspects of his personality that had tripped him up in the earlier years became strengths in his ministry. The imprudent loudmouth became a powerful voice for God, the man so confident in his own opinions became a humble, Spirit-led leader, the cringing denier became a fearless witness in the face opposition and in his bold approach to death. At the end of his life, no inconsistency remained. He gave his life for the Christ he loved, leaving me a widow. I miss him bitterly but am full of memories of a great and multi-faceted man who allowed Christ to transform him into a greater man and servant of God whose life and writings still inspire transformation in others who are willing to be as honest as he about their failings, accept God's forgiveness, and learn to trust in the power of God instead of in themselves, just as Peter did.

DISCUSSION QUESTIONS

1. Simon Peter is the disciple about whom we read the most in Scripture, so we know more about him than about any of the others. There is also more record of Jesus talking to him than to any of the other disciples. We know more about his humanity and failures than about those of any other. Drawing on your study of the Bible, and reading these stories featuring Simon Peter, share your impression of the kind of person you think he was.

2. What insights can we glean in terms of spiritual growth and maturation when we focus on the consistent inconsistencies of Peter's life. What does this tell us about the sanctifying work of the Holy Spirit in the life of a person?

3. Despite his "consistent inconsistencies," Peter had great natural abilities as a leader. From your reading of the Gospels, and what you know about Simon Peter's life, what was it about Simon Peter that made him such a great leader of men and of the church?

4. This story was written from the perspective of Peter's wife. Knowing what you know about Simon Peter from the Gospels, the book of Acts and the Epistles, what do you think his home life might have been like? What do you think he might have been like as a husband and possible father?

5. It might be fair to say that more people can identify with Simon Peter than with any other disciple. What is it about Simon Peter's life that helps people identify with him? What qualities about Simon Peter do you like or dislike? Are there any ways

that you can personally identify with Simon Peter in our own life?

6. What can we learn from Simon Peter about how God deals with all of us as disciples who start out with rough edges or as "diamonds in the raw"?

7. What are some of the principles, ideas, or truths you can take with you from this story today that can be of help to you in your life and work for God?

6

PETER

His Mountaintop Experiences
A story developed from various scriptural passages

I have lived such a rich and fulfilling life that I hardly know where to begin trying to tell you about it. Since I met Jesus, it seems as if hardly a day has passed that hasn't been full of meaningful and often life-changing experiences. Examples crowd into my mind as I start to isolate some events that I would call the "mountaintop experiences" of my life.

When I am the topic of conversation, most people cite my walking on water, the night I denied Jesus three times, the occasion when Jesus called me to be a "fisher of men," or maybe my experience at the home of Cornelius when the Holy Spirit came upon the Gentiles, or even the sermon I preached on Pentecost. There is, however, a whole lot more to my life than these often-recalled moments that people think about most.

One of the first instances that comes to my mind is the time that Jesus took James, John and me to the home of Jairus, a leader in the synagogue. He had sought us out, pleading with Jesus to come and heal his daughter who was near death. Moved by the earnest plea of this desperate father, Jesus went with him, and we all saw a wonderful miracle. Since then, we have witnessed several people being raised from the dead but observing such a supernatural miracle for the first time left an indelible impression on me.

When we went to Jairus' house, the crowd of mourners ridiculed us as we passed because Jesus told them that the girl was not dead but sleeping. I didn't know what to expect that day when we shut the door behind us and went with her parents into the room where the dead girl was laying. I looked at her still, pale features and two thoughts impressed me – one, that she was undeniably dead and the second, how beautiful was her innocent, young face. I couldn't help but notice her parents' desperation, yet I caught a trace of hope passing across her father's face, as his eyes beseeched those of Jesus. Silence enshrouded us all, occasionally broken by a quiet sob expressing the broken heart of her mother who felt as if the removal of the life of her child had deposited a crushing weight on her own life that was too heavy to carry.

No one spoke. No one knew what to say. Jesus broke the silence with firm but gentle words. Taking the dead girl's hand, he said, *"Little girl, I say to you, get up."* The moment hung in suspension as we all looked at the child's lifeless form, yearning for her to obey, unable to imagine it, and not knowing how to react if she did. Then she opened her eyes, and we heard her gasp, drawing life-supporting air into her lungs. In a matter of moments, color returned to her face, and she shuffled to sit up in her bed. Even though I have since witnessed other resurrections – the son of the widow at Nain and the raising of our friend Lazarus, this first wonderful, awe-inspiring experience was a first such high point in my life.

Another day, James, John and I went with Jesus to the top of Mount Tabor and saw Jesus meeting with the long-departed Elijah and Moses, two spiritual giants of our people's past. I am aware that this too is often referenced when people talk about me. That experience was so out-of-this-world that I can't even describe it to you in meaningful terms. I regard that moment as a rare experience of the soul, allowing our threesome the privilege of seeing something of what our future life in heaven will be like. We saw glory! It glowed and radiated from Jesus, Moses, and Elijah. Just to be in their presence was totally captivating, but also a fearful and humbling encounter for mortals such as us. The vivid recollection of that foretaste of glory is a memory to relish that generates hope and joy in my soul. While a mountaintop experience in a literal sense, Jesus permitted me to ascend to the summit of one of human experience's highest peaks. Just to tell you about it revives the euphoria I felt at the time, a rare experience this side of heaven, to be sure, as well as an exciting expectation of what awaits us there.

A wonderful mountaintop moment came after the crucifixion and resurrection of Jesus from the dead. In some ways, it is difficult to separate two experiences that seemed to merge into one in terms of the emotion they caused. The first Sunday evening after Jesus' execution, ten of us were gathered in an upper room. Judas was dead, and Thomas was not present on that occasion. Our mood was one of utter defeat, and we feared for our very lives. In one sense, therefore, that evening was one of the most difficult and lowest times I have ever known. But everything changed in an instant when Jesus suddenly appeared among us. At first, we felt a shudder of fear thinking that a phantom had appeared. We soon came to realize, however, that it was none other than Jesus himself standing there. The fear we had allowed to cower us, and the gloom and hopelessness to which we had succumbed melted away in the warmth of his presence. Joy replaced sorrow and fear and hope replaced hopelessness.

There was yet another experience that had an even greater personal impact on me. After the crucifixion of Jesus, we were all broken men, but I more so than the others, feeling such deep guilt over my having denied Jesus in the courtyard. Tucked into the first hours and days of Jesus' post-resurrection movements was a very private meeting with me. Apart from the fact that it happened, no one knows much about it. It was an experience so deep and personal that I chose to ponder and cherish it alone in the innermost parts of my soul and to keep it totally to myself. That conversation, however, completely transformed me as a person. While in a different way, I think this meeting with the resurrected Jesus was as profound in meaning and as deeply significant spiritually as my being present on the mountain of his transfiguration.

What I have already shared with you would be enough to have made my life worth living, but these examples are only a few of the "mountaintop" experiences I have known. One day, as many of us were gathered on a different mountaintop, we witnessed another eye-popping miracle that I shall never forget. After giving us his final instructions, commanding us to go and wait for the coming of the Holy Spirit and telling us that we would be his witnesses to all the world, right before our eyes Jesus began to ascend into Heaven. We stood there gaping at the sky, our eyes transfixed by the figure of Jesus growing smaller and less distinct as he took his extraordinary departure by ascending heavenward into the clouds!

After Jesus had disappeared from our sight, an angel appeared and told us that Jesus would return one day in the same way that we had just seen him leave. Just like the time on the mountain when Elijah and Moses came, we found ourselves once again on a literal mountaintop, and just as before, beholding a divine wonder became a figurative spiritual mountaintop experience for us. Of course, I was sad when Jesus left, realizing that we wouldn't see him physically again, but the privilege of being present to watch him ascend to heaven was a truly exhilarating spiritual moment of my life.

Not many days later, on the day of Pentecost, I preached one of my first sermons. The Holy Spirit came upon us in a wonderful way. After I had stood up that day and preached, around three thousand people believed in Christ as their Messiah, Savior and Lord. This was for me the first manifestation of the power of the Holy Spirit that had been shed abroad in all our hearts. It gave me a glimpse of what the future ministry was going to be like for me and for us all. As long my memory is sound, I will never forget how my soul rejoiced at seeing so many embracing Jesus. Yes, I must add that to the list of mountaintop experiences of my life.

The Holy Spirit who had flooded our life with spiritual power at Pentecost would show that power in many ways in the years to follow. It could be that as God used me as an instrument in many marvelous spiritual acts through the years of my ministry, my excitement over healings and other amazing divine interventions became a little dulled. However, the first experience of a wondrous act of God has a special impact on one's life. For example, there was our experience when Jesus sent us out two by two, and we saw many miracles happen. That experience was, however, wrapped in the broader ministry of Jesus himself. A particular healing that really stands out in my mind though is one of the first of my post-Pentecost ministry…

We went to the temple one sabbath and saw there a crippled man who had been unable to walk since the day of his birth. He followed us with his eyes, hoping for a small charitable contribution.

Sensing the Holy Spirit moving in my soul, I met this beggar's gaze. He quickly looked away, neither accustomed to, nor wishing for, such engaged interest from a stranger. Then, as I felt the Spirit prompting me, I said, *"Neither silver or gold have I, but what I have I give to you, stand up and walk."* I reached down and took him by the hand to help him stand for the first time in his life. His legs were restored and fully functioning. His joy and excitement were uncontainable, and I too felt the same elation in my heart. As I said, there would be many such examples in the following years, but the first time always has the greatest impact, imprinting itself on one's memory as "a mountaintop experience" with God.

Of course, my fame spread everywhere, and people brought their sick to be healed or sought other favors from me. At times, I felt as if I were reliving the years that we had traveled with Jesus when the sick people were brought to him for healing. Some of you might recognize the name Tabitha, or maybe her Greek name, Dorcas. People knew that I was near where she lived, so when she died, they immediately sent for me. When I arrived, the room where they had laid her was full of weeping widows. Those who knew her told me wonderful stories about Tabitha's life, indicating that she must have been a remarkable believer in the Messiah. Empathizing with their deep sorrow, I thought about what Jesus must have felt when he went to be with Martha and Mary after Lazarus had died. He cried that day. I didn't cry, but I keenly felt their pain and sorrow. I pondered the situation before me, and then asked everyone to leave me alone with the body of this wonderful woman.

I prayed, asking God what he wanted me to do. A deep assurance in my soul confirmed what I had to do. I rose from my knees and looking at Tabitha's dead form, I commanded in just three words, "Tabitha, get up." My mind returned to that day many years earlier when I had waited with bated breath to see if the daughter of Jairus would get up when Jesus asked her to. Once again, I waited... then saw the same telltale signs I had seen when Jesus gave a young girl her life back. Tabitha gasped as air entered her lungs again, the color began to return to her face, and she opened her eyes and looked at me. What a glorious, unforgettable moment that was, another divine "mountaintop" experience of my life!

Please don't think that I am proud and trying to brag. Far from it! I defer all credit and glory to God as the author of the wonderful acts that have enriched my life's experience. My examples would not be complete, however, without another very special instance that I'd like to share, but in a way, this was also one of the valleys of my life. It took place after I had been arrested and was sitting in prison awaiting a possible execution the following morning.

King Herod had just executed James and had had me arrested. King Herod sent two soldiers to guard me in my cell and others to guard any entrance to or exit from the prison. As the night wore on, I must confess that as any other human being, I struggled with the thought that I might be executed. We all share the human will to live. Despite my circumstances and chilling fate, I felt an uncommon peace allowing me finally to fall into a deep sleep. Without going into many details about that night, for that is another story to be told, an angel came and awoke me, and opened the prison doors, having put the men guarding me into a sound and deep sleep. We escaped the prison with angels, delivered from almost certain death. But when thinking about what happened that night, it is not the fact that I was delivered that amazes me, but the way God did it! His grace, his ways, and his timing, of which this is another stellar example, always astound me so. Let's add this to my list of "mountaintop" experiences too.

There is always more that I could add. How privileged I have been to see God at work. Each experience evokes a deep sense of awe within me, and I know that I have been with him in a way that reminds me of our literal mountaintop experience with Jesus, Moses, and Elijah on Mount Tabor. Not only have I been privileged to have been allowed these glimpses of such a holy and awesome God, but each one has helped me know Him a little better, has humbled me and moved me to worship, and has wrought great changes in my life. The memory of them brings me joy and excitement and are solid proof of God's goodness and power that I can retreat to even in the darkest moments of my life, just as God told the Israelites never to forget what he had done, but to remember his mighty working in their lives and history.

DISCUSSION QUESTIONS

1. Peter would witness several people being raised from the dead during his lifetime. The first time we experience a new and significant event in our lives always creates within us first reactions and impressions that often overshadow subsequent occurrences of that same event. In the story above, seeing the daughter of Jairus raised from the dead was listed as one of the "mountaintop" experiences in Peter's life. Try to place yourself in Peter's place and then describe what you think he might have felt and thought and how he might have reacted when witnessing someone being raised from the dead for the first time in his life.

2. Reflecting on the first question, how differently do you think Peter might view subsequent experiences of others being raised from the dead? Do you think it ever became somewhat "normal" and lost its sense of amazement for Peter?

3. Again, try to enter into Peter's experience as he was there on the mountain when Jesus spoke to Elijah and Moses. He and the other two disciples were given a glimpse of glory and what we will be like in Heaven. What do you think Peter might have felt and thought when he witnessed this appearance of these two Old Testament saints and saw all three of them, Jesus, Elijah, and Moses, in their transfigured state? How do you think you might have felt if you had been in that same situation?

4. We know that the initial emotional reaction of Peter and all the other disciples was fear when Jesus first appeared to them after his resurrection from the dead. Try to place yourself into that moment and describe what you think that experience might

have been like, and how do you think you might have felt and responded.

5. The Bible tells us that Peter and Jesus had a meeting together after Christ was resurrected from the dead. The Bible doesn't tell us anything else about this meeting. It seems to be clothed in total privacy and obscurity. Why do you think the Bible is so silent about this meeting? Why do you think Peter never talked about it when writing his epistles, nor Mark when writing Peter's story in his Gospel? What do you think Peter and Jesus might have talked about during this special meeting?

6. In the same spirit as is reflected in the previous questions, try once again to place yourself in the experience Peter (and all the disciples) had that day as they witnessed Jesus being taken into Heaven. There must have been several conflicting feelings in the lives of these men. If you had been there, how do you think you might have felt and reacted to seeing Christ taken up to Heaven and the angel appearing and telling you that Christ is going to return in the same way you just saw Him go?

7. On the day of Pentecost, Peter preached and it resulted in over 3,000 people responding to his message and becoming followers of Jesus. As far as we know, this was one of the first (perhaps the first) sermons that Peter preached. How do you think he felt and thought at this kind of response to his sermon?

8. Peter had seen people healed at his command, at least during the time when Jesus sent the disciples out "two by two." It appears, however, that one of the most significant and perhaps one of the earliest miracles that he would perform following Pentecost was the healing of the man who was crippled from birth. How do you think this healing might have been different in the mind of

Peter – if it was – from some healings he had been "responsible" for a couple of years earlier when Jesus had sent them out "two by two." If this was the first post-Pentecost miracle Peter performed (or among the first), how do you think this might have shaped Peter's way of thinking for the ministry that lay before him? As many people were healed by Peter in the years to follow, do you think the luster, glow, and excitement of seeing people healed ever faded over the subsequent years of his ministry?

9. In one of the previous questions, we talked about Peter having seen many people raised from the dead. But being a witness to an event is different than being instrumental in something happening. The raising of Tabitha (Dorcas) from the dead was probably the first time that Peter was responsible (as God's instrument) for restoring someone to life. What do you think Peter might have felt and thought when this happened? Do you think his reaction, feelings and thoughts were any different than they might have been when he witnessed similar resurrections as a bystander and now as the human instrument in bringing about the resurrection?

10. What do you think Peter might have been thinking and feeling when he was put in prison by Herod who had just had James executed, and it appeared that Peter was almost certainly going to be executed the next day? Does the fact that he was able to go into a "deep sleep" give us any hints about his mental and emotional condition during this imprisonment?

11. How do you think Peter felt and what might have been some of his thoughts when the angel came and delivered him from the prison? If we assume that Peter heard (or knew) that the guards

would be executed because of his "escape," do you think Peter felt any guilt or remorse over their fate?

12. Just thinking about this story as a whole and knowing what you do about Peter's life from your knowledge of the Bible, do you think there were any other events that occurred in Peter's life that you might have included as a "mountaintop" experience if you had written this story?

13. Again, based on your own knowledge of the Bible and the events in Peter's life, what do you think might have been some of the low points in Peter's life? How might it have helped him to recall the mountaintop experiences?

14. Describe your view of what kind of a person you think Peter was and how you feel about his life? In what ways can you identify with Peter? Think of your own "mountaintop" experiences with God. How have they impacted your life or the lives of others with whom you have shared them?

7

PETER AT THE PASSOVER

John 13: 1-8

Note: The other two stories about Peter were told by his wife and brother. This story attempts to take the reader inside the mind of Peter during his experience of the Last Supper and share some his possible thoughts as that night unfolded. It is written as a psychological Bible study rather than a historical recreation of Peter's life.

Boy, am I full! That was a delicious meal and, as usual, I ate too much of it. I never seem to know when to stop!

I have always looked forward to and enjoyed the feast of the Passover because it brings me a little closer to my past. Passover was so important to us as a family and has always been a special time in our home with my mother busily preparing all she could to make this a significant and memorable day in our lives. My father really liked telling us about the exodus of God's people from Egypt. The nostalgia evoked by taking part in today's Passover celebration makes me feel so close to my parents, as if they were somehow present with us – and I miss them here tonight.

Ever since I started following Jesus, I have missed the day-to-day life and activities I shared with my parents. I enjoyed fishing with my father and was close to him, learning so much from being with him day by day. How bereft and hurt he must have felt on the day that Andrew and I left, and for a long time afterwards, I am sure. I have often thought about that.

At times, I still ask myself what it was about Jesus that made us drop everything for him. He just came up to us one day and said, *"Follow me, and I will make you fishers of men."* That was all he said, and had it been anyone else, we wouldn't have paid much attention, but Jesus was so compelling and his personality so magnetic that we wanted to know him more, so we went with him, and thus began three years of spending time with him and all the while, I have been watching everything he has been doing and listening to everything he has been teaching.

Sometimes, I think I have his teaching all figured out, and at other times, I am not sure I really get what he is saying at all. What I am certain about is that I respect him a whole lot, more than I have ever respected anybody. Never has he given me the slightest reason to alter my respect. He is clearly unique, has done amazing and wonderful miracles, shown boundless compassion and unequivocally condemned untruth and unrepentant sin. When, at Caesarea Philippi, I was able to recognize and declare that he is God's Son, I felt good about getting that right!

It's been quite a night, an unusual Passover in many ways. Take Andrew, from the look in his eyes, I suspect that he might be thinking about home as well, about the times over the years when we shared this Passover with our mother and father. Tonight, they are doing exactly what we are doing. It would be good if they could have done it with us. I wonder if they are thinking about us too, missing us as much as we miss them. I suppose they too have just finished eating the meal, reaching the same point in the celebration as we have.

Looking at Jesus sitting there at the table, he looks no different from any other man. His difference does not lie in his appearance. Often, I wish I could understand more about who and what he is. As well as the divine miracles he has performed, seeing him in a transfigured state with Elijah and Moses up on the mountain really displayed for me, while raising a myriad of questions, the "otherness" of the man I have been following for these past three years. As I look at him now, what do I feel? There are moments when doing life with him is wonderful, but there are other times when it is frightening.

It seems to me that Jesus is so serious, even solemn tonight, as if something might really be bothering him. He's been quieter than usual, and when he speaks, his voice carries tenderness and urgency. In fact, it has been that way for a while – since his visit with Elijah and

Moses on the mountain. He's been different, and his tone has changed. He has talked about going to Jerusalem to die. It is true that there have been many threats on his life of late, but it seems to me that he will never die. I could not imagine life without him.

John is sitting next to Jesus. Those two have really become close. I have really learned to love Jesus too, but sometimes I feel uncomfortable around him, just like the time in the boat when I felt so sinful in his presence that I asked him to leave. He was too good for me to be around, so much of a better man than I. He seems pure and righteous, and I often feel sinful and inadequate, especially when we're together. That might seem like a strange thing for me to say because I was always so proud. Able to out-fish and out-fight them all, I had quite a reputation in Capernaum. As I sit here watching him, I recall how he can read the minds of others. He's looking at me, and for some reason that is making me uncomfortable. I wonder if he knows what I am thinking.

Jesus is getting up, and I am unsure what he is going to do next. He's reaching for a towel. Perhaps he's going to wash himself again. No, he's coming my way. I am wondering what he is up to, but wait, he has stopped, there by James. He's kneeling and washing James' feet. Who does James think he is? Oh yes, I remember well enough how James and his brother wanted to sit at Jesus' side in Heaven. James has been a proud man too. But this, who ever thought he would allow something like this, not saying anything to Jesus, but just letting him wash his feet? I would never do that! I wonder if James thinks he's better than Jesus, or something.

Now Jesus is going over to Matthew, the tax collector. Matthew has always thought he was important, but I never thought he would let Jesus do this to him. Wait until Jesus comes to me, I will show them! He's not going to wash my feet! Not Jesus; not me! He's the Teacher; don't they have any respect for him at all? We followed *him*, and we ought to wash *his* feet. What's wrong with them? Well, here he comes. Now I'll show them...

"*No, Jesus. We followed you, not you us. You're the Master. You shouldn't be washing our feet like this.*"

"You don't understand, Peter, why I am doing it, but someday you will." Oh, I understand all right. I'm not proud like they are. What would it look like if he washed my feet? *"But Peter, if I don't wash your feet, you can't be my partner."*

Why is he looking at me that way? It seems as if he's looking right through me. His tender eyes seem to be filled with sorrow tonight. I see tears moistening his cheeks. I can't look anymore; I must turn my head. There he goes, looking right into my heart again. I don't understand what he said, something about not belonging to him, not being his partner if he couldn't wash my feet. What is happening to me? I don't know, but I do know that I love him, and I certainly want to be with him.

"Lord, if washing my feet is what you ask to belong to you, then Jesus, not just my feet but my hands and my head as well." As I look down at him tonight, memories are clustering in my mind. I remember how much he loved so many people, how he raised the dead and walked on the water. I remember that he even helped me to walk on the water as well. Right now, my heart is pounding hard. This experience with Jesus is filling the moment, pushing thoughts of the others away. There's nothing but him. He's here, *kneeling before me.* I remember the times when I fell and knelt before *him.* I remember the times I worshipped him, whether on the mountain with Elijah and Moses, or at the tomb of Lazarus, but this? God, why is he doing it? Why me? I don't deserve it; I should be washing *his* feet.

There, he's done, and I'm glad. He cares, he really cares – not just for the multitudes that are hungry, not just for the sick and the sorrowing – he cares for me! I know I am loved tonight, such a warm feeling inside. I know I am unworthy, but I feel so good that he did that for me. I wonder how he feels. In response to his love, my heart is reaching out to him, He's fixed his gaze on me again, in that way he has of laying bare my heart.

"Peter, one who has been bathed all over needs only to have his feet washed to be entirely clean. Now you are clean, but that isn't true of everyone here..." I'm clean all over. What does he mean, I'm clean? I don't understand! Oh, God, I don't understand. What's going on here

tonight? What is he doing? Why doesn't he explain what he means? Something, however, is happening to me tonight.

"Peter, you seem moved and uncertain. Do you understand what I was doing? The rest of you as well, do you understand what I am doing? You all call me master and Lord and you do well to say it, for it's true. And since I, the Lord and teacher, have washed your feet, you ought to wash each other's feet. I have given you an example to follow. Do as I have done to you. How true it is that a servant is not greater than his master, nor is the messenger more important than the one who sends him. You know these things, now do them; that is the path of blessing."

Do the same unto others! To John and James? Does he mean that I should be willing to wash their feet as well? I remember how they wanted to be given special treatment in Heaven, and thought they were better than I. Jesus, surely you don't mean that I should lower myself to that degree, do you? – or *do* you? ...I guess I do understand. I am to do that even to them, even to the least of them. Help me God, it's so hard!

Jesus continued, *"I am not saying these things to all of you. I know so well each one of you I chose. The Scripture declares, one who eats supper with me will betray me, and this will soon come true. I tell you this now so that when it happens, you will believe in me. Truly anyone welcoming my messenger is welcoming me, and to welcome me is to welcome the father who sent me."*

What is he saying? That one of us will betray him? Who of us would betray him? He's done so much for us. We have walked with him for three years and have stood with him through many things. Why in the world does he think we're going to betray him? Look at him! Look at his face, it's troubled. I have never seen him like this before. What's happening, God? What's happening to him? What's happening to me? He looks disturbed and distressed. Does he really believe one of us would betray him?

"Yes, it is true, one of you will betray me." That frightens me. I wonder who it is. Surely, I am not the one! No, not me. I love him. I would never do that. Listen to them, look at their faces. They all seem shocked, confused, their faces reflecting fear and doubt. I have never seen them like this before. I wonder who Jesus thinks will betray him.

Ah, John, you're looking my way. John, why don't you ask him? You're his closest friend and you're right there beside him. That's it, John. Yes, he understood my nod and he's asking Jesus right now.

"John, it is the one I honor by giving the bread dipped in the sauce." The one he gives the bread to. There, he's breaking the bread and dipping it in the sauce. I wonder who he will hand it to. Look at them, all of them, their eyes fixed on him enquiringly, just like mine. He's reaching out to Judas, yes to Judas! Judas took the bread...but wait, he's dipping it again and he's handing it to... to me! I can't believe it. Why would he hand that piece of bread to me? Why me? I would never betray him. I'm scared, because something is so different here tonight, something I don't fully comprehend. Passover was never like this at home. But then, I had never met a man like this before. Now he's handing a piece to Thomas and even to my brother Andrew. I wonder why he told Judas to go and to do what he had to do. Perhaps he had to pay for the supper, or maybe he had to go and make the temple donation. He'll come back, no doubt. It looks as if Jesus is going to speak again.

"My time has come; the glory of God will soon surround me, and God shall receive great praise because of all that happens to me. And he shall give me his glory, and this is so very soon. Dear, dear children, how brief a time before I must go away and leave you. Then, though you search for me, you cannot come to me. Just as I told the Jewish leaders, and so I am giving a new commandment to you now, love each other just as much as I loved you. Your strong love for each other will prove to the world that you are my disciples."

Love. Yes, God, I felt love tonight. When he washed my feet, I felt he loved me. I even understood a little of what he was saying about returning that love to others. When I pause to think about what he just said, I realize it's a hard thing to do. Maybe it's not so hard to say that I love Jesus, but what about John, James, and Matthew at times, and what about the Pharisees and the high priest? Certainly, he doesn't expect me to love them, too, does he? Or *does* he?

Love. If he really loves me tonight, why does he talk about going away somewhere else? It sounds as if he is leaving us. He said we couldn't come, yet I have gone with him everywhere these past three years, even to the mount where he was transfigured. Why can't I go along this time...?

"Jesus, Master, where are you going?"

"Peter, you can't go with me now."

What does he mean I can't go with him now? Why I am even ready to die for him.

"Die for me, Peter? No, three times before the cock crows tomorrow morning you will deny that you even knew me."

No, God, no – a thousand times no! I will die for Him. I know I will. What is he saying? Doesn't he even trust me? Haven't I proved my love to him yet? What does he think I am, a doubled-minded man? His words have hurt me. I thought he had reason to trust me. What does he mean that I will deny that I ever even knew him? Why, I left my father's home, and I left the fishing nets of Galilee to be with him! I would never deny him, never God, never...

He will see, for I will show him. I wonder why he gave me that piece of bread after he handed the first piece to Judas. I wonder what he meant when he said that the one who would betray him would receive bread dipped in the sauce. Why did he say I would deny him? Every time I think I am beginning to understand him, something like this happens. I wonder what Andrew is thinking tonight. I wonder what happened to Judas who hasn't returned yet. I wonder where Jesus is going that I can't go with him. I love him, but he has left me wondering so many things tonight. I guess that time will tell and that one day I will understand.

DISCUSSION QUESTIONS

1. In the story above, Peter reflects on how special the Passover was to him in his years. Discuss how Christmas, Easter, birthday celebrations, or some other special family time creates remembrances for you of the earlier years of your life. What makes these times so special to people?

2. The story suggests that Simon (Peter), even after three years of walking with Jesus, seeing all he did and hearing all he taught, was still confused at times trying to figure Jesus out. [This story occurred before the resurrection of Christ and Pentecost.] Describe what you think might have been some of Peter's thoughts as he reflected on the three years he had spent with Jesus. Do you think he had reason to wonder at times about who Jesus was, even though he had experienced so much?

3. Even though, after the experience on the Mount of Transfiguration, Jesus talked about his impending death, do you think Simon (Peter) or any of the other disciples really grasped how true the words of Jesus were, or how close his death really was?

4. The story portrays Jesus as sometimes making Simon (Peter) – and probably the other disciples – uncomfortable because of his nature and person. Do you think it is accurate to say that Jesus did at times create feelings of uncertainty or confusion in the minds of the disciples?

5. Why do you think Simon (Peter) felt uncomfortable with Jesus washing his feet, and why did he object to that?

6. What do you think we can learn about Simon (Peter) as a person when, after at first objecting to Jesus washing his feet, he went on to ask Christ to wash not just his feet but his hands and head as well?

7. What do you think might have been some of Simon (Peter)'s thoughts when Jesus said that they were to wash one another's feet just as he had washed their feet? Do you think any of the disciples might have felt some reservation when they thought of people they didn't like or struggled to get along with?

8. Describe what you think Simon (Peter) might have felt – or any of the other disciples for that matter – when Jesus said that one of them was going to betray him.

9. Describe what you think any one of the disciples might have thought and felt as they watched Jesus dip the bread after he had said that the one who would betray him would be given that piece of bread?

10. Describe what you think the mood might have been in the Upper Room the night of the Last Supper. In doing so, try to think about positive and negative happenings of that night that might have contributed to the way the disciples were feeling.

11. It is obvious that the disciples never understood that Judas was the betrayer. They all thought he had left the room to care for some business related to the feast. If that were the case, to what extent do you think they all still found themselves wondering about the idea that one of them was going to betray Christ?

12. Describe how you think Simon (Peter) might have felt when Jesus told him he was going deny him three times that very

night? How do you think the others felt about the statement that Jesus made to Simon (Peter)?

13. During the dialogue in the Upper Room, Jesus told the disciples that he was leaving, and they couldn't go with him. After they had forsaken all to follow him, how do you think that statement made them feel?

8

PETER WEEPS IN THE GARDEN

A Psychological Bible Study
John 18: 15-18
As told by an unnamed observer.

> *"And immediately the cock crowed. Then Peter remembered that Jesus had said "Before the cock crows, you will deny me three times... And he went away, crying bitterly."*

It's been a cold night, Peter, and a long and anxious one. Although you may not have realized it, I have been watching you through the passing hours. It's those tears, and the remorse and bitterness you're feeling. Do you remember John and his ministry on the banks of the Jordan River? He often preached in those earlier years about repentance, sorrow for sin and the need to repent of it to be fit for the Kingdom of God.

Many things have happened in these past three years since you first met this Jesus. You remember when you were cleaning your nets, and Jesus walked up beside you and cried out to you and your brother, *"Come, follow me, I will make you fishers of men."* I was on the shore that day and heard him call you and saw the look on your face. I wondered what you would do. You see Peter, that call to follow him also pierced my own soul. I too have heard him say, *"Come, follow me and I will make you a fisher of men."* I noticed how quickly you responded. I wasn't so certain, not sure at all that I was ready to respond as quickly as you did.

It's strange, Peter, but there is something compelling about Jesus. Once you see him, your life is never quite the same again. From that first moment when I really began to understand that this was God's Son, I could never forget. How often, when I would hear him say, *"Come, follow me,"* I wished I had responded as quickly as you did back then.

You met him that day for perhaps the first time, or at least it was the first time I had seen the two of you together. I can still remember that hour when, like you, I finally decided to leave the past and begin to follow this strange Galilean. I certainly didn't understand it all, but there was just something special about him.

Peter, you have been chosen to be one of the twelve. I have walked in the shadows, observing your life and your relationship with Jesus Christ. I have seen how your love for Jesus has grown. But I have also seen the weakness of your life that has brought you to this moment of bitterness and tears.

There were times when I drew very near to our Christ, perhaps not physically close like you, but I drew close in my heart and soul. Then there were times when I would find myself among those other followers who "followed afar off." In fact, there were times when I wondered whether I was following at all. As you do now, Peter, I felt so completely alone, so miserable, and empty inside. I could never quite forget him, and it seemed that from time to time he would come so close again and say, *"I still love you and I want you to love me."* I felt so warm to know that he still cared, but so miserable to realize that in my own soul I had moved so far from him.

Peter, think back to those earlier years. I remember standing there one day, watching out across the sea of Galilee. You had been fishing. This same Jesus came and wanted to use your boat, and you let him. He taught the people, you recall, and there was something enthralling about his ways. It wasn't only the way he taught. It was him! He spoke as one who had authority, and you knew that he was more than a mere man. I too felt that way. I didn't always know what it was, but one thing was for sure: when I was with him, I felt so unworthy and unholy. I knew that so much of what I did was the opposite of what I saw in him.

Remember that day on the mount when we sat at his feet and listened to him teach. He said so many wonderful things. He told us how we ought to love our enemies. I could only think about the many times I felt full of bitterness and hate. He told us that we ought to pray and be the salt of the earth, but I know, even as he shared these life-changing principles, I felt that the kind of life I lived would never meet that standard. He even said, *"be perfect as my father in Heaven is perfect."* I stood there in all my imperfection and felt so guilty.

Peter, I remember your reaction. It was out there in the boat a bit later when he performed a miracle and calmed a terrible storm that was threatening to sink the boat you were in. You were moved, Peter, and you stood there... until finally you had to fall on your knees before him. I still remember those words, *"Master, leave me, I am too sinful to be in your presence."*

I understand why you responded that way. There were times when he drew near to me that I felt so torn inside. I couldn't understand his love, but I knew I needed it. I wanted it more than anything else. But like you, there was all that sin making me feel so unworthy to stand in his presence. In that moment, I began to understand and to feel what real love was. In all my unworthiness, he still loved me, he still stayed, and he still cared. Like you, Peter, I *had* to follow him. My whole heart began to reach out. What about the horrible guilt of my sin? I just told him of my worthlessness and began to reach towards him.

Do you remember what it was like, Peter? In that moment, he just opened his arms to accept you. I remember the moment when I felt him reaching out to touch me. I vowed that day never to leave him again, and I meant it. Just like you a few months ago, I wanted to stay there on the mountain with Christ, to build a tabernacle there.

I have been watching you over the years. I often wondered what you must have felt like on those occasions when he rebuked you in front of the others. You were wrong Peter, but I really believe you thought you were right. I can understand. I too remember how I often rationalized my wrongs and tried to find natural reasons for the things I did. But when he came close, I always knew that all my reasoning just did not stand up. Like you, it was as if he would say, *"Get behind me Satan!"* I know, Peter. I wanted to do what was right, but so often found that I was frustrated in my desire, because my actions were wrong, and the very sins that I had learned to detest, I found present in my life. Like you Peter, I too have often said, *"Lord I will do anything for you. I will even die for you,"* and I meant it. I think you did as well.

I learned something from your life last night. I watched you there in the courtyard. You didn't know it, but I saw that young girl as she came near to you and began questioning you. I wondered what you would do. It's that pressure of being different, isn't it? Of standing alone, being persecuted, talked about, knowing that honesty now would mean rejection and scorn to come.

Peter, I think I can understand why you said, *"I have never known him."* I also think I know how you felt inside, for I have felt that way so often. I wanted to love him with all my heart and all my soul, with everything I had inside of me, but many times I found myself doing as you did, denying him and yielding to the pressures of my own fears and doubts. You were miserable last night. I could see it written all over your face. So was I. Only God knows how true this was of both of us! Like you, I didn't want others to know what was really going on inside. Like you, Peter, I just kept warming my hands while my heart was in confusion and doubt. It's a horrible experience! Deep inside, I really wanted to be there with him. I wanted to share his life and if need be, even his death, but it seemed that something just stood in the way. There was still a part of me that would not yield. I have often tried to understand it, but I could not.

Last night, the others helped you to confront yourself and see who you really are. It was painful wasn't it, Peter? If your heart was like mine, it was being torn in two. I loved him, Peter, and I wanted to serve him and walk with him more than I wanted anything else in the whole world. I don't think I have ever loved anybody or anything as much as him in all my life. I never knew before what it meant to be willing to do anything, to be so completely obedient in spirit. Yet, like you, there was an awful realization that even though I wanted to be true with all my heart, I was not doing it. I was unable to accomplish it to the degree that I longed to do.

I loved him, Peter, but I doubted, and I sinned, and I found my love so impure and so shallow as I saw the demonstration of his love. Last night I was watching as he walked out of that hall. You remember, he was already showing the signs of physical pain. But even in his personal agony, I could feel how much he loved us. His face still bore his look of love. He loves us, Peter, and we failed him so miserably last night. When he needed us most, we all left him! He told us we would scatter like sheep without a shepherd, but we never believed him. He was so alone and yet he loved us. I saw him coming down the hall, and I noticed the look on your face.

Your love for Him was still there, Peter, I could tell because it was written all over your face. I remembered my experience as well. It was awful: those months and then those last days as I waited and longed for him. I wanted him so much. I wanted just once more to be sure that I was his follower and to know that our relationship was what it ought to be, but I felt so far away. I had tried, Peter, but somehow, he seemed so distant. I really wondered if I would ever see him again, or if I had finally walked so far at a distance that he was gone forever. Perhaps you felt like that as well. I think that maybe you did, as you warmed yourself there beside the fire last evening. Not just once, but three times you denied him. Each time, it was like a knife cutting into your soul. There was just something there that made you go against everything you knew to be right.

I watched you, as they led him out. Perhaps it was the look on your face, or the shifting of your body. I shall never forget that look. Remember, as you stood there by the fire, he looked right at you. He singled you out and looked deep into your soul. I remember because he saw me too. He looked right into me too. I knew in that moment that I stood before him without any front or excuse. He knew it all, and then I knew that I wanted him more than anything else in my life. Nothing else mattered. The way He looked at us caught it all. I have never seen anything like it before or since. It pierced my very soul.

The rooster crowed, you remember, for the second time last night. Just as he looked at you, the words came flooding back into your soul, just as he had said the night before. Not just once, but three times you had denied him, but it was that look that he gave you. It was still the look of love. I could see it as well. His heart was breaking, and he was deeply hurt. You could see it in his eyes and in his expression, but beneath all that, you could feel it again, as if he were silently saying, *"I love you anyway."*

I think, Peter, that you must have felt as I felt. Never in all my life have I been so broken. Never have I ever wept like that. For like you, I wept bitterly. Only God knows how broken I felt. Weep on, my friend, weep in remorse, weep in repentance. I did too! The hours passed. I prayed, I confessed, I told him everything. I opened my heart for the first time in years and it just poured out of my soul. The others that stood nearby didn't matter. Nothing else mattered now. He understood the cries of my soul. At first, they were bitter tears of remorse, but it wasn't long until they became tears of joy. Before, I never really knew what it meant to repent like this. I thought I did, but now I understood for the first time in my life what real sorrow is.

True repentance became a sweet balm for my soul. I learned that Jesus was nearby. The hours passed. I was being honest with him and with myself in a way that I had never experienced before. I was beginning to really see who and what I was and, Peter, I didn't like it! Those tears, those bitter tears… but then I heard him say, *"It was for those tears that I died."* Then those tears became sweet again. He looked at me again, and they turned into tears of joy and peace.

That second look reached into the very core of my being. It was as if I heard him say, *"Son, it's alright, I understand."* But more than that, he assured me that it need not be like that any longer, that he was going to send the Comforter, that I might have the power to walk with him, not far off as before, not as in the garden beside the fire. But this time Peter, we will walk together to the very end of the world.

For the first time in my life, I was truly free. I had walked with him, like you did, only for me, Peter, it was not just for three years but for longer than I care to remember. I may have wept bitterly that night, but let's remember, there is a day of resurrection coming and even beyond that, there's Pentecost. Tonight, weep on, weep until you know that every part of your soul has been opened to him, until there is nothing left. Weep, Peter, until he gives you that second look that no longer pierces your soul with guilt, but that says, *"I freely forgive."*

Peter, it's been a long, cold night, but even now I feel the warmth of acceptance, assurance, and forgiveness, and I feel the dawn beginning to come.

DISCUSSION QUESTIONS

1. This story is told from one observing Peter's reactions and finding points of identity with him and his experiences. As you read this story, did you see any places that you felt you could identify with Peter?

2. The story contains the account of Jesus calling Peter and his becoming one of his followers. Share briefly how it was that Jesus brought you to Himself.

3. This story talks about some of the high and the low point of Peter's spiritual. Share some of the high points in your Christ experience and perhaps some of the low moments.

4. When you did experience some low moments, how did God help you. Were there any particular people that He brought into your life at those times?

5. The admonishment to "love our enemies" is embedded in this story. Share a time when you really struggled with someone and how God helped you work through that experience.

6. Share a time when you felt especially close to God, when you sensed his love in a unique or special way.

7. Peter betrayed Christ out of fear. Can you relate to his experience? Was there a time when you struggled with identifying yourself as a follower of Christ?

8. This story is different than many of the others. It is more personal and introspective in nature. How did you feel when

you were reading this story? What were some of the emotions you felt?

9

JAMES

A Man of Ambitious Zeal

Note: This story is being told as if the interviewer were talking to John, the brother of James, who shares experiences and insights concerning his brother. Though the Bible is not clear, there seems to be strong reason to believe that Salome, the mother of James and John, was a sister to Mary, the mother of Jesus, making James and John first cousins to Jesus. This is a position taken by several scholars. This story embraces that possibility.

I am more than glad to talk about my brother, James. In fact, I never tire of talking about him. I only wish that he were still alive for you to interview in person, but he died far too young, having hardly experienced more than four decades of life. I must always remind myself of the old saying that it isn't the length of one's life that counts, but how one lived it that really matters. If I use that as my criterion for the definition of a good life lived by a good man, my brother James stands tall in my eyes.

We enjoyed a good home life, loving and being loved by our Parents, Zebedee and Salome. Like so many people in our village of Capernaum, we were fishermen. Perhaps you would better understand our family life if you understood the context of our trade. I will try to avoid political statements which, apart from providing background to our way of life, would probably serve no one well. Our industry is highly controlled rather than being run on a free market philosophy. It seems that the economy of our area and, I suspect, throughout the whole of the Roman Empire, is a system that serves the interests of the powerful. We are regarded as little more than peasant fishermen, and we are given no say or control over the fees we pay for our fishing licenses, or the taxes imposed on our daily catch. We also have no say on the toll fees we must pay to transport our fish to one of the many markets in the area or to the fish processing plant at Magdala. There is very little we can do to rise above our humble position in the scheme of life in the eyes of the more elite and even of the religious leaders who themselves seem to have so much control over our Jewish society.

Don't get me wrong, everyone knows that we provide an essential service that meets a critical need for fish, a staple food for our whole population. In that sense, we have a secure profession, but security doesn't elevate our social standing. Most of us are not highly educated. To say that we are not the most refined and polished of men would be a true assessment. It is certainly true of me. I think that most of the upper classes would see us as little more than country bumpkins or even ruffians, best left to ourselves. Perhaps the "Sons of Thunder" nickname that was given to my brother and me captures the essence of who and how we were. Of course, I realize that title was given to us because of our flaring tempers in our younger years, but to tell the truth, it speaks accurately of the general manner of so many of us who were fishermen. Just look at our friend Peter, for example, and you will soon notice his rougher edges.

As I am thinking about our social status, I can't help reflecting on how many of the twelve men chosen by Jesus to be his disciples were fishermen just like me. In fact, except for Matthew and Judas Iscariot, none of us were from the more respectable elements of our society. Through our business dealings over the course of time, our family had contact with and developed a working friendship with some of the higher levels of society in Judea. Our family fared well in the fishing industry and were some of the wealthier business people in our area, perhaps as wealthy as was possible at our level of society. Unlike so many others, our family business had expanded to the extent that we owned more than one fishing boat and needed hired workers to help us maintain our operation at the level that brought us this financial success.

My brother James was a highly motivated and ambitious person, and a rather outspoken individual. He was always ready to share his thoughts and stand up for what he believed. Perhaps that is what led, in part, to his early death as the second martyr of our wider Christian group. He was beheaded by Herod shortly after the death of Stephen. I think that James probably stepped on too many toes with his bold preaching and forthright manner.

But before jumping to the end of his story, I'll talk about my wonderful older brother's life. We were close friends with the family of Simon Peter and Andrew. Being first cousins of Jesus, we sometimes had family interactions with the young Master as we were growing up.

Sometimes I wonder why my brother and I, along with Simon Peter, were selected by Jesus to be in his more intimate group of disciples. On several occasions, we were chosen to experience some very special moments in the life of the Master. We were present at the raising of the dead daughter of Jairus. We accompanied Jesus during that sacred moment in the Garden of Gethsemane as he prayed on the last night of his life. But above all else, it was the three of us who were with him on the mountain when Elijah and Moses came! We saw the very glory of Heaven itself displayed before our very eyes! It was so wonderful that we wanted to stay there forever! Why did Jesus choose us for those experiences? Was it because of our family connections? Or was it because of our character and person? Perhaps it was a combination of the two that cemented our lives together in this special union. Or did Jesus have some reason and purpose of which we were unaware at the time?

I often wondered how the others thought and felt about the three of us and our apparent privilege of being allowed to witness some of the most remarkable moments in the life of the Master. At times, Peter's brother Andrew was included, but often it was just we three. Yes, I also wonder what Andrew thought and felt. At times part of the inner circle, did he feel excluded at other times when he was not? I wonder if he was content enough with doing his own ministry with the gifts and in the place that God had given him and knew his worth through that.

But let's talk about the raw material of our personalities that must sometimes have been a handful for Jesus to deal with. Do you remember how angry James and I became after some of the Samaritan people spurned us and kicked us out of their village? We could only see this as a rejection of us as persons and of the message we were trying to bring to them. Looking back on that incident now, I would have to say that we reacted like two hotheads. We brought our anger to Christ and said, *"Lord, do you want us to call down fire from heaven to burn them up?"* Shaking his head at our pitiful attitude, Jesus just looked at us and reminded us that he had come not to destroy men but to save them.

Then there was the time that our mother came to Jesus, asking that the two of us be given a special place in His Kingdom, one to sit at his right hand and the other at his left. To be fair to my mother, as his cousins we were the only two of the twelve that were blood relatives of Jesus. Perhaps my mother felt that blood ran thicker than water, and that we, above the rest, had a closer connection and therefore a more natural right to such an honor.

I can tell you that our mother's request didn't sit well at all with the other ten disciples! It was something that James and I had to live down for a long time. To be quite honest, there were always squabbles and tensions among us over who would be the greater in the Kingdom of Heaven. Nothing, not even our suspicion that this must have annoyed Jesus, ever put an end to our bickering, at least until Pentecost. Even on the final evening as we gathered in an upper room, the last night we would spend together with Jesus, this hankering after prominence was still on our minds.

That day when my mother asked for a special place for us in Heaven, Jesus put a personal question to James and me: *"Can you drink from the cup that I am going to drink?"* Somewhat nonchalantly, we vowed that we were able to do that. Looking back, I realize how little we understood! How shallow our answer was! James would be the first of us to taste the bitter cup of death, living only another fourteen or fifteen years after that day.

If James were still alive and available for you to talk to in person, I think he would say, as do I, that the day on the mountain with Jesus, Moses, and Elijah was the most significant single event we ever experienced in all the years we walked with Jesus. I will never forget that day, and I am sure my brother carried the glow of it with him until he took his last breath. Perhaps, as the executioners readied themselves to behead him, the remembrance of that glorious experience of glimpsing into Heaven buoyed up his spirit with a vision of a coming glorious reality that took away the fear of the sword and the dread of his impending death.

Those were good years for both of us, but we were thorny stalks in a prickly bunch. Change didn't come overnight; refinement of character was a slow process. That is, until the day of Pentecost, the unique event in all our lives that brought about the greatest change of all. From then on, we understood why Jesus had told us to wait for the coming of the Holy Spirit upon our lives.

I think for some of us, Pentecost was an emboldening experience, giving us new courage to step up and out where we were once hesitant. But for James and me, it may have had the opposite effect. Our need was more for sedation than greater animation in life! When I think of my brother before Pentecost, I would say that he could be impulsive, outspoken, easily provoked to anger, with hair-trigger responses. In some ways he and Peter were similar, although Peter tended to limit himself just to speaking and acting impulsively. My brother, and I to a lesser extent, lent a more deliberate tone to our outbursts, reflecting something of our untamed spirits.

Jesus, as you know, was crucified and buried, but rose again from the dead. We were all there, except for Judas the betrayer, and we watched Jesus ascend into Heaven. Then, as I mentioned a moment ago, we did as He asked us to do and waited in Jerusalem for the coming of the Holy Spirit. His coming worked a spiritual transformation in us all. Some became bolder and more outgoing, others more refined and controlled. Each of us was empowered to carry out the work that Christ was asking us to do.

On the day when Jesus Christ was taken back into Heaven, he told us we were going to be his witnesses, starting right at home in Jerusalem and fanning out into all the world. My brother was faithful to that commission, never relinquishing nor lagging in any way as he carried out the divine command. He served his Savior well for the next fourteen years of his life.

In the providence of God, I am still alive. Since the death of my brother, the first of the twelve to die for Christ, several other members of our group have also met untimely deaths. I won't go into that now, but we could talk about that later. I remember how hard it was for me when I was told about my brother's death. I missed him so greatly that it seemed as if a part of me had died as well, my deep grief lingering long afterwards. Of course, along with my keen sense of loss, I was able to rejoice when I thought about the new life James was enjoying, his fiery disposition tempered, and his rough corners smoothed. In my mind, I pictured him in Heaven, not only seeing Jesus, Elijah and Moses as we had done here on Earth, but this time, he was included in the conversation!

DISCUSSION QUESTIONS

1. As noted in the opening comments of this story, many Bible scholars believe that James and John may have been first cousins of Jesus, their mother and Jesus' mother being sisters. Assuming this might be true, do you think this had anything to do with James and John being part of the inner core of three that seemed to have a special place in the life of Christ?

2. When thinking about the possible blood (family) relationship that may have existed between Jesus and James and John, do you think this might have been the reason their mother set the two men up to request a special place in Heaven? Do you think she might have thought they were more worthy than the rest because of these family ties?

3. We know that several, perhaps six or even more of the disciples of Jesus were fishermen. This story tells about their social standing as one of the lower levels of society, seen as important but not socially acceptable among the more polished levels. Jesus talked often about the poor and identified much with common people rather than focusing his ministry on the rich and influential. What does the fact that so many of the disciples were fishermen (from a lower social status) tell us about Jesus, his attitude, and his ministry? What lessons might we learn from this in our own lives and ministry?

4. Woven into the story is an overview of the political structure at the time of Christ. In this system, fishermen (and other lower classes) were locked into their social level by political control. There was little they could do to rise in status (almost a type of caste system). How does this relate to our society? What social

similarities and differences are there between the times in which they lived and the times in which we are living?

5. Thinking about question number 4, do you think the fact that they were locked into a social status in life made it easier to follow Jesus and leave their trade as fishermen, seeing this as a possible way to escape a system that was hard to rise above?

6. Do you think the social milieu in which James and John lived had anything to do with their being brash, outspoken, and known as "Sons of Thunder"?

7. It appears that James and John were also very close friends with and possibly even business partners with Andrew and Peter. If so, and if James and John were possibly first cousins of Jesus, we can assume that they had a long-standing friendship and relationship as a group. We know that three of those four were part of the inner core of three that had experienced special times with Jesus during his ministry. How do you think this long-standing friendship and relationship might have affected their relationship with the other eight disciples? Do you think any of this played into the constant conflict the disciples had over who was the greatest in the Kingdom of Heaven?

8. We know that changes in life are often slow, a process taking time. Yet there was a marked change almost instantly and significantly in the lives of the disciples on the day of Pentecost. Discuss ways in which you see some of the disciples being changed slowly by natural processes and more suddenly and supernaturally by the infilling of the Holy Spirit?

9. The Bible says that Herod arrested James and ordered his execution. When he saw how this pleased the Jews, he had Peter

arrested as well. How much do you think the possibility that James, in his boldness, may have spoken against Herod might have had to do with his arrest? Knowing something about James and John's personalities as hotheads (Sons of Thunder), might that have played any part in James being perhaps bold and outspoken about Herod? Is there any possible parallel between Herod arresting James and his arresting John the Baptist for speaking against his marriage to Herodias?

10. When Jesus asked James and John if they were able to "drink from the cup from which he had to drink," referring to his death, they responded that they were able. How do you think John might have felt and thought about their response after his brother became the first of the twelve to be martyred?

11. In the story, it is stated that the transfiguration of Jesus Christ (with the appearance of Moses and Elijah) that Peter, James and John witnessed, may have been the single most influential day in their lives, at least in the three years of walking with Jesus (although Pentecost may have later superseded that day in importance). They all saw so much happen during their three years with Jesus: the raising of Lazarus, Christ walking on the sea, the feeding of thousands from hardly anything, etc. Do you think it was accurate to say that the transfiguration experience might have stood above all the rest?

12. In the course of time, all the other disciples were martyred and John alone lived to old age and died as an old man. His brother was the first to die, he the last. How do you think John might have felt and thought in the later years of his life as he pondered the death of James and all the others?

13. Share your overall feelings about James as a person? What do you see as some of his strengths and weaknesses? Are there any ways in which you can identify with James?

10

MATTHEW

Saved from Himself
Matthew 9:9-13

I will gladly share my story with you. I suppose others of our select group that are known as the disciples of Jesus would speak of the change that came to their lives when they met the Master. But perhaps I, more than all the rest, can say that my relationship with Jesus *saved me from myself*. At least that is how I feel when I look back on the life I once lived.

I was born in Galilee, as were the other disciples, except Judas Iscariot from Judea. For this reason, I shared many things in common with the other eleven, such as having lived and worked in Capernaum, being born and raised in a Jewish home, attending the synagogue school, and being trained in our Jewish ways. In those ways, I was no different from the rest, but my inquisitive mind motivated me to achieve a higher level of education than the others in our group. I mastered not only our ethnic languages of Aramaic and Hebrew, but I also spoke Greek fluently. There were times that my polylingualism was helpful, as we interacted with different cultural groups that inhabited or passed through Galilee. One big difference, however, separated me not only from my fellow disciples, but from all the rest of my fellow Jews. I was a tax collector.

I can't tell you exactly when the idea of becoming a tax collector first entered my mind. Of course, I knew what Jewish people thought about tax collectors. They were hated and despised. But I also realized something else about tax collectors: they were a wealthy group of men. Sometime during the earlier years of my life, money's appeal tugged on my heartstrings. I wasn't satisfied to work hard every day merely to make a meager wage or just sustain my life. I believed that I had greater potential than that. Now, since the Lord has helped me realign my priorities, I look back on my life and my attitudes and see how sinful and wrong they were. In fact, as I look back over the span of my life, I think it is fair to say that *the Lord indeed saved me from myself.*

The quest to become wealthy is never achieved. A man whose goal is to be rich never has enough, no matter how much he possesses. There is always a little more to be had. That desire for money began to shift my moral bearings and resulted in my learning how to twist things I once believed were wrong to become in some way morally acceptable. Indeed, I became a wealthy man, but my riches came at a high price.

My moral compass slowly became faulty as I began to give up the values that I had once held dear, the first being my sense of identity as a Jew. I was still a Jew at heart, to be sure, but in the eyes of almost all with whom I rubbed shoulders, I was not worthy of being called a Jew, not fit to be associated with them in any activities that gave us our national and religious identity. Although I basically worked for Rome, the Romans also considered me to be an ethnic outsider. So, although a Jew at heart and an employee of Rome, I felt like a man without a country as I went about my daily life. Even my own family rejected me, seeing me as a traitor not only to my nation but to my very kin as well. My fellow tax collectors were the only people with whom I could really feel at ease and be myself.

The world I walked out into every morning as I left my house, and that I experienced every hour of every day as I sat at my tax collector's booth, was one of constant cold glares, abusive language, expressions of hatred and rejection. I cannot find the words to describe how excruciatingly unpleasant it was to feel so shunned.

At first, I tried to hold onto my religious identity, maintain my temple connections, and not forsake my spiritual mooring. But this became almost impossible. It didn't take me long to realize that I was not welcome in the synagogue. There was no sympathy there for a tax collector and a Roman sympathizer. So, I quit going to the synagogue and finally gave up any spiritual pursuits, except for some feeble attempts at private adherence to faith in the seclusion of my own home.

So it was that I lived with epithets such as "collaborator with Rome, traitor to Israel, robber, thief, crook, swindler, unworthy to be called a Jew," although these were some of the better words used in my presence! Others are unrepeatable. I can't say that I ever got used to these insults. I just learned to build an emotional carapace around me and, to the best of my ability, insulate myself against the relentless vilification.

As I have already explained, no one wanted to be identified with me except for other tax collectors. When we were together, we could relax and enjoy our own bond of mutual understanding around our common wheeling, dealing and being reviled for our ways. This was a special "club" with membership limited to those of our kind. It was only here and in our own homes that we were spared from expressions of contempt.

My chosen career cost me my morality in other ways too. The system within which I worked bordered on dishonesty, and the key to my financial success was the ability to work that system. Rome allowed a tax collector to lawfully pocket fifteen percent of what was owed, but my Roman supervisors never cared how much more a tax collector took from his own people as long as Rome received its dues. Increase the amounts and take twenty percent, twenty-five, why not? The more I take, the more I have. Rome turned its face the other way, and my fellow Jews couldn't do anything about it. I began to reason in my heart, *"Why not? A few extra dollars from each one won't hurt them, but it will help me achieve my goals in life."* Little by little, my moral compass was setting a new bearing as this way of thinking clouded my vision and motivation for living: push the deal to its limit to profit the most in the situation.

I am so glad that my story doesn't end there! This might have been the story of my whole life if it hadn't been for Jesus. Yes, let me say it again. *I needed to be rescued from myself,* and I don't believe there was anyone else that could have changed the course of my life if not for Jesus. I had attained a level of material ease, but now that I have been freed from my former life, I have come to realize how dearly I paid for what I wanted my life to be.

Without wanting to brag, I think I had some things to offer to people and, eventually, to use for the Kingdom of God as well. I believe I have a keen mind, am adept with figures and am a capable businessman. I know how to think, analyze, and organize well. And, even though it came by questionable means, I had been quite successful in my business as a tax collector. I was, in fact, quite a wealthy man.

But I wasn't necessarily a happy man, for there was an emptiness in my soul. Money cannot buy everything, and I had a deep yearning for something more significant and satisfying in my life.

As I sat there daily at the tax booth, I would hear news and gossip as people passed the time of day. They had begun talking about a teacher and miracle worker who was now living among us. His name was Jesus from Nazareth. I didn't think much of it at first, but the more I heard, the more evidence there seemed to be that his teaching was new. That piqued my curiosity. As I was hearing from others about the change he was making in their lives, I desired to hear him for myself. Something was happening in my soul. Maybe my emptiness and longings were becoming a search, but I didn't dare believe that this new teaching could in any way be an answer for me, a tax collector. I was still the scorned outcast living on the edge of society. Why, I thought, would he care about me?

The most transforming day in my life started out as any other normal day, normal that is, until Jesus walked up to my tax booth! He looked straight into my eyes in a way that made me feel that he saw into the deepest recesses of my soul. I felt uncomfortable at first, wondering what kind of harsh words would come from him, perhaps some condemnation of my avaricious way of life.

I shuffled a bit, trying to avoid his penetrating stare. I was already building up my emotional defenses for what I expected to come my way... but there were no harsh words, rebukes, or condemnation from this stranger. Gradually, instead of building up another layer of protection, I began to relax a little, my cold, hardened spirit warming in the rare presence of kindness. Even though he had not yet spoken a word, I sensed love and acceptance emanating from his spirit. What was this? His whole countenance was unlike that of any man that I had ever known.

He began to smile, and he spoke just three words: *"Come, follow me!"* Now I knew how to handle insults and abuse, but I didn't know how to respond to this kindness, love, and warmth of spirit that was melting my heart. It wasn't just his words, but it was his whole way of being that was removing any rampart of fear or rebellion that I might have wanted to raise in my soul.

It slowly began to dawn on me that this person did in fact want me, that I was important to someone outside of my small circle of professional friends. It was such a long time since I had felt wanted! This was also the first instance in such a long time that I had not felt dirty, but clean! It is hard to explain what happened next. I closed my book, stood up and walked away from my business and, as I would soon come to realize, from my whole former way of life.

I am sure all my friends wondered what had happened to me. Why, they thought, would he give up his rich life of ease to become an itinerant preacher? Of course, none of us realized at first what following Jesus was going to look like, but as we accepted Jesus' invitation to follow him, we were becoming a select group of men that became known to others as his disciples, or the "Apostles." It is a tremendous and humbling honor to bear those names and to know that we were chosen by Him to be his closest friends.

Would you be surprised if I told you that the first thing I did after I made that decision to follow Jesus was to host a large banquet for all my tax collector friends? I wanted to introduce them to Jesus. I never even gave a thought to whether he would want to attend this banquet. He was a Jew after all, and I was inviting him into a circle of "sinners." I was so excited and full of energy that I didn't even think about what he might feel about that.

He came to my banquet, and I think he enjoyed himself. I didn't detect in him any reservations or regret that he had accepted the invitation to eat with us. The religious leaders criticized him for coming, but their comments didn't seem to bother him at all. He just told them that he hadn't come to invite the righteous but sinners into his Kingdom.

Although it was not my intention when I organized my banquet, that event became something of a going away party for me. I would never again return to the tax booth nor to the secluded, emotional refuge of my marginalized group of friends.

I have already told you that I felt *"rescued from myself,"* rescued from my money-hungry way of life and my misplaced faith in the philosophy that "money talks."

For the next several years I went on to follow Jesus everywhere that he went, until the terrible day when He was crucified. But that dark time was followed by his glorious resurrection.

I have spent the rest of my life, even to this day, telling others about the man who saved me. I even wrote a book where I recorded many of our wonderful experiences with Jesus. I didn't want anyone to ever forget the words, actions and sacrifice of my Lord Jesus who came to this world to save sinners such as I. I am honored to be counted as one of his disciples and known as his follower. I know that one day my earthly life will be over, but I have no doubt that even on my death bed, I will be able to look back and say that ever since the day when he said, *"Follow me,"* my life has been truly worth living – rich, full, and abundant in every way.

DISCUSSION QUESTIONS

1. It seems that Matthew was different from all the other disciples. They were all "blue collar" workers, and he was more of a businessman. It also appears he may have been better educated than the rest. Do you think these differences were ever a source of problems or tension between him and the other disciples?

2. Knowing what we do about the social ostracism that came with being a tax collector, do you think the decision to become a tax collector was possibly a difficult one for Matthew to make? What do you think we can learn about him as a person, knowing that he made this decision to be a tax collector?

3. Knowing what we do about the life of a tax collector, what do you think might have been the hardest part of that lifestyle?

4. No mention was made in the story about the possible attitudes of the other disciples, at least at first, toward Matthew because of his former profession. Do you think there were initially some negative feelings toward him from the others, and that his vocational choice was the source of any personal tensions between him and the others?

5. How do you think Matthew might have felt about his being rejected from the synagogue?

6. What can we learn from Matthew about the pull of money in the life of a person?

7. The subtitle of this story is "Saved from Himself," and on several occasions the expression that he was being "saved from

himself" occurs. Do you think this is an accurate description, and in what ways was he "saved from himself"?

8. The statement was made in this story that no matter how much a man has, it is never enough, referring especially to those who are wealthy. Do you think this is an accurate statement and if so, how does that dynamic manifest itself in a person's life?

9. In what sense did Matthew's lifestyle require him to compromise and surrender some of his moral bearings in life?

10. What do you think life was like for Matthew (and other tax collectors) living with constant verbal abuse and being the recipients of the hate of their own people? How do you think they learned to live with this?

11. Do you think that some of the qualities of personality that made Matthew a successful businessman and tax collector were able to be used effectively as an Apostle? Give some examples of how this might have happened?

12. Knowing what we do about the life of a tax collector, how do you think Matthew might have felt and thought when Jesus said, "Follow Me"? What might have been some of his emotional responses to this invitation?

13. What do you think were the reasons he accepted that invitation and followed Christ?

14. Though many things may have played into Matthew's willingness to follow Christ, how much do you think the fact that Jesus was willing to accept him as a man and a fellow Jew may have been a part of that decision?

15. What do you think was Matthew's reason for and what motivated him to give the banquet and invite all his friends (other tax collectors) to come to that banquet where he introduced them to Jesus?

16. Do you think it bothered Matthew that Jesus was criticized by the religious leaders for attending the banquet?

17. Do you think Matthew ever missed anything about his former life as a tax collector, the comfort of living as a rich person and having material possessions, a secure job, et cetera?

11

JOHN

The Aged Apostle

Perhaps you didn't expect to see such an aged man, but you must remember that I am now in my nineties. I am unable to walk any longer and am dependent on others to carry me where I want to go. I am content to stay at home these days, except for being taken to the church to worship. I am humbled by the respect that is always given me as the sole surviving disciple of the Master, the last contact the world has with those of us who are often referred to as his disciples, or as some rightly call us, the Apostles.

Over the years, reports have slowly filtered back to us of the horrific martyrdom of all the others. My brother James was the first of our group to give his life for the Master. I never completely got over his death and I still miss him greatly, even at my advanced age. I do not know why, in God's sovereign will, I was spared a similar fate. It is true that they tried to take my life, but having other plans for me, God supernaturally spared me. Allow me to reflect on the wonderful life I have been given, not just to relive my past, nor to indulge in nostalgic geriatric ramblings, but to talk about how God changed and used me.

You already know about my early years, as you have read what James, my elder brother, had to say. I was the youngest of the family. For that matter, I was also the youngest of all the twelve disciples. All the others recognized that Jesus seemed to hold me just a little closer in his affections than the rest, and they often referred to me as the "one the Master loved." Maybe my youth had something to do with that. I cannot say that it didn't make me feel rather special, and I hope I didn't take advantage too often of that honored place.

Our home was loving and stable. My parents, Zebedee and Salome, always put the welfare of their children above everything else.

Of course, we were aware of our cousin Jesus, but he and his family lived in Nazareth and we in Capernaum, so we did not spend much time together in our youth. When I think back to the years before I got to know him, I do wonder what kind of a young man he was while he was growing into manhood.

In our culture it was expected that I would follow my father into the fishing business, and that is indeed how I began, but in many ways, I was no different from so many other young people who sense a restlessness stirring their heart. I could not clearly identify my aspirations but knew that I was longing for something greater and more fulfilling in life.

I heard through the grapevine that a prophet was preaching in the wilderness region of Judea, baptizing people in the Jordan River. Having asked my father for some time off, I went south to listen to this new preacher, taking my friend Andrew along, and together we walked about a hundred miles to listen to this young prophet that was creating a stir in all the land. We were both immediately captivated by John's preaching and became his "disciples," beginning a completely new chapter of life. For me, it was a spiritual rebirth as John's preaching touched my deep-seated longing. We remained there longer than we had planned.

This was followed by an unexpected but singular experience that would set the course for the rest of my life. Jesus came down to the River Jordan, and John the Baptizer was visibly moved to see him. *"Behold the Lamb of God,"* John said, *"the one that will take away the sin of the world."* I felt an inner confirmation of the truth of John's statement. I knew the Holy Spirit was speaking to my soul. At the time I could not have told you that it was the Holy Spirit, but I was convinced that Jesus was all that John said that he was. Both Andrew and I did not hesitate to become followers of Jesus. What a turnaround in our lives that brought! In a short time, we became part of the group of men who would remain with Jesus until He was crucified.

I was still a very young man, with most of my life still before me. On that day I began a remarkable journey that, although I did not know it, was going to transform me not only spiritually but emotionally as well. Today, they all call me the "Apostle of Love." The definition is accurate. As I talk, write, and interact with people, I seek to live out the principle of love in all that I do. That is what the Master wanted. He once said that we would be known as his disciples by the love we show to one another, and even to those who are our enemies.

Looking back from the vantage point of great age, to say that I mellowed over the years is an understatement! There was a reason that my brother James and I were called "the Sons of Thunder" as young men. It is well known that we wanted to call down heavenly fire on an inhospitable Samaritan town. Jesus rebuked us that day, and rightly so. I must confess that our angry outburst was not an isolated one, for there was also the time that I reported to Jesus that while out on a ministry assignment, I had forbidden a non-disciple to cast out demons in Jesus' name. Jesus had to remind me that those who are not against us are on our side. These are just two examples that give some insight into the younger John.

A transformation in our souls was needed before James and I could learn how to control our tempers. That came about as we learned to apply Christ's principles to our own lives, but the coming of the Holy Spirit on the day of Pentecost accelerated that transformative process. You cannot change a "son of thunder" into "an apostle of love" all by yourself. Such deep transformation is a work of God's Holy Spirit.

Another area of my life also needed a deep transformation if I was going to become the man I believed God wanted me to be. I needed to learn humility. Many remember our notorious request, at our mother's prompting, to be granted a special place of honor at the right and left hand of Jesus when He came into his kingdom. That sums up the young John! Now, I want to be known for my humble heart. Sometimes, I reflect on the words of King David who said, *"I would rather be a doorkeeper in the house of my God than to dwell with sinners."* I no longer covet a special place at Christ's right hand. My happiness is to know that I will soon be with him again.

Why did Jesus choose me to be special to him? I cannot say. Perhaps it was on account of my youth, or maybe some aspect of my temperament and spirit. In the same way, I cannot explain why Peter, James and I became an inner trio in the life and ministry of Jesus. We got to see and experience many special moments of which the other nine were not privileged to be a part. We were present when Jesus raised the daughter of Jairus from the dead, and I will never forget the day when we saw Jesus and his heavenly visitors, Moses and Elijah, transformed. We were the three disciples that Jesus took to be with him during one of the most intense and agonizing nights of his life in the Garden of Gethsemane.

We all agreed that the three years spent with Jesus were a special experience and time of learning. We had our ups and downs, moments of inexplicable awe and exaltation and of trouble and extreme discouragement. Through all our experiences, we learned, sometimes slowly, deep truths that Jesus wanted to instill in our hearts. Above all else, we learned to love unconditionally the one we called Lord. Lord was not the only term we used to describe him. Sometimes we referred to him as Rabbi, at other times as the miracle worker, but mostly we affectionately called him by his name, Jesus.

We had no idea how short our time with Jesus was going to be. I said that we had some difficult times, but for me no moment was heavier or more sorrowful than the day I stood with Mary, Jesus' mother, at the foot of his cross. Mixing inexpressible emotional agony and horror, it was one of life's dark moments, traumatic in its effects that the mind can barely assimilate and comprehend. Only the passing of time would bring healing to our souls.

I embraced the shaking and sobbing Mary, her heart wrenched and torn as she watched her son suffer an extreme form of torture that few are ever forced to endure. As he was dying, Jesus looked down at us from the cross. Love and tenderness softening his pain-ridden face, he commended his grieving mother into my care, a commission that I took very seriously. I cared for her as my own parent until her death.

After his death, we had to learn how to live without the Master. Even though I was the youngest, the others were noticing me. I was aware of growth in my heart towards emotional and spiritual maturity. Before long, I became a recognized leader – a "pillar" – in the growing congregation in Jerusalem. For a while, I ministered alongside Peter, enjoying some wonderful experiences together such as when we were instrumental in healing a lame man at Solomon's Porch in the Temple.

The two of us went together to Samaria to visit the new believers there. We were even thrown into prison together, but God quickly set us free.

Ultimately, we disciples scattered to different parts of the world, all remaining faithful to Jesus and finding ways to share his love and truth with others. It was difficult for me each time one of us was martyred. Finally, I was the only one left. As I grew older, I often wondered why God was sparing my life.

When I was arrested and sentenced to death, I thought that my time had come to join the others as a martyr too. I felt something like our friend Paul when he said he was torn between the desire to stay on this Earth to continue serving God, or to go and be with the Master which was far more desirable. However, in the end, I was exiled to the Isle of Patmos. Why, I wondered, should I be spared harsher persecution and difficulties?

My exile began during the reign of the Roman Emperor Domitian. Patmos is a small, rocky, barren, and desolate island where many criminals of Rome are sent to serve their prison terms by working in mines. This is no "paradise island." Nor was exile a pleasant experience, but I am not grumbling about our harsh living conditions in a cave. More than anything else, the isolation and separation from other believers were the most difficult aspects of exile.

It was during those dark and grim days of just trying to exist that I had one of the most blessed experiences of my entire life. It happened when I was worshipping alone on a Sunday "in the spirit," my soul focused on thoughts of my Savior, that Jesus himself came and talked to me!

Anyone who can fully grasp how hard life was on this island will understand why I began my account of Jesus' visit with these words: *"I, John, your brother and companion in the suffering and kingdom and patient endurance that are ours in Jesus."* However, I chose not to dwell on my human suffering, for I was given a vision of Heaven and saw what no mortals are ever privileged to experience on this side of eternity. The closest to this revelation was on the day so long ago when James, Peter and I saw Jesus, Moses, and Elijah in their heavenly state, but this time, I saw more than those two heavenly visitors; I was given a glimpse right into God's Heaven! People now call my description of the vision Jesus gave me "The Revelation," God's blueprint for the last days and our glorious future with God. Maybe this is the reason that God kept me alive, to have time to share this glorious revelation and my other writings about Jesus and what he taught me about life, love, and light with the churches as they face threats, challenges, and sufferings of their own.

DISCUSSION QUESTIONS

1. Do you think John may have pondered why he and he alone was spared and permitted to live to be such an old man? If so, do you think he may have felt any guilt at being the only one of the disciples who did not die as a martyr?

2. How do you think John felt about being the "one that Jesus loved"? How do you think the other disciples felt about the special attention Jesus paid to John? Do you think John ever took advantage of that special place he had in Christ's life?

3. There was a marked change in John's life from "the Son of Thunder" to the "Apostle of Love." This change certainly didn't happen all at once. In reflecting on John's long life, talk about some of the things that may have happened to help make this significant change in his life.

4. The story talked about the "restless spirit" John probably experienced in his younger years. Can you identify with this in your own life? If so, how did that "restless spirit" help you to become the person you are today? How do you think that "restless spirit" might have motivated John to make changes in his life?

5. What do you think we can learn about John as a person from his becoming a disciple of John the Baptist and his quick willingness to follow Jesus when John the Baptist pointed him out as "the Lamb of God"?

6. We know that pride was a problem for the young John (asking for a special place in Christ's Kingdom), yet at the end of his life we are told he was a humble man (according to his disciple

Polycarp). What may have contributed to this change of attitude and character?

7. John is known as the Apostle of Love and he wrote so much about love in all five of the Biblical books attributed to him. What may have been some of the factors that helped John focus on love as a part of his character? How is love really shown and lived out in the life of any of Christ's followers?

8. Try to envisage the part of the story when John and Mary stood at the foot of the cross during the crucifixion. How do you think John might have felt and what might have been some of his thoughts as he watched Jesus dying on the cross? What do you think he might have thought when Jesus committed Mary into his care from that day on?

9. We know that John quickly became a "pillar" in the Jerusalem church, working very closely with Peter for a time. What might have been some of the qualities that others saw in John's life that helped him to rise so quickly to this position of authority?

10. Do you think John being the youngest of all the disciples was in any way problematic for the other disciples, especially as he was rising so quickly to a predominant place in the life of the Jerusalem congregation?

11. It appears that Peter and John had very different personalities and character traits. Yet they were part of the inner core of three disciples while Jesus lived, and John and Peter formed a ministry team in the early years of the new church. In what way were their differences both a strength and a weakness in their relationship and their working together in ministry?

12. How do you think John felt and what might have been some of his initial thoughts when he was sentenced to be exiled on the Isle of Patmos? This was a place for some of the worst of Rome's criminals and a place of hard labor and very few comforts. It was probably expected that John would die on the island. Do you think John ever became discouraged or felt abandoned during his time of exile?

13. We know that in John's early years, he seemed to have struggled with pride. Do you think he had any problem with feelings of pride after he was "taken to heaven" and given all that we know now as the Book of Revelation?

14. Compare John's experience and possible reaction to seeing Heaven with Paul's experience when he "knew one who was taken into the third heaven," and then later said God gave him a "thorn in the flesh" so that he wouldn't become proud. We know that God had to do something to help keep Paul humble after that experience. Do you think God had to do anything special in John's life to make and keep him the humble man he was known to be?

12

PHILIP

The Pragmatist
John 1:43–51; John 14: 1-11

Please forgive me for my slow response to your questions. You have clearly picked up that I am a bit distant and slow to open myself up. I don't intend to be rude, nor do I lack interest in the questions of others. My initial holding back and the time I take to consider my responses will already tell you something about me. After all, that is what you want to know, isn't it? You want to better understand me as a person and to hear about my time spent with the Master.

Well, let me just start by saying that when you really get to know me, you'll find that I am a very practical person. You might call me a pragmatist, and you wouldn't be the first person to pin that label on me, because that part of my personality is quite evident to people. You might want to ask any of my three daughters about the kind of person I am, as I think they would all agree that what I am telling you is true. I am slow to trust others and to embrace anything new and different. My type – or quirk – of personality needs to be sure of something before I make a commitment to it. I have been that way all my life.

I cannot put my finger on anything in the earlier years of my life that helped form the personality that I have, nor do I see anything wrong with being a person that needs to know and understand before making an emotional or intellectual commitment.

I think you already know that I grew up in the city of Bethsaida, as did some of the other twelve men that followed and became the closest disciples of Jesus Christ during his three years of ministry. I grew up around Peter and Andrew and knew some of the others from my earliest years. If there was anything that distinguished me from the others, it was that I had come under more Gentile influence than they did. You'll remember that Galilee was a mixture of cultural groups. You are also aware that my name, Philip, is a Greek name, that I speak Greek and had developed a friendship with many Greek people that came to our area to live and work.

In other ways, I was no different from some of the others. We heard about a man who was preaching and baptizing in the Jordan River near where it merges with the Dead Sea. I was one of those who went down to hear him preach and spend some time with him. It took me a while to make up my mind about the legitimacy of his person and ministry, but in time I was convinced that he was a man sent from God. I became one of John the Baptist's disciples and I spent a considerable amount of time with him on the shores of the Jordan River. While I have explained that I need to think about what I choose to believe and do, once I am convinced that something is true and worthy of my commitment, I will stick with it to the end. I don't see myself as fickle but rather as a trustworthy person you can count on as a loyal friend.

As far as my relationship with Jesus is concerned, I still remember the day that I first met him. John was preaching, and Jesus came and asked John to baptize Him. Usually, I would have been hesitant to accept that Jesus was "the Lamb of God," that John proclaimed him to be, but by this time, I had such an unshakable trust in John and what he said that his endorsement of Christ was enough to give me an instant assurance that he was indeed who John said he was.

Planning on returning to Galilee, Jesus came by where I was standing and said, *"Follow Me!"* You can be sure that I was far too cautious to be swept off my feet by some fly-by-night evangelist or preacher! Usually, I would have taken a good look at all the data I could find about a person and weigh the pros and cons before deciding to accept such an invitation. So, what I did next came as a surprise even to me.

As I look back on it now, I think it was a combination of John's endorsement and something about the person of Jesus Himself that gripped my heart without much forethought on my part. That was so unlike me! I must tell you that it wasn't I who found Jesus; it was he who found me. I immediately did as Christ had asked, and I have never turned back from that decision.

I was so convinced that he was the Lamb of God that John had said he was, that the first thing I did was to go and find my friend Nathanael, whom we sometimes called Bartholomew. I was excited about my new discovery and immediately I told him, *"We have found the one Moses wrote about in the Law, and about whom the prophets also wrote – Jesus of Nazareth, the son of Joseph,"* That happened many years ago, but I recall my disappointment at Nathanael's response. He just looked at me doubtfully and said, *"What good thing can come out of Nazareth?"*

There was a time when Nathanael's statement might have caused me to do some further investigation, driving me to prove that I could be sure that Jesus was who John claimed him to be. Not this time! I was utterly convinced that He was indeed the promised one. All I said to Nathanael was, *"Come and see for yourself!"* I didn't try to convince or persuade him, I just challenged him to come and make up his own mind about who Jesus was, just as I had done. Nathanael too would be convinced that my initial evaluation of Christ was correct, and he also became one of the group of twelve who became Jesus' closest disciples.

I had so much to learn after I started following Jesus that day. After my initial encounter with Jesus, we often talked together. I had many down to earth questions for him, and He patiently answered them all. I grew in so many ways, and as the years passed, believing became easier. However, my cautious nature remained.

For example, I remember the day when we were with Jesus as he taught a very large crowd. I recall that there were about 5,000 men plus all the women and children. By the end of the day, we knew they would be hungry, and something had to be done. Either we had to send them home or take responsibility for feeding them. Jesus asked us how much food we had. Almost instantly, my questioning and heedful mind began reasoning, quickly leading to my conclusion that no matter how much food we had, it would not be enough to feed this huge crowd of people. Andrew brought a little boy who had a sack lunch with him: some bread and a couple of small fish. Jesus turned to *me*, not to

Andrew who had brought the young boy to Him, but to me, and he asked me a very practical question. *"Where are we going to buy bread enough for all these people?"* My first thought was, we can't, we don't have the financial resources available to us to buy enough food for this massive crowd. Then another thought flashed through my mind – that Jesus, I thought, agreed with me that the little boy's lunch was not worth mentioning. It seemed to me to be so logical. I wondered, however, why he had put that question to me rather than to Andrew. I hope that by now I have matured enough to realize that this was not a question that required a practical answer from a man with a personality that always needed to reason things out, but it was asked with the intention of moving me beyond the practical realm to that of faith.

My response to Jesus' question was that it would take more than half a year's wages to buy enough bread for each one to have just a bite! How much more practical could I be than that? It seemed to me to be just an obvious statement of fact.

You can't imagine my amazement at what happened next! Jesus took that little boy's lunch and with it fed the entire mass of people. There was nothing "practical" about what Jesus did. What I saw unfold before me that day was a leap from the doable to the impossible!

That is just one of so many stories I could tell that happened as we accompanied Jesus over three years. A tremendous time of growth in my life, those years passed so quickly, and our time with Jesus was ending. It was near the close of his earthly life that something happened on what many now call Palm Sunday.

A group of Greeks wanted to see Jesus but they couldn't get near him. They came to me asking for help. You ask, why me? Well, that was not a surprise. As I mentioned, I had a Greek name, I spoke Greek, and I already had connections with the Greek community in Galilee. So, it was quite natural for them to come to me first. But my personality would again stand in the way of solving their problem of finding a way to get them to see Jesus. I immediately perceived two difficulties. First, I saw the same thing they saw, the large crowds that prevented us from getting near to Jesus. I was ready to give up before starting, recognizing that we had a problem too large to solve. Then secondly, I remembered that Jesus had told us that he had come only for the household of Abraham, not to have a ministry to the Gentiles. So, I approached Andrew with my problem and doubts. Andrew wasted no time in finding a way to get them to meet Jesus. He succeeded where I saw only an impossibility.

Perhaps I can share about another time that helps illustrate what I have been telling you today. It happened only a few days later, when we had all gathered with Jesus in an upper room for the last Passover feast that we would share together.

Jesus was talking to us that night about his leaving us and going to Heaven. He imparted precious counsel about another comforter, the Holy Spirit, that he was going to send. Jesus was talking about knowing the Father when Thomas interrupted him with a question we all had, *"How can we know the way if we don't know where you're going?"* Jesus answered him with these words, *"I am the way and the truth and the life. No one comes to the Father except through me. If you really know me, you will know my Father as well. From now on, you do know him and have seen him."*

Those words had barely crossed his lips when my practical mind began wondering how all this could be possible. Why, I wondered, was he talking about going to the Father, about knowing the Father, and what did he mean when he said that *"we had seen him"*? I had never seen him, nor had any of the rest of us, I reasoned. So, I made what I felt was a very constructive request, *"Show us the Father and we will ask no more."* Could there be anything more practical than *"show us the Father"*? Just two simple words seemed to me to summarize it all, *"Show us!"* That was how it was with so much in my life: *"Show me! Prove it to me! Do it or show it in a way that makes common sense! Deal with us in a way that is visible, tangible and totally explicable and practical!"* *"SHOW US THE FATHER,"* I said. Nothing more, nothing less, and that will satisfy us.

The answer Jesus gave was so simple, so practical, so down to earth – just like my request. He said, *"Look at me. Anyone who has seen me has seen the Father."* Remember the feeding of the 5,000, Philip. Remember the raising of Lazarus from the dead. Remember the many miracles I performed in your presence. Remember the healing of the sick and the casting out of the demons. *"Philip," he said, "you have seen me, you have seen the Father!"*

I have tried to be as honest as I could with you today about my life and the kind of person that I am. But there is one more thing that I need to say. All that I have told you happened many years ago, and during the years since then, I have remained loyal to Jesus Christ. I have served him with all my heart and soul, and He has worked through me in so many ways in his Kingdom, showing that Jesus can use people like me for His glory. My personality is not a hindrance, but just a different tool in His hands to reach a certain group of people that perhaps have personalities like mine. If it is not rooted in lack of faith, such commitment to honest enquiry and examination of the facts can become the foundation for a true, deep, and abiding faith. When my probing mind has sought answers and reached a conclusion, I have such a strong reason for what I believe that Hell itself cannot shake it.

DISCUSSION QUESTIONS

1. Having read (or listened) to this story, discuss the role between reason and faith. When is faith without reason dangerous and when is the need to "know" before believing dangerous?

2. When viewing the ministry of Jesus while he lived on earth and the interplay of the disciples with Jesus, what do you think a personality type like Philip's might have added to the interaction between the disciples? What kind of a contribution do you think Philip might have made to the group?

3. Philip had a Greek name, perhaps spoke Greek, and it was to him that the Greeks came when wanting help to see Jesus. Do you think this set him apart in any way from the others? Do you think this gave him a special role among the twelve in any way?

4. What are some of the advantages to having a personality like Philip's? What are some of the disadvantages?

5. Do you think it a bit "surprising" that Philip was so quick in responding to Jesus asking him to "follow him"? What do you think might have been some of the factors that led up to and prepared him for his uncharacteristically quick response to Jesus' invitation?

6. How do you think Philip might have initially felt when he told Nathanael about Jesus and he received Nathanael's negative response asking what good thing can come out of Nazareth? How do you like and what do you think about Philip's short answer, "Come and see for yourself"?

7. We know that Philip at first questioned their ability to feed the "five thousand." He correctly noted that they didn't have enough money to buy even a taste of food for this many people. What do you think might have been some of Philip's first thoughts when the food began to multiply and when they were able to feed that large group of people?

8. What might have been some of Philip's first thoughts when he saw the young boy's lunch and realized that was all the food they had?

9. Even though it was Andrew who brought the young boy to Jesus, it was to Philip that Jesus addressed the question about how they were going to feed the crowd. Why do you think Jesus might have specifically singled out Philip for this question rather than putting it to Andrew or any of the other disciples?

10. Thinking about when the Greeks came to Philip, wanting to see Jesus, why do you think Philip took the problem to Andrew? What do you think Philip might have thought Andrew could do that he couldn't?

11. It seems there were two possible problems Philip faced when the Greeks came to him asking for help. One was a physical one, the size of the crowds and the difficulty of getting a group close enough to see Jesus. The second was theological and spiritual (Jesus didn't come to minister to Gentiles, but to Jews). Discuss how both were a potential problem for Philip, a problem he didn't know how to solve by himself?

12. Thinking about the exchange between Jesus and Philip during that last Passover: Jesus talked about knowing the Father and Philip asked Jesus to "show them the Father" and then they

would ask nothing more. Do you think this was an unreasonable request on Philip's part?

13. Thinking about the previous question, how do you think Philip felt and what might he have thought when Jesus said, "You have seen me, you have seen the Father"? Do you think Philip grasped and understood immediately what Jesus was saying?

14. Can you in any way identify with Philip? Discuss points of similarity you may have with him.

13

THOMAS

The Pessimist

I am sorry if I came across as a little harsh or distant in my initial reaction to you and your inquiries about my life. Please understand that by nature I am a person who does not trust people quickly and am always slow to make quick judgements and commitments. I have been like this for as long as I can remember, and the passage of time has not totally eradicated some long-standing characteristics of my personality. Mind you, I do not always see this as negative. I think this trait has protected me from some situations that others have rushed into with their quick reactions and responses. On the other hand, my cautious nature can make people think I am standoffish or not interested in them. I could share so many stories to illustrate this personality trait, but perhaps none stands out more than the time when I said that I would not believe in the resurrection of Jesus unless I could put my finger into the wounds in his hands and place my fist into the gaping wound where a sword had pierced him on the fateful day of his crucifixion. Ever since I said that I have had to live with a label that I feel is undeserved. Every time someone talks about me, they usually begin with, "Thomas, the doubter." In my defense, I should like to remind them – and maybe the whole world – that I was not the only one to question the resurrection of Christ from the dead.

On the morning that Christ returned from the dead, he appeared to Mary Magdalene, Joanna and Mary, the mother of James. It is to their credit that these women believed immediately, but let's not forget that they had talked to an angel that morning. They ran back to where the disciples – except Judas and me – were huddled together. Judas had hung himself after betraying Jesus, and I had other things to do that morning. As I was not present, I can only tell you what I heard, but I understand that all the others initially doubted what the women were telling them, considering such a report of his resurrection to be nonsense. It was not until Peter and John ran to the tomb themselves that they believed he had risen. They tell me that Jesus appeared among them, and all their doubts vanished. So why don't people call them doubters as well? Was I so different than they? It just took me longer to believe than it had taken them. Today, I have no doubts at all, and honestly, I resent always being defined as a doubter.

I have come to peace with myself and have a good grasp of what kind of person I am. A word that more appropriately catches the essence of my person is "pessimist." All too quickly, I see the dark side of a situation. Almost immediately, all the possible scenarios of what might go wrong play out in my mind. So, I am cautious and weigh the pros and cons of a situation before responding to it. That explains my reluctance when I heard people talking about Jesus coming to life again after being dead. No, I would not call it doubt, but just my need to have tangible evidence before I could embrace a truth as radical as this.

If I were to try to put into words my feelings and personality, I would describe myself as the most melancholy and stubborn of all the disciples. I am sure the others would say that I am too negative and depressive, and they would be right, for that is my tendency. But even if I honestly share these glimpses into how I am, none of that makes me a doubter. As you can tell, I do resent that title.

Let me share another example. Do you remember hearing about the time that Jesus raised Lazarus from the dead? That glorious day occurred just a few weeks before the Master was crucified. By that time, we all knew we were living under a cloud of suspicion and hate coming from the religious establishment. We all feared the way things were going. Life was more uncertain, and none of us doubted that the religious leaders wanted to silence Jesus. What would that mean for each of us? We were thinking about that when we received word that Lazarus was very sick, and his sisters wanted Jesus to come immediately to Bethany. We all felt uneasy about going to Judea in the prevailing political climate, knowing how the authorities felt about Jesus and his followers. The others kept their thoughts and feelings to themselves. I was the first to express what I felt – what we all felt collectively. I remembered the two failed assassination attempts, and I had no reason to believe that this time would be any different. Little did I realize how prophetic my feelings were, and that within a few days Jesus would die on a cross.

I sensed danger for us all if we were to go again into Judea. I might have covered my deep feelings by saying I was concerned about what they might do to Jesus, and I was. Even deeper, however, was the ominous fear of what they might do to me – or to any or all of us. I said, *"Let us also go, that we may die with him."* While my words spoke for us all, they also expressed my melancholy, gloomy and depressed outlook on life, devoid of hope and resigned to fate. This was not an isolated instance of this attitude of heart for me, but more my philosophy of life in general – but I also spoke of my willingness to stay with Christ no matter what might await us.

Not very long after Lazarus was raised from the dead, we were gathered for what would become our last meal with Christ. Of course, none of us realized at that moment what terrible events were about to burst upon us, plotted in the shadows while we ate our meal. We were all having difficulty understanding what Jesus meant as he talked about going away to Heaven, preparing a special place for us, and returning to take us to be with Him. The pieces did not seem to fit together. I felt as if I had as many questions as answers, so I spoke up saying, *"Lord, we do not know where you are going, and we do not know what road you're going to take."* I was trying to ask him how we could go along with him, wherever he was planning to go. I may have been slow to make decisions and commitments, but once I made them, they were deep and solid. I did not want anything to come between me and Christ, but I just could not fathom His going somewhere without me, without all of us. I know now that he was talking about Heaven. I understand it all now, but that night nothing made sense. Jesus answered my inquiry by telling us that He is the way, the truth, and the life. He was telling me not to go down any other road in my life, but to stay focused on him no matter what happened. In that moment, a cross overshadowed our gathering, but none of us foresaw it. That shadow would soon become a shocking reality.

The day of his crucifixion saw us in utter despair, evaporating every hope and dream we had carried for the past three years. A cloud hung over us during the following two days, depressing us so much that we could not express our agony. The painful memory of his death replaced all others. All the negative thoughts and imaginings that I generated so easily had taken the form of a stunning and horrible reality. How could it have come to this?

That was all before the Sunday morning when Jesus appeared to Mary and then to the two disciples walking to Emmaus. Later in the day, he also appeared to ten disciples gathered in the secluded room. Reports of his resurrection were multiplying, and evidence was mounting to prove that Jesus had truly come back from the dead.

Being absent from the group showed me how much I missed the others. My uncertainty and deep seated need to be sure of things had robbed me of the blessing the others had experienced. I felt like an absentee father who missed his son's first words or failed to see him take his first step.

Reflecting on that experience, I believe I can honestly say to you that it was not doubt that made me question the resurrection of Christ from the dead. No, it was a defense mechanism that was trying so hard to prevent me from once again experiencing something as soul shattering as the crucifixion of Christ. I could not face another disappointment of that magnitude. I had believed that He was who He said He was... and then all I had believed in and hoped for had died with him on the cross! Emotionally, I locked the door and threw away the key, shielding my heart from ever experiencing anything like that again. I am sure that this emotional barrier prompted me to insist that unless I could touch him, put my finger in the nail prints, and my fist into his side, I would not lower my emotional guard by opening my heart to another round of disappointment and emotional collapse.

When people call me a "doubter," they are suggesting a lack of faith, a willful decision not to believe. No, that was *not* the battle waging in my soul. It was not so much about spiritual failure, but rather a symptom of a fragile emotional state that did not want to go through such deep personal sorrow and emotional pain again. I had to be sure and could not be *"unless I can put my hands in his side and my fingers in his hands."*

Just a week later, Jesus invited me to do just that. In his grace, he came to me as the physician that could heal the sickness in my spirit, giving me the assurance that I needed to overcome the fear that had taken hold of me. Today, I know He is alive, and I want to tell you that I have not, even for a moment, looked back again. In so many ways, I am the same man I was before, with the same basic personality traits that I have always had. However, the Spirit of God has beautifully refined them, even helping me turn my "negative" characteristics into something useable for the cause of Christ. In outward appearance, I may not seem to be very different, but inside, I am no longer the man I once was, and Jesus is still in the process of making me the man he wants me to become. Some might say that *I had to touch him,* but I would say that *he had to touch me* and my life has never been the same.

DISCUSSION QUESTIONS

1. Thomas was presented in this story as having a personality that was slow to make commitments, not quickly trusting people, and needing to be reasonably secure in the decisions he had to make. What are the advantages and disadvantages of this type of personality?

2. Discuss what you think might have been the factors that motivated Thomas to say he needed to put his finger into the nail scars and his fist into the side of Jesus before he would be convinced that he was risen from the dead.

3. People always called Thomas a "doubter" because of his saying he would not believe in the resurrection unless he could put his finger into the nail scars and his fist into the side of Jesus. Remembering that the word "doubt" suggests failure to believe, which is more of a moral problem, while wanting to be sure of something before you commit to it is more of a personality pattern. When comparing these two different concepts, which do you think might more likely have explained the behavior of Thomas?

4. Reflecting on the previous question, do you think Thomas deserves the label "doubter" that is always attached to his name?

5. The Bible clearly tells us that initially all the disciples doubted the account of the resurrection that was brought to them by the women who had been at the tomb early that Sunday morning. Why do you think we separate Thomas from the rest of the disciples and call him a "doubter" while we overlook the initial reaction of the others?

6. In this story, Thomas is said to identify himself as a pessimist, having a tendency always to see the dark side of a situation or to quickly analyze all that could go wrong. Discuss the difference between being a "doubter" and being a "pessimist."

7. What are the advantages and disadvantages of a person with pessimistic tendencies?

8. We make our evaluations about Thomas two thousand years after he lived. How do you think you would react if someone came to you today and told you that someone you knew who had recently died had just come to life again? Do you think you would initially doubt what you were being told?

9. The disciples rightly feared that the religious establishment wanted to silence Christ, and therefore were afraid of going into Judea because of that threat. When they received word that Lazarus was sick, and that his sisters wanted Jesus to come, they all feared going to Judea. It was Thomas who said they should "all go with Christ and die with him." What can we learn about Thomas as a person from his statement?

10. Despite the portrayal of Thomas in this story as always needing to be sure of things, slow to react, and reserved in his responses to life's situations, he appears to have been as loyal and dedicated to Christ as any of the disciples. Do you think it fair to say that he may possibly have been "more loyal" than some of the others because he had already weighed in his mind and heart what it meant to follow Christ? Did his personality ultimately result in an even deeper sense of commitment than he might otherwise have had?

11. During the last meal that the disciples had with Jesus, it was Thomas who, while listening to Christ talk about going to Heaven, made the statement, "We do not know where you are going, and we do not know what road you are taking." He then asked Christ to clarify what he meant so that they could go along with him. What does all this tell us about Thomas as a person, his personality and disposition?

12. If Thomas had the personality traits expressed in this story, do you think the crucifixion of Christ was even harder for him to accept and work through than it was for the others? Do you think he might have felt as if he knew this was going to happen?

13. For whatever reason, Thomas was not with the other disciples on that first Sunday when Jesus appeared to them. We can assume he heard others' stories that testified to having seen Christ alive. What do you think some of his thoughts and feelings might have been during the week that elapsed between that first appearance and the following Sunday when Thomas was with the others, and Christ appeared to them again?

14. This story was built on the idea that it was not doubt that caused Thomas to question the resurrection of Christ, but rather his fear of being hurt and disappointed again if he did believe what he was hearing. Which do you think was the likely motivation for Thomas's reaction to the resurrection: spiritual doubt or psychological protection from being hurt again, or was it a combination of the two?

15. This study begs the question of how much the refining process of God's Spirit in our lives changes our personality, or how much we retain the same personality traits while he transforms our character. Discuss what you believe is changed in a person's

life when he or she commits his or her life to Christ and submits to God's control.

14

THOMAS

Meeting the Risen Christ
John 20: 24-29

As I stand here outside the door of the upper room, I don't know if I can go in there again. Sometimes I wish I had never been born. Perhaps Judas is better off than I, for at least he is not experiencing what I am going through. This has been the most awful week of my life. I know that if I go through that door again today, all I am going to hear from Peter and the others is the talk about Jesus being alive. I am so tired of what they are saying, yet I wish I could believe them. Because I won't believe them, they call me a doubter. I don't think it would really help to try to tell them why I feel the way I do. It isn't that I doubt so much as that I can't stand the thought of being hurt again. Why can't they understand where I am coming from?

Three years ago, I met Jesus, and for the first time in my life, I had something worth my belief and commitment. I had never met a man like him before and I really believed that he could help me. The three years spent following him have been the three most precious years of my life as I spent time with him listening to what he had to say. His messages touched my heart. The parables were so meaningful to me and, I believe, to the others as well. Today, in contrast, I feel nothing but grief and despair.

I wish I could find a way to relive some of the times we shared with Jesus. One such time was when he came to us on the sea when we were afraid of losing our lives. I can still remember his words, *"Peace, be still!"* and everything becoming calm. I still remember what I felt on another occasion when he told us to feed thousands of people – my sense of utter amazement as I took a loaf of bread and some small fish and kept passing the food around and around to those seated on the ground on the shore of Galilee. Every time someone took some food, more just seemed to appear. At first, I wondered if there would be enough for that massive crowd, but always, the loaf was as big as before. In fact, there were baskets full of leftovers. I saw that miracle and did not doubt.

I remember standing there as He said, *"Lazarus, come forth!"* I certainly thought that the Master was going a little too far this time. I waited to see what was going to happen, then amazingly, I saw Lazarus standing, bound by his grave clothes, at the mouth of the tomb that had held his dead, decaying body. I have often wondered about that. I can't understand what happened, and I don't know how his decaying body was able to revive and function again. I wondered what Lazarus was experiencing in that moment when life returned to him. When I saw him standing there, I was able to believe. I did not doubt.

During these past three years, I have believed so many things I would never have thought remotely possible before I followed the Master. We walked and talked together. For the first time in my life, I had something worth living for, something worthy of my belief. As those years passed, I came to the place where I thought my life would never be the same again. He had his own special way of saying my name, *"Thomas...Thomas."* I remember him warmly laying his hand on my shoulder as He would ask things such as, *"Thomas, why are you so afraid?"* or *"Thomas, can't you see?"* or *"Thomas, don't you understand, don't you believe what I am saying?"* I wonder sometimes why he thought I did not believe, but then he said the same to Peter and the others.

A few days ago, all of that changed. I guess I should have known better. Now, I am not sure I can trust myself again. I need to be sure about things in life, not because I doubt, but because I need a solid basis for what I believe. As I seek to understand myself, I believe some of my need for proof comes from having been hurt before. I allowed myself to believe something, only to be disappointed when it turned out not to be true. Is it a fault that my type of personality does not trust easily? Is it a sin to need to be sure about something before accepting it as true? Having been deeply hurt in the past, I don't want to believe anything without a sound basis for doing so. When they say, *"He is alive,"* on what can I base that belief?

For three years, I followed Christ and believed the things he was saying and doing. After I first met Jesus, it didn't take long for me to decide to follow Him. That was the first time I had made such a deep commitment to anyone. I surrendered myself to him and trusted Him to make me into the kind of person I longed to be. I firmly believed in the Master and what He stood for. I felt secure in that belief.

Where are all his promises now? What did they mean? He talked about establishing his kingdom, yet He lies dead in a cold, damp tomb, his body decaying. What is left of his promises now? Were they empty? I wish with every fiber of my being that what the others are saying could be real. I wish I could believe their stories. I wish there were something on which to base my faith.

I saw them arrest the Master. Flashbacks play out in my mind of the horrors of these past days when they nailed him on a cross where he died! No one will ever know the intense pain I felt! It was not just that he died, but that *part of me also died with Him.* When He drew his last breath, what I had believed in died as well. The others expect me to trust them when they say He is alive, but how can I know it is true?

I placed my hope in what the Master promised to do. Now that he is dead and gone, what hope do I have left? The hope of a grave like his? I cannot even continue to believe what he told us would happen after we die. How can I know if any of his statements are trustworthy about what life will be like after death? Maybe he was just a man like everybody else. Maybe it doesn't really matter anyway. Maybe in the end I am a doubter after all… or maybe I am a realist.

What am I going to do with the rest of my life? Now that it has come to this, what is left? To go look for another cause to fill the rest of my days on earth; to make enough money to eat and have a place to sleep and get up in the morning; to go to work and come home to a lonely house at night? For what? That was the pattern of my life before I met Jesus. He replaced the humdrum emptiness and made life worth living, but now that He is dead, my life seems just as empty as it was before I met him, and maybe even worse, because before I knew him, I had no idea about what life could be like spent in his company. Having lost that, I am not even sure I want to go on living.

The others are so different from me. I look at them and wish I had their faith. I wish I could believe that what they are saying is true. I don't doubt they believe what they are saying. I can see it in the radiance of their eyes and the enthusiasm of their words. Mary said she saw him and talked to him in the garden. What if all of this is real? Inside, I am yearning for it to be real. Oh God, if only it *could* be real!

I too wish I could believe again with the faith I used to have. But what if their claims aren't real, and once again, I set myself up to be deeply let down? I meant what I said to Peter and the others that, *"unless I can put my finger in the nail holes in his hands and my hands into his broken side, I will not believe."* No matter what they say, *"I will not believe."* I will not take a chance on being let down again. I could not stand another disappointment like I had the day they crucified the Master. My life fell apart that day, and I will never let it happen again. I will try to pick up the broken pieces of my soul and will guard my feelings so tightly that nothing will ever hurt me like that again. Do you understand my reason for saying that unless I can touch and hear and see with my own eyes, I will never believe?

What should I do? – Join the others or turn and walk away? I know the disciples are inside rejoicing and talking about Jesus being alive, but I am afraid that as soon as I go in, my heart will be torn into a thousand pieces. They will say, *"O Thomas, can't you believe when we tell you that we saw Him alive?"* Part of me will say, *"I want to believe; everything in me wants to believe."* However, can I take a chance? I cannot bear the thought of being let down another time. They will say, *"Thomas, what a doubter."* You know, God, that it is not a question of doubt, but of fear of hurt and avoidance of pain that is so deeply seated that I must be sure about where I place my faith.

I have no reason to go through that door. They do not know that I am standing here with my broken heart and shattered spirit. And yet, something brings me back to this place. I wonder what it is. Is it the companionship I enjoyed with these men, a longing for kindred spirits tugging at my heart? Is it a place to belong when loneliness couches around me? Is it desire for a sense of security, drawing emotional strength from our shared experiences? Or is it because I honestly want to believe what they say about Jesus being alive?

At first, our shared doubts and fears huddled us together in unity in this room. Now, however, the others believe, and I do not. If Jesus is alive as they say, and appeared to them all, I wish he would come and talk to me as well. If the Master really is alive, why *doesn't* he come and talk to me? Is there something different about me? Am I not important? No, that is not it at all! It is about my being unable – or unwilling – to let myself believe. As I stand here, I continue to ask myself what brought me back here today.

They said He arose a week ago and came and talked to them. Why did I leave them that day? Oh God, why didn't I stay a little longer? So here I stand, confused, afraid, hungry for the fellowship that I once knew with Jesus, so lonely since He has gone. This must be the worst week of my life!

I know I cannot stand here forever. I think I will slip into the room. Shutting the door quietly behind me, I don't think they have even noticed I came in. Yes, hello John, hi James. They are still talking. I stand here beside them listening to what they say. It feels good to be back, even if I feel like an outsider having missed the last days of shared experience. Look at them – *they* don't look sad or confused. In fact, I have never seen them look so happy! I wish I could share their joy. Part of me is glad I came, and part of me wishes I had stayed away. They appear to have something I lack – or to have seen something I have not seen. They say it was Jesus, alive from the dead.

No, my God, it cannot be! Jesus just came through the wall!! The door is locked. I locked it myself when I came in. His appearance is different, but it is clearly Jesus! He is looking my way, right at me. Even as I fight back a sense of fear, I am beginning to feel the profound beauty of this moment. Fearful yet marveling, a deep sigh expresses my wavering heart, balancing on the line between doubt and faith. How I yearn to know. Can this really be Jesus? Can dead men live? If only I could hear Him speak his words to my doubts as well. A different thought arrests me. Maybe he is a ghost, or perhaps I am hallucinating, seeing things that are not there. Could it be that I want to believe so badly that I am imagining that Jesus is here?

I have no time to entertain these thoughts before the silence is broken by His words. *"Peace be unto you."* Just a few words, but enough for me to recognize without a doubt that it is his voice! This is the moment of truth. I find myself mentally affirming that the others were right after all, from the moment just a week ago that Mary claimed to have seen Him early that morning as she stood in front of His tomb.

I begin to wonder what the others are going to think about me as a person. They all know how uncertain I have been about their reports. Shame spreads over me like an ink stain on a blotter – because of my unbelief, my fear of being hurt, my unwillingness to hear and accept what they have been telling me. As I fret over the potential rejection by my peers, I am even more distressed by what Jesus might think of me. Does He know what I said about needing proof, and how I failed to embrace the truth of his resurrection? I am so relieved that he does not know, and that He was not there to hear when I said I needed to touch Him before I would believe.

I let my eyes meet his as he starts walking toward me, stretching out his hand. I see the hole where the nail pierced and tore his flesh. *"Thomas, put your finger here in the nail hole in my hand. Come on, Thomas,"* he says, *"touch me. This is what you wanted, this is what you asked for, now here I am, and I want you to come and touch me. Thomas, I want you to believe just like the rest of them have believed that I am alive."* Now I realize that he knew all along what I had been thinking and feeling. But it doesn't matter because I know He accepts me despite my thoughts and doubts. He is willing to forgive even my unbelief. Tears are flowing onto my cheeks, and my knees are buckling beneath me. I feel love, but I cannot tell if it is his love for me, my love for him, or a mixture of both, I cannot express my feelings right now because I am too deeply moved by the scene. *"HE IS ALIVE!"* My heart opens in wonder to this newly realized fact: he *is* alive! So, I too can believe! Praise God, I can believe! My entire being swells with a chorus of joyous affirmation. All doubt is gone! HE IS ALIVE! I now want to embrace that truth more than anything else in the world.

He can read my heart and my tear-stained face. *"Thomas, not only in my hand, but as you asked, put you hand here in my side where the spear pierced my body. Come on, Thomas, I do want you to believe. Place it here."* I want to say, *"Jesus, just by touching you, I have certainty, I am sure now, I feel your love, I have hope again."* With assurance at last, I freely and sincerely declare, "JESUS, MY LORD AND MY GOD!"

DISCUSSION QUESTIONS

1. How do you think Thomas felt about and related to the other disciples during the week between the two appearances of Jesus? Do you think he might have struggled to be with them?

2. What do you think Thomas may have been thinking about during that week? Do you think he was relieving the good experiences, or fixating on his loss, or perhaps a mixture of both?

3. Thomas was there when Jesus raised Lazarus from the dead. This must have confirmed to him that a dead man could be brought back to life. Yet he struggled when confronted with Christ's resurrection. Why do you think he might have had reservations about the resurrection of Christ despite what he had previously witnessed?

4. When Jesus was crucified, Thomas, like all the rest, must have experienced extreme disappointment and a sense of loss and defeat. What do you think was the hardest for Thomas (or any of the disciples) to face? What might have been their greatest loss, and what was their greatest frustration when Christ died?

5. How do you think Thomas felt about himself and about his fellow disciples when they were embracing the resurrection of Christ, but he still needed further proof before he could believe that Jesus had been raised from the dead?

6. How close to utter despair do you think Thomas might have come when Christ was crucified? Do you think he (or any of the others) might have looked at Judas and felt that he was better

off dead than they were living with pain and despair after the crucifixion?

7. During the days between the crucifixion and resurrection of Christ, do you think Thomas (or any of the others) might have had difficulty believing what Jesus had been telling them? Do you think they had any doubts about who he was and what he had taught?

8. It is possible that Thomas might have recalled the life he had lived before meeting Christ. Do you think he envisaged that that previous lifestyle would become the pattern of his life again now that Christ was dead and gone?

9. The other disciples must have been rejoicing and praising God after Jesus appeared to them on the day he was raised from the dead. Thomas, who was absent on that occasion, must have felt different from them because he did not accept their testimony or believe what they said they had seen and experienced. Why, therefore, do you think Thomas wanted to come back and relate with the group again, after at least a week of emotional separation from them and their professed experience in having seen the risen Christ?

10. When the other disciples testified to having been with the risen Christ, do you think Thomas wondered why Christ hadn't also sought him out and appeared to him as He had done to the others?

11. What do you think might have been some of the first thoughts Thomas had when Christ appeared in the room where he and the others had gathered the week after his resurrection from the dead?

12. Do you think Thomas might have wondered at first what Jesus thought about him as a person since he had questioned the reality of his resurrection?

13. How do you think Thomas felt and thought when Jesus told him to put his finger into the nail prints and his fist into his side? Thomas must have realized at that moment that Jesus knew what he had been saying.

14. At some point, Thomas must have embraced, both cognitively and emotionally, the truth that Jesus was indeed alive from the dead. What do you think might have been some of his first thoughts and feelings when this truth finally gripped his mind and heart?

15. What does his confession (My Lord and My God!) tell us about Thomas as a person and what was happening in his life?

15

NATHANIEL AND JUDAS

Those Less Honored

I, John, the only one of us that is still alive, already had the privilege of telling you about myself. As I said, I have often wondered why I alone should be the only one not to be martyred for our faith.

All that transpired during the three years we spent with Jesus occurred over half a century ago. The perspective of an old man recalling cherished memories is different than living those events in the zeal of younger years. I hope that the passing of time and life's refining processes have brought the former days into clearer focus.

Now I turn to the lives of the "lesser disciples" in the sense that they did not exercise leadership roles like some of us had. Isn't that the way life is? Some rise to positions of authority and recognition – without the reason always being apparent – while others remain in the shadows. In my old age, I have come to realize that how others perceive a person's value does not tell the whole story. As the years went by bringing me news of the death of one or another of our group, I would realize that he too had died in the service of the Master. Each martyr had been as faithful as I in discharging his duty to be a witness to Christ to the ends of the earth. I cannot help but wonder what Heaven will reveal when we have a clearer picture of the impact each of us has had on others. Didn't Jesus tell us that "the first shall be last and the last shall be first"? My brother and I had once sought a privileged position beside Christ in his Kingdom but now, I am content to be one of the chosen who will share equally the blessings of Heaven.

A handful of us disciples lived in the spotlight of public acclaim, becoming leaders of the new movement that emerged out of Christ's life and teachings. But God forbid that in reflecting on the spiritual success of some, I should in any way diminish the accomplishments of those who worked behind the scenes.

Let's begin with Nathaniel, often referred to by his last name, Bartholomew, which means "Son of Tolmai." We disciples used his first name, though some of us nicknamed him "the dreamer," or at times, "the visionary," names he earned because while we would be talking, Nathaniel would drift off to some other world, as if not present with us at all. Had we not known him better, we might have thought he was not paying attention or was not interested. In time, however, we came to understand that was not the case. No, in those apparently absent-minded episodes, he was dreaming dreams, envisioning what might be, but we would just wonder where his mind was wandering. He was a dreamer, unconstrained by concrete reality, imagining possibilities that did not yet exist. Now, I wonder something else: how many times were ideas that changed the world born in the mind of men like Nathaniel?

Nathaniel displayed the behavior of an introvert, finding it a little harder to mix with people. His cautious nature wanted to get the "feel" of a person before he was willing to trust or commit himself. His first encounter with Jesus is a good example.

When Philip became a follower of Jesus at the Jordan River, the first thing he did was to go and find his best friend Nathaniel. *"Nathaniel,"* he said, *"We have found him!"* *"Found who?"* replied the dreamer. Philip said, *"We have found the Messiah, of whom Moses wrote in the law. The prophets wrote about him as well – Jesus of Nazareth, the Son of Joseph."*

It seems to me that Nathaniel only heard the word "Nazareth." He was from Galilee too, but from Capernaum. In the minds of many, Nazareth was a little country town that amounted to nothing more than a hill of beans. It was as if Nathaniel was thinking, *"Nazareth? Never! Maybe Jerusalem or Bethlehem, as the prophet had said, or perhaps even Capernaum, but not Nazareth!"* He questioned, *"What good thing can come out of Nazareth?"* – revealing what he really thought.

Our group was amazed at what happened next. As Philip and Nathaniel were walking toward him, Jesus spoke: *"Behold an*

Israelite," Jesus said, *"in whom there is no guile."* We all noticed the questioning look on Nathaniel's face and knew what he was thinking: *"How do you know anything about me? We have never met."* Jesus told Nathaniel that he had been sitting under a fig tree. That was enough to convince Nathaniel, who instantly embraced Jesus as the true Messiah.

I got to know Nathaniel very well as we spent three intense years together with Jesus and then had time together after the Master was taken back to Heaven. Without reservation, I can tell you that the words Jesus had spoken about Nathaniel were prophetic. Nothing could have described this man better. Of course, he was as human as any of us with our shortcomings and failures, but when it came to living a godly, righteous life, Nathaniel was indeed a man without guile, a good and upright person. Everything about him reflected godly character. While he never rose to what people would consider an exalted position, I have no doubt that he stood tall in the eyes of the Master. I admired him and cherished his friendship.

Nathaniel wasn't the only good man to follow Christ and yet remain in the shadows. Another I would like to tell you about is Judas. Now I don't mean the Judas who betrayed Jesus, for there were two disciples with that name. The one I am talking about is sometimes referred to as "Judas the Less" or Thaddaeus, his last name. So, I am talking about Judas Thaddaeus. I am not sure he appreciated being called by his last name, but after the other Judas placed the kiss on the neck of the Master in the garden – to betray him – I am not sure anyone would want to be called Judas anymore.

It's so sad that whenever anyone speaks the name "Judas," everyone immediately thinks of the traitor. But I do not, for I remember the other Judas that was so faithful, loyal, and true to the Master. I like calling him "the steady one" whose faith did not waver. We all had a momentary lapse of faith at the time of the crucifixion which shook us to our core, but fortunately those few days of doubt were erased by Jesus' resurrection. We went on to serve Christ by faith for many years, and Judas the Less was no exception, remaining faithful to our Master until his own death as a martyr.

My memories of this loyal follower of Christ are many, such as the last meal we shared with Jesus on this earth, as we celebrated our last Passover together. The night was tense, filled with many emotions. We all felt the heaviness settle upon us. Jesus explained well what was about to happen and how He was going to send the Holy Spirit in his place, but we failed to grasp his meaning or the seriousness of the situation. It is only with hindsight that we now understand what he was saying.

Jesus said, *"If you love me, show it by doing what I've told you. I will talk to the Father, and he will provide you another Friend so that you will always have someone with you. This friend is the Spirit of Truth. The godless world can't take him in because they don't have eyes to see him, they don't know what to look for. But you know him already because he has been staying with you and will even be in you."* He added, *"I will not leave you orphaned. I'm coming back. In just a little while the world will no longer see me, but you're going to see me because I am alive and you're about to come alive. At that moment you will know absolutely that I'm in my Father, and you're in me and I'm in you. The person who knows my commandments and keeps them, that's who loves me. And the person who loves me will be loved by my Father, and I will love him and make myself plain to him.'*

We became quiet as we thought about his unusual and very interesting words. No doubt each of us had questions about what we had just heard, but it was Judas (the Less) who broke the silence by asking a question that was at the forefront of our minds. *"Master,"* he said, *"why is it that you are about to make yourself plain to us but not to the world?"*

We all understand now that Jesus will come again one day, descending on a cloud in great power. He told us about that later, when we had all gathered on the Mount before we watched him being taken back into Heaven. Yes, one day he will appear for all the world to see, and every knee will bow before Him. In that special moment as we huddled together in the upper room, Jesus had just us in mind. He was concerned for those of us who had given up everything to follow Him. He knew what lay ahead of each one of us. For some, there would be great suffering and pain. He wanted us to know that no matter what we went through, we were not alone. He was going to send His Spirit to be with us, to comfort us and give us the grace we would need for all that life brought our way. All of us disciples, except Judas the traitor, went on to serve the Master. Not one of us deserted, even though everyone but me paid the ultimate price for his faithfulness.

Sadly, we have all seen far too many people start to follow Jesus and then, for whatever reason, fall away and lose their faith. I am grateful that this was not the story of these disciples of Jesus, my fellow workers who had shared three years of living with the Master.

When people talk about us as a group, I am sure that not many will mention either Nathaniel or Judas the Less, but instead think of prominent characters like Peter, my brother James, and even me. Some remember Matthew because, being a tax collector, he seemed an unlikely choice to be a disciple. The inclusion of each individually chosen disciple shows that Jesus did not see things the way we do. I have no doubt that he saw in Nathaniel a godly man with "no guile" and he saw in Judas the Less a faithful spirit, and the unwavering love and loyalty that was so characteristic of his life.

Now let me ask you a question. Do you think these two men stand any lower in the eyes of the Master than I do, or Peter, or James, or any of the other men that were part of our unique group? Does the acclaim and praise of men somehow give some of us a greater standing in the eyes of God? Would it be correct for me to say today that a man without guile, a godly and holy man and a man of unwavering faith might not be equal, if not superior, to some of us who caught the eye, esteem, and imagination of men?

DISCUSSION QUESTIONS

1. In the opening statement of this story, John said that he has seen his perspective of life's experiences change as he aged, seeing them differently in old age than when he lived them in the younger years of his life. Share some examples of how your view of life and attitudes toward things that happen may have changed as you have aged.

2. The earlier paragraphs of this story talk about how some people rise to greater positions of fame and importance in the eyes of men because of certain things they achieved in life. Yet the story of both Nathaniel and Judas the Less tells of the faithful and godly lives of these two disciples who are hardly ever talked about and of whom little is shared in the Scriptures. Reflecting on this idea, discuss how you think God views the status of different persons and what might be some of his criteria for greatness and renown.

3. Nathaniel was portrayed in this story as a "dreamer" and a "visionary." He is described as seemingly uninterested in what is happening around him and disengaged from the conversation and interaction of the group. Do you know people like that, and if so, how do you feel about them?

4. Where is the balance between being socially engaged and personally interactive and being motivated by ideas and dreams that seem to make a person "disengaged" and uninterested in social interaction? What are the advantages and disadvantages of both types of personalities?

5. Think about people who are either introverted or extraverted. What do you like and dislike about either type of personality?

Where do you think you fit as a person? Do you think it is better to be one over the other?

6. We usually think of pastors and church workers as more extraverted people who can relate to and enjoy being with and working alongside people. Yet God calls all kinds of people into his service. How do you think a more introverted person can be used effectively in God's Kingdom?

7. It is obvious that Nathaniel had some deep-rooted prejudices and negative feelings toward citizens of the little village of Nazareth. Yet Jesus said he was a man that had "no guile" in him. Today, we would recognize prejudice toward another group of people as a moral problem. How do you reconcile those two statements, that Nathaniel said, "nothing good comes out of Nazareth" and yet Jesus said, "he was a man without guile"?

8. The Bible tells us much about the life and character of men like Peter and James and John. Especially when looking at the life of Peter, we see a man with so many human faults and failures of character, yet he became the predominant leader in the early church and among the disciples. Nathaniel was a man "without guile" and yet he is hardly talked about in the Gospels. What can we learn about people from the lives of these two men? Which do you consider in the end to be the greater of the two men, Peter, or Nathaniel? What makes a man "great" in the eyes of men and "great" in the eyes of God?

9. Before reading the story, what did you think about or what was your perception when you heard someone mention the name "Judas the Less" as one of the disciples?

10. In the dialogue above, it was noted that all the disciples at times had personal failures and at least at the time of the crucifixion of Christ, there was a corporate lapse of faith. Yet all these disciples, except the traitor, were faithful and productive for the Kingdom of God. Talk about the place where normal human failure occurs in a person's life and when it is "sin" verses just being human. How difficult is it for you to accept the failure of another and to look beyond it to see the good in the person despite their failure(s)?

11. How many Nathaniels and Judases have you known in your life, people who live for Christ but somehow seem to fail to rise to acclaim. Who are some such people who come to your mind?

12. Has the telling of the story of these two men helped you view any differently people that might have personality traits like these two had?

13. Are you more comfortable with one type of personality over the other (introverted or extraverted)? Do you seem to quickly respect the one more than the other?

14. If you had a choice and could pick the kind of person you would like to be, which disciples would you most like to pattern yourself after? Why?

16

JAMES AND SIMON

The Faithful and Zealous

    During our last time together, I, the aged apostle John, shared with you about two faithful men that I referred to as "those less honored." I used that term because it seems to me that some of us, for whatever reasons, rose to positions of authority and public importance in the new church that was born at Pentecost. Some of us wrote letters and books that have been collected, and others seemed always to be at the center of attention. There were also some disciples who just faithfully served Christ in the background and seem to have been almost forgotten. They were devoted, never wavered in their faith, and became martyrs for what they believed. Something that I have shared with the world speaks volumes about the lives of us disciples, including those all too often overlooked:

    When I was exiled on the Isle of Patmos, I was granted an exceptional visit to Heaven. In my vision of the Holy City, I saw the names of all twelve disciples engraved in the foundation of the walls of the New Jerusalem and not one of us was more important than any of the others! I was reminded that Jesus had told us that we were all going to have an equal role in Heaven. I can still remember his words as he was addressing us as a group. He said, *"Truly I tell you, at the renewal of all things, when the Son of Man sits on his glorious throne, you who have followed me will also sit on twelve thrones, judging the twelve tribes of Israel."* There was not the slightest hint that Peter, I, or any one of us might have a superior position over the others.

    So once again, let me talk about two more of the chosen men with whom I lived and worked during our three years with Jesus. We have already considered Nathaniel and Judas, and now I will talk about James the son of Alphaeus and Simon, sometimes referred to as the Zealot. So, here are four men that I refer to as "those less honored" by people – but equal to any leader in the eyes of God.

Many of Christ's followers, in listing the names of the twelve Apostles, might forget about the other James. They easily remember my brother James, the leader in the early church and the first martyr, while this James often fades into obscurity. That is why, when talking about him, I sometimes refer to him as "James the forgotten." People always talk about the main characters in a play but seldom mention the supporting actors and the backstage helpers essential to making the drama a success. Can you imagine what it would be like if we only had the main actors without the supporting cast? James played his part well, making an important contribution to the cause of Christ.

James was one of the younger members of our group and a man of small stature. Maybe that is why we sometimes referred to him as James the Less. But regardless of his physical stature, I believe he stood equal to the rest of us. When I think about him, I am reminded of God's words to the prophet Samuel, that He does not look at the outward appearance but at the heart and soul of a person. James laughed with the rest of us, and his heart broke with ours when our Master was crucified. He was with us on the day that the Holy Spirit came upon us, and he became all that the rest of us became. As I reflect on this fellow disciple, he was not "less" to me in any way. I see him as equal, if not more.

Sometimes, when thinking about these four often forgotten men, I ponder the words of Jesus that, *"The last will be first and the first will be last."* I imagine that in some ways James will stand head and shoulders above many on the day when all the secrets of men will be revealed, and I have no doubt that my friend James the Less, James the son of Alphaeus, heard the words that we all hope to hear, *"Well done, good and faithful servant."*

Then there was Simon the Zealot. No doubt, many people wondered why Jesus chose him to be one of his closest disciples and friends. "Zealot" has a negative connotation for most people who only remember the political movement aiming to overthrow the Roman tyranny under which we have lived for such a long time. Simon was certainly sympathetic to that way of thinking and may have been more involved than many of us would want to say. But if so, those thoughts were totally altered when he became one of us. The Master talked about loving our enemies and turning our cheek when we were wronged by others. It was Jesus who said we should give to Caesar what belonged to him and to God what he had a right to have. All of this countered the deeply rooted convictions Simon may have held in the younger years of his life.

There was, however, another way in which the term "Simon the Zealot" fit this special disciple. The same (possibly misdirected) zeal of his youth continued to be a part of his personality. No matter what Simon did, he did it with all his heart and soul. He was "zealous" in his love and devotion to Jesus, in his service and commitments. So, I prefer to think of that term "zealot" in the latter sense. There was never a time when his zeal was not obvious to us all. I was not surprised when I learned about his missionary endeavors and death for his faith. I have no doubt that he was just as engaged in the cause of Christ on the last day of his life as he was on the day when he decided to follow Jesus. For my co-worker Simon, I use the term "zealot" or "zealous" as a badge of honor.

I am not trying to downplay any association Simon might have had with what so many see as a radical movement, but I do not believe that his background defines the man he became. Those who criticized us – and there were many – often picked on both Matthew and Simon. Matthew, because of his being a traitor to his people and Simon, because he threatened the delicate balance our nation had with Rome. Yet both these men, with such different backgrounds and goals, became close friends and co-workers in God's Kingdom. Isn't that a wonderful example of what the Spirit of God can do in people when their lives are open and pliable? Where a person came from does not matter; what is important is where a person ends up. This is just one of the many lessons we can learn from these "men of lesser honor." All of them, though largely forgotten by most, made significant contributions to the cause of Christ.

God needs people like Simon, people who are dedicated to His cause and willing to give it their all. So many people spend endless energy and "zeal" serving life's much lesser causes instead of following Simon's example of putting his zeal into what really matters.

There are others who seem to be forgotten by the world, life's "lesser" people. They serve quietly, often in the background, working faithfully and steadily to make this world a better place. A few people will notice what they do, especially those who are touched by their love and generosity, but the majority will never even see what they accomplish so unassumingly.

Perhaps what I saw on the Isle of Patmos has engraved deeply on my soul the thoughts that I am sharing with you today. I saw the martyrs in Heaven crying out to God, asking him how long it would be until he would avenge their death. I saw the great and small alike, drawn from every nation and every tongue and every race extolling God together in one great chorus of heavenly praise. They were all there, and they were all standing equal before God. Whatever crowns of glory any of us might have earned here on earth, we all threw them down at the feet of Jesus in Heaven. Those things did not matter there. Just being with Jesus, forever, was the only reward that counted.

Now in my nineties, I await my turn to join the others of our band who have gone ahead as martyrs to Heaven. While I wait, I have a vision of God's Spirit going back and forth across the earth. Nowhere is beyond his reach, and no secrets are hidden from him. "Forgotten ones" are concealed everywhere – laying in unmarked graves all over the world, in the depths of the sea, in vanished graveyards. I envision God's spirit hovering over a desolate cemetery in some distant place, remembering the unknown and long forgotten people buried beneath the weeds. These too were saints of God, yet nobody remembers them now. Some died horrible deaths, martyred for God's cause, but their stories are forgotten… except by those who wait in Heaven where no one ever forgets. In God's presence, no one is unknown; no one is insignificant. James the less is as important there as Paul the great leader. All who were faithful to God's calling in their lives share together in the glories of heaven.

I believe God's Kingdom still needs men like Simon. There are many people like him alive today, who get excited about a cause, expending great energy with purpose and direction, giving their all to try to change society by pursuing the goals in which they believe. Often, their energy is directed to a wrong cause, but their level of dedication is commendable. Or sometimes, a person strives for a good cause, but not always for the best one. As a young person, Simon resembled so many who dedicate their time and unbounded energies to political causes, hobbies, sports, and other pursuits vying for their attention, time, and resources. But when Jesus called Simon to follow him, he obeyed in an instant, and his life became reoriented to the cause of Christ, a cause *worthy* of his efforts and zeal. In the same way, I believe that God calls each of us to follow Him and to channel our energy into activities that are worth the investment, for the greatest cause on earth.

As an old man now, I cannot lay claim to energy and exertion any longer, but I hope that my spiritual zeal and love for the Master have not waned. I am well respected by all the believers, even venerated as the only Apostle still living, yet I know in my heart of hearts that I am no better than any of the others. I am just a man like them who tried to live the way I believe Jesus wanted me to live. Soon, I will join them in the place where no one is overlooked, and no one is more exalted than another, but each an important, recognized member of God's family. They might have received "lesser honor" in the eyes of men, but as my brothers in Christ and coworkers in faithfully and zealously spending themselves to carry forward the great mission Christ entrusted to us, they are indeed "good and faithful servants."

DISCUSSION QUESTIONS

1. The opening paragraph of this story talks about some who rise to positions of authority and predominance, while others who are equally faithful and loyal to Christ seem to remain in the shadows with little recognition. What do you think are some of the factors that contribute to this?

2. How do you think God views this discrepancy? What role does God have in gifting some and working in ways that promote them to a more "exalted" position while other very faithful Christians do not reach places of honor? How do you think all of this will be handled in Heaven?

3. Remembering the words of John, that in Heaven we will all be given "our rewards" but will then cast down our "crowns" at the feet of Jesus, do you think this is part of a process that both permits a just recognition of earthly achievements while maintaining a "leveling" experience for all of Heaven's citizens?

4. Discuss what you think Jesus might have meant when he said, "the first shall be last and the last shall be first." How does this fit into our thoughts about some of the disciples who did not receive the public acclaim on earth that some of the others received?

5. Do you think the four Apostles discussed in the previous story and this story (Nathaniel, Judas, James, and Simon) ever felt resentful or jealous of those who were given greater public acclaim and seemed to be the ones always recognized and talked about?

6. Though we do not know for sure, some Bible scholars believe that his being referred to as "James the Less" may have been in part because of his possibly being short in stature. If that were true, do you think his physical appearance might have contributed in any way to his not being as involved in leadership as some of the others? How do you think one's physical appearance and self-perception affect performance and status in life?

7. Describe possible dynamics and reactions when a person's role is to play "second fiddle" to others in the group? How can we overcome some of the possible negative reactions that might arise when we are placed in such a situation?

8. When we think about Simon the Zealot, we tend to focus on his identity with a political group called the Zealots who wanted to overthrow Rome. Josephus says that this group did not become a clearly identified and named movement until after the time that Christ lived. It is quite possible, therefore, that Simon being referred to as a "Zealot" may have referred rather to the concept of "zeal" for other causes in life. Is it possible that Simon might have been called a "zealot" because he had exceptionally significant "zeal" for the cause of Christ? If so, does this change your attitude toward Simon?

9. Thinking about the previous question, even if the Zealot group was not clearly identified and named until later, its activity might have been in its early stages during the time that Christ lived. If so, and if Simon were a part of the early beginnings of this group wanting to overthrow Rome, why do you think Christ picked him as one of the disciples? How do you think the other disciples might have initially related to him, especially Matthew who was working for Rome?

10. Some personality traits are deeply rooted. This may have been true for Simon who had a personality that was very committed to what he believed in, displaying exceptional commitment to those causes. Thinking about that, how do you see people who are committed to something before they know Christ taking that same kind of zeal and enthusiasm into their new Christian experience? To what degree does becoming a Christian "temper" or "change" or "utilize" such types of personal qualities?

11. It appears that Matthew and Simon came from totally different philosophical and political positions, yet they became friends and co-workers. It probably did not happen without some personality struggles, but they bridged whatever philosophical differences they had between them. What can we learn from their lives and examples that we can apply to our own lives?

12. People today are "zealous" for many types of causes. It is important that we become "zealous" for the causes most worthy of our time and energy. How do we decide what are the most important causes to which to give our time and energy? Do you think a lot of people come to the end of life knowing that they chose "wisely" and feel satisfied, or realizing that they spent all their energies on things that really will not matter much in the end… and feel regret?

13. Recalling what John described in the Book of Revelation about all the saints praising God, and what appears to be equality between people, how should that truth affect our thinking and attitudes while living our lives on earth? If that picture truly gripped our soul, do you think it would affect the way we view other people socially, economically, racially, politically?

14. How significant are the labels that are sometimes attached to our names (like Simon the Zealot and Matthew the tax collector)? Neither of these two men remained associated with the labels that defined them, both having walked away from their former lives to follow Jesus. To what degree can such labels become either a positive or negative influence on our lives and the attitudes of others toward us?

15. Once we have a "label" attached to our names, how much does that label motivate us to fulfill the image it conveys about us, either positive or negative?

17

JUDAS

A Life That Went Wrong
Recounted by the Apostle John

Here in Ephesus, we are a long way from Jerusalem, and in terms of years, we are a long distance from the events I am recalling. I was in my early thirties when we all, including Judas Iscariot, walked with Jesus as he travelled. I am now in my nineties, but I remember well so much that happened during that time. When talking about Judas Iscariot, now often labeled "the betrayer," I must be careful to distinguish between the two members of our band who shared that familiar name.

It was Judas Iscariot that did betray the Master, but I prefer not to focus merely on that part of his life. I knew him as a man, a fellow disciple, and a friend. The many positive memories of our good times together have, however, been tainted by his final act.

If we were in Jerusalem today, I could take you outside the city to a burial ground that people now usually refer to as the Field of Blood, but sometimes as the "Potter's Field" because of its rich clay, formerly used by the potters. Judas hanged himself in that field, and the religious authorities used the money he returned to them, after they had paid him for his betrayal, to buy this piece of land. Now it is used as a cemetery for foreigners and for those who are not seen as faithful and loyal Jews. I share this with you because Judas' betrayal of the Master and his horrible death is what most people remember about him. Just hearing his name creates a negative reaction and atmosphere of uneasiness in many people. I often hear people portraying him as dressed in black, lurking in the shadows, his face twisted in a ruse, with menacing eyebrows and unruly hair, their personal epitome of a criminal.

The Judas I knew really wasn't that kind of villain at all. In fact, for the three years that we lived together, he didn't appear to be any different than any of the rest of us. Nothing about his demeanor or character ever suggested any of the evil inclinations that we later discovered concealed the darkness of his soul. When I think of the Judas I knew, I would say that he was neither a devil nor a saint. He was just one of us, sharing the ups and downs of discipleship that we all experienced together.

If there was anything to set him apart from the group, it was his town of origin. His name was Judas Iscariot. His last name identifies him with the city of Kerioth which was located about ten miles south of Hebron in Judea. The rest of us were from Galilee, so he was the only one from Judea. We often teased or joked with him about his distinctive accent, but we all dressed in the same way and did not feel that his place of origin made much of a difference.

Many of us began following Christ even before he went up to a mountain to spend a night in prayer before choosing twelve of us from among his many followers. We twelve would become the special group into whom he poured his life during the three years we spent together before his crucifixion. Since Judas' betrayal of Christ, I am forced to remind myself that it was Jesus who chose Judas to be one of our number. Jesus never treated him any differently than he did Peter and James, Philip, or Nathaniel. Judas heard the same things we heard, and he saw and experienced the same things all the rest of us did. When Jesus sent us out on a mission two by two, Judas cast out demons, preached, and healed the sick along with the rest of us.

We all enjoyed Judas as a person. Of course, twelve men living together almost every day for three years will inevitably have differences and disagreements from time to time, but they were nothing more than signs of normal interaction within a group of people. Judas never seemed like an outsider in our group but blended in well.

I cannot tell you when Judas' heart began to change. The night that he betrayed the Master, none of us suspected that anything deceitful was happening. When Judas left the upper room that evening, we all assumed he was going to take care of some unfinished business, or perhaps going to give something to the poor on that most sacred day in our religious year. With the clarity brought by hindsight, we later recognized the indications that something was wrong that we had not been able to discern in the mix of emotional experiences assailing our senses that evening, even though Jesus had begun to hint that something momentous was about to occur.

I remember the first reference being quite close to the end of our time together. Many people were turning against Jesus, even to the point of wanting him killed, the main proponents being those in power over our land and our own religious leaders. That ill will was growing in intensity and becoming more evident as time passed. Many of Jesus' earlier followers abandoned him because of this pressure, coupled with their difficulty in accepting some of his teachings.

One day, Jesus asked us pointedly if we were going to leave him as well. Peter, often the spokesman for our group, replied, *"Lord, to whom shall we go? You have the words of eternal life."* It was then that Jesus told us that even if he himself had chosen the twelve of us, one of us was "a devil" who was going to betray him.
We were stunned and speechless! How could we believe that any one of us would do such a dastardly thing? He never named the one to whom he was referring, so we were left wondering who the traitor could possibly be.

Of course, now I know that Jesus was referring to Judas Iscariot. I often wonder if Judas was even aware, at that moment, of the evil for which he would forever be infamous, or how wicked thoughts were not only birthed but were allowed to grow to manifest themselves as fully developed sinful acts. I honestly believe that at first Judas' desire to follow Christ was as real as it was for any of us. I have never entertained the idea that he might have come to us with a hidden agenda or evil intent. On the contrary, I believe that his intentions were true and sincere.

At some point, however, there was a change in his life and soul. I can only guess about what might have motivated him, but from observing what began to unfold, I think it is reasonable to say that the desire for money was one of the underlying incentives that began to steer his choices. Later this became obvious when we discovered that he, our group's treasurer, had been taking advantage of his role to steal money from our collective funds.

The attitude towards money growing in his heart began to show one day when we were all invited to a special dinner where Mary, a friend of Jesus, took a large quantity of expensive perfume, poured it over Jesus' feet, and wiped his feet with her hair as an act of worship. Suddenly, Judas objected, *"Why wasn't this perfume sold and the money given to the poor? It was worth a year's wages."* We might have been caught off guard at the rashness of his statement, but to be honest, we were wondering the same thing. It did indeed seem to represent a large amount of monetary value to pour out in just one moment. Judas' reaction, however, was of far greater intensity than ours. I now believe that Judas saw his potential for personal advantage if this money had been given to us "to use to help the poor." I can see now that Judas' willingness to take the thirty pieces of silver offered to him to betray Christ was consistent with the growing greed that was by this time taking over his soul, even if he artfully kept it hidden from us all.

My long life has taught me that a person's descent into sin is composed of many steps. The fall of a godly man is a gradual process, and no doubt that this was true of my friend Judas. Did he ever realize what was happening to him? At some point, he became a man of double motives. Expressing concern for the poor, his true motive was covetousness. Showing outward acts of piety, his inner desire was greed, hidden under the cover of good works. He said the right words, but did the wrong deeds… or sometimes, no deeds at all.

There came a point at which Judas crossed a moral line, opening the door, outside which sin was couching, to Satan… who wasted no time in walking right through it, enjoying a special moment as he took advantage of my friend's accommodation of sin. Satan's sole desire was to destroy Christ, and it seems that he saw in Judas the instrument to help make that happen. While I don't want to diminish Judas' role in this, he was an actor in a greater spiritual drama playing out on a cosmic stage, an altercation between heaven and hell, good and evil, where Satan was using Judas to achieve his own ends.

Until now, I have been explaining what I perceived to have been happening in the life of Judas. Now, I come to the tragic ending of his life. I can guess with some level of accuracy what might have been going on in the mind and soul of Judas too, but only he could have known what it felt like to experience such a personal hell during the last couple of days of his life. Throughout our ministry, we had encountered (and dealt with) demon possession and seen the horrible physical and spiritual turmoil inflicted on the demon possessed, but I doubt if there are many who have known Satan to take personal control of their life. I can only imagine the destructive tsunami of fearsome wickedness and evil forcefully and chaotically crashing through a personality, leaving wanton destruction in its wake.

Together with those seeking to take the life of the Master, Judas came to the garden where Jesus was. It is beyond me to imagine what thought processes were now captivating his mind and heart as he placed a seemingly warm kiss of friendship on the cheek of Jesus, the treacherous sign of betrayal that identified the Master to his enemies. Can any observer truly portray the thoughts and heart of another?

After Jesus was seized, brutalized, tortured, put on trial, and ultimately murdered by crucifixion, during each moment of that chain of events, Judas too must have found himself inevitably pulled towards his end. Jesus chose how to bear and react to his ordeal; Judas was sucked down into an emotional and spiritual vortex. Doubtless he was smitten with guilt at the thought of his part leading to such a cruel death for the Master he had once loved. What did it feel like to betray the person to whom he had once vowed his allegiance? Whatever thoughts possessed him in those hours are now buried with him.

It is obvious that the weight of Judas' guilt, a burden too heavy for him to carry, was stressing his spirit to its breaking point. We know that his guilt incited him to return the money paid to him, indicating a recognition of his wrongdoing, and at least in some measure, a gesture of remorse. That was not enough, however, to alleviate the sense of guilt and self-reproach plaguing his soul. Wreaking havoc on his psyche, his emotional turmoil hauled him into an abyss so dark that he had no more hope of the possibility of redemption or deliverance from the personal torture to which his choices had pushed him. There seemed to be only one way out. So it was that Judas went and hung himself.

Even though more than half a century has passed, talking about Judas makes me sad. Sad, of course, because I lost a friend with whom I lived, worked, and shared a chapter of my life. Sad too, as I think about his eternal destiny. I am also cautioned when I realize how easily Judas' story can happen to others. It is sobering to remember that Judas did not start out as a villain. He was fallen, like all of us, to be sure, but in the face of the same feelings, desires, loves, failures, and temptations that we all experience, he made a series of choices that not only wrecked his life but led to an ignominious end.

The parallel journeys of Jesus and Judas during the days from Judas' betrayal to Jesus' crucifixion and Judas' suicide could not have played out more differently. Jesus, ever in control, chose to suffer and die through the wickedness of others for the sins of others and was vindicated through resurrection. Judas, ever losing control, suffered, and died because of his own chosen sin, and discovered that Satan is never kind to those who allow him to use them.

DISCUSSION QUESTIONS

1. Most people only think of Judas as the one who betrayed Christ. This story attempts to show him as a man who made some very tragic decisions. Did the overall flow of the story make you think any differently about Judas than you did before reading this story?

2. Do you think it fair that the one major event of his life (betraying Christ) defined totally who Judas was?

3. Putting aside the betrayal of Christ and pondering what kind of a person Judas might have been like for the early years of his life, what image comes to your mind?

4. Are there any positive thoughts that come to your mind when you think of Judas?

5. Why do you think Jesus chose Judas as one of his disciples? He had spent the entire night praying before choosing the men He would have as his closest followers (disciples). Do you think Jesus knew, when he picked him, that he would betray him?

6. Thinking about the previous question, if Christ knew when he picked Judas that he was going to betray him, do you think he treated Judas any differently than the others throughout the three years they spent together?

7. Is it possible that Judas was at first a person of good, solid character? If so, what might some of the dynamics have been that led to his spiritual and moral decline?

8. We know that Judas was the group's treasurer and that he was stealing money from the group. Do you think Jesus knew what Judas was doing? If so, why didn't He address this problem and confront Judas with his behavior, perhaps helping him to change direction before he reached the tragic end of his life?

9. Even to the very last night when Judas betrayed Jesus Christ, none of the others had any idea what was happening in the life of Judas. What does this tell us about Judas and the way he was living his life?

10. Judas had been effective in healing people and casting out demons, etc. when Jesus sent his disciples out on a ministry tour. There is no indication that Judas was any less effective in doing all that the other disciples did. Does this tell us that the decline and moral deterioration of Judas came over time, and that to start with, he was as committed and usable as all the other disciples?

11. The one thing that might have made Judas a little different from the others was that he was the sole disciple from Judea while all the others were from Galilee. Do you think this might have made Judas feel like an outsider or "different" from the others?

12. The disciples didn't perceive any problem with Judas before he betrayed Christ. Do you think that after the fact, they were able to see some indicators of Judas' decline?

13. Jesus indicated very near to the end of his life that one of the twelve was going to betray Him. How do you think the other disciples felt when they heard Jesus say this and He failed to identify to whom he was referring?

14. Thinking about the previous question, why do you think Jesus failed to confront Judas with his intention to betray Him?

15. The death of Christ involved a spiritual battle between Heaven and Hell. The Bible tells us that Satan himself entered Judas. Judas is responsible for opening his heart's door by his sinful decisions, but at some time Satan took advantage of this. Do you think there came a point in this spiritual battle that Judas lost control of his own will and was totally under the control of Satan?

16. What do you think Judas might have felt and thought when he placed his kiss on the cheek of Jesus?

17. What, in your opinion, caused Judas to hang himself?

18. Do you agree with the summary, "[Judas] was fallen, like all of us, to be sure, but in the face of the same feelings, desires, loves, failures, and temptations that we all experience, he made a series of choices that not only wrecked his life but led to an ignominious end"? How you see and feel about Judas as a person?

18

THE RESURRECTION OF CHRIST

Dispelling the Doubts

Although some of us disciples have now died, when we were living, we agreed as a group that there were three events that we experienced that had a transforming influence on us. None of these three events occurred to any one of us individually apart from the group, but we all shared in these experiences. No one can fully understand how we were transformed into the kind of group we became without talking about how these three events affected us.

What three events are these? It is no surprise that I am referring to the resurrection of the Master, His ascension to Heaven, and the coming of the Holy Spirit on the day of Pentecost. Each one of these events had a deep and lasting impact on us all, one being that we were transformed from being individuals called by Christ to a team of recognized Apostles in the church. Today we speak with authority and are honored by all the believers, but it was not always that way.

At the end of our three years of living alongside Jesus, we were anything but a confident and effective band of men. When Jesus was crucified, our world fell apart. Everything we had hoped for and believed in now seemed nothing more than futile, broken promises. What was there left to hope for? As we hunkered down together in fear of our lives in the days following the Master's death, our assurance had left us. We were a completely broken and shattered group. One of our members, Judas Iscariot, had tragically committed suicide. Those of us who were left were a disillusioned band. With the loss of everything to which we had dedicated ourselves, those dark days removed even the hope and cheer of a new dawn. We tried to encourage each other as best we could but what comfort could such demoralized spirits offer to each other? We were numb, drained to empty and without hope.

We were in mourning for one we had loved so dearly, traumatized by the horrific way in which he had died, and felt deceived because it had all come to nothing. It was only as we recognized the darkness in our souls that we began to understand the impact upon us of the first of those three events. Looking back after the fact, we can remember many times when Jesus had prepared us for his resurrection by telling us that it would happen, but none of us had really understood what he was saying. When we witnessed the raising of Lazarus from the dead, we should have understood better, but instead we considered that amazing event as a stand-alone miracle. We had looked on in awe yet failed to connect the reversal of Lazarus' death with Jesus' teaching about his own resurrection.

One Sunday morning, our hopelessness was turned into joy! Like a bright light bursting forth into dark, desolate caverns, transformational hope illuminated our souls. It was as if we, so emotionally and spiritually dead, experienced a resurrection of our spirits. It was not just Christ who was alive, but new life was breathing into us as well. Once again, life had a purpose, and we were being transformed to carry it out.

On that first Sunday after His resurrection, we were all, except for Thomas, huddled together, fearful, and secluded, unaware that several women had gone to the tomb to anoint Jesus' body. I remember Mary Magdalene running in to tell us what she and the other women had just experienced. At first, she talked about the possibility of grave robbers having stolen the body of Christ, but soon the other women added that an angel had appeared to them and told them that Christ had been resurrected from the dead. It was almost too much to believe! Their haste to bring the news to us and their excitement about such an astonishing experience was hard to assimilate in our depressed state.

Peter and John were quick to act on what the women had told us. Without skipping a beat, they immediately left the room that we were using as our "hiding place" and ran to the tomb to see for themselves; to confirm or negate the reports that the women had brought to us. After they returned, it was obvious that John had no doubts whatsoever about the reality of the resurrection of the Master. He seemed transformed, a man who had found hope again and his reason for living. His darkness had turned to light!

Peter, on the other hand, was not as confident and at peace as John about it. Later, Jesus would meet privately with Peter, removing all doubt for Peter by that encounter. The other eight of us, however, had to sort through our own feelings about what had occurred and weigh for ourselves the validity of the testimony of those claiming to have seen either the angel or Christ himself. Their excitement and vibrant mood certainly impressed us, but a claim so massive as a rising from the dead is difficult to accept. And what if they were mistaken? We would be setting ourselves up for a big disappointment. Over the next hours, we each had to work through our reactions, our tendencies to believe or doubt, as we weighed the reports that we had heard.

As the sun was nearing its hour of repose, the day about to fade into the early hours of evening, something unbelievable happened! We heard a knock at the door. When we opened it, we found two other followers of Jesus standing there. They were excited and eager, barely into the room before launching into the story of their encounter with Christ. I hope that our tempered reaction did not dampen their enthusiasm, for some of us still doubted the reports. Even in the light of multiple testimonies, some things seem almost impossible to believe. The difficulty of embracing something as improbable as a resurrection from the dead, together with a fear that it might turn out not to be true, was a formidable hurdle for some.

Peter was struggling with it. He slipped out into the twilight, perhaps to weigh for himself the full impact of what he was hearing. He was a man who had to sort out his own thoughts and find truth for himself. It was at that point that Jesus met him. Whatever doubts Peter had entertained were dispelled forever by his encounter with the living Christ. When he returned to our group, we all saw a different look on his face. Joy had replaced the haunting look of pain and confusion that all of us had displayed.

Before Peter had had time to share much about his encounter with Christ, Jesus himself appeared among us. He did not enter through the door, but just appeared. He told us not to be afraid. He ate some fish with us that night to show us that he had indeed come in bodily form, not as a ghost or spiritual apparition. He showed us the nail prints in his hands and talked to us about the ministry that we would all have. He talked about sending us into the world as his ambassadors, to represent Him to a lost and dying world. He did not stay long, vanishing as suddenly as he had arrived.

As for us, we would never be the same again. Any lingering doubts were now dispelled forever. Nothing, not even the threat of persecution or ultimate death, would shake our belief in the living Christ. As the darkness of the night descended outside, the inner light of assurance, faith, and fact-based hope burned brightly in our souls.

The following Sunday, we were once again gathered in the same room, this time with Thomas. He had heard our stories about having seen Christ. The changes in our spirits were evident too. However, doubt still lingered in Thomas's mind, and unbelief chained his spirit... until Christ once again suddenly appeared in the room with us. This time, he had his moment with Thomas, knowing just what was needed. *"Put your finger into the hole in my hand,"* he told Thomas, *"and your fist into the gap in my side."* That was enough to convince Thomas. His reservations evaporated in the warm reality of Christ's presence.

Thus, once again, we had become a united band of believers; not one of us doubted the truth of the resurrection of our beloved Master. With our renewed faith and full assurance came new spiritual struggles as well. What were we to do with our lives? Was it enough just to believe in a resurrected Christ? How were we to assimilate the great truth of the Master's resurrection into the way we lived our lives each day? What did Christ want or expect from us now? We thought about these things and often discussed them together.

The Master had specifically commanded us to return to Galilee, telling us we would see him again there. We were so excited about that. We did not know, however, that Christ would soon be leaving us. I think we were all hoping that we would once again walk with him, enjoying his presence as we had before. It took part of the week to make the long trek to Galilee from Judea. As we walked the many miles, our discussion was animated. Many questions came up about our future and what it would be like to live in the presence of the resurrected Christ. We waited, wondering when He would appear to us again.

The next time we saw Christ was when some of us had returned to fishing on the Sea of Galilee. Jesus had prepared a breakfast for us on the shore, and then made himself known to us. We immediately brought the boats to land and enjoyed another special time with the resurrected Lord. This moment was especially meaningful for Peter. Jesus had a conversation with him that centered on Peter's love for him. Three times Jesus asked Peter if he really loved him, and each time Peter reaffirmed his love for his Master. Even though the dialogue concerned the two of them, each of us affirmed in our hearts our love for Christ that day. We did not know that this would be our last personal and intimate time with Jesus Christ as a group.

We would learn later that Jesus had also appeared to his half-brother James. That moment transformed James, and for the first time, he embraced Jesus as more than just a member of his biological family. He accepted him as his Savior as well. Soon, the entire family of Jesus would make that same commitment to their sibling, now recognized as their Savior and Lord.

Christ appeared just once more, this time to approximately five hundred of his followers. After that, anyone wanting to deny that Jesus was alive would have to negate the testimony of a very large crowd of witnesses.

Not only did the resurrection of Christ prove his divinity and display his absolute power over death – in his own case and for anyone who believes in Him – but it was also the first of three events to transform us radically – individually and as a group. Our human despondency and hopelessness were replaced with joy and hope inspired by the living Christ and a Christ-filled purpose and future. So, the resurrection was the first key event to prepare what was to come. Two more were to follow.

DISCUSSION QUESTIONS

1. How do you think the disciples felt, and what do you think they did between the crucifixion of Christ and his resurrection?

2. Develop a list of words that describe how the disciples might have felt:
    a. before the resurrection of Christ
    b. after the resurrection of Christ

3. "Hopelessness" probably best describes the disciples' feelings immediately after the crucifixion (and before the resurrection). Try to put yourself in the disciples' shoes and talk about what it would have been like to experience this type of hopelessness.

4. In the story, the statement was made that during those three days between the crucifixion and the resurrection, the disciples tried to encourage each other as "best they could." What might they have done to try to encourage each other? Do you think any of this worked?

5. We know that the disciples doubted the firsts reports of the resurrection, brought to them by the women who had gone to the tomb on that first Easter morning. How do you reconcile their having witnessed the resurrection of Lazarus, yet doubting the resurrection of Christ? Do you think that one reason that Lazarus was raised might have been to give the disciples a basis for belief in the resurrection from the dead?

6. The disciples appeared to be in confusion during the few hours between the first report of Christ's resurrection by the women earlier in the morning and Christ's personal appearance to them late in the afternoon. During that time, Jesus appeared to the women, the two disciples on the road to Emmaus, and ultimately to Peter. John, apparently, was the only one to

believe initially. The others wavered between doubt and belief. Why do you think it was so hard for them to believe even when so many people testified to having seen Jesus alive?

7. Thinking about the previous question, even after the other ten believed in the resurrection, Thomas continued to doubt for another week. Why do you think Thomas had such a hard time believing in the resurrection given the growing number of eye-witness accounts?

8. On hearing about the empty tomb, Peter and John immediately ran there to see for themselves. Why do you think the other eight (Thomas not included) did not go with them to see for themselves what had happened?

9. When the two visitors that had been walking on the road to Emmaus came and reported to the disciples about the risen Christ having joined them on the road, how do you think the disciples received them and reacted to their report? Do you think they immediately believed what they were saying?

10. Peter, it appears, had his own struggle with believing in the resurrection. It seems he may still have doubted its reality until Christ appeared to him, probably shortly before he appeared to the twelve later that afternoon. Try to enter Peter's experience and describe what you think Peter might have been going through before Christ appeared to him for a "private meeting."

11. Why do you think Jesus ate some food in front of the disciples the first time he appeared to them? What did this prove to them?

12. After his first appearance, Christ did not appear to the disciples for another week. Do you think the disciples expected to see Christ again? What do you think it was like for the disciples during the week between the two appearances of Christ?

13. How do you think the disciples might have felt about and responded to the fact that Christ just suddenly appeared among them without knocking or coming through the door, and then disappeared the same way?

14. Why do you think Jesus told the disciples to return to Galilee where he would appear to them again? Remember that later they would return to Judea when Jesus would ascend to Heaven in their presence. Why do you think Jesus did not just let them remain in Judea for that brief span of time between the resurrection and the ascension?

15. After Christ appeared to them following his resurrection, he did not initially tell them he was going to leave them (although he had talked about this before his crucifixion). Do you think the disciples might have expected a whole new chapter to begin, once again living with, following, and ministering with the now resurrected Christ?

16. How do you think the other disciples felt during the dialogue between Jesus Christ and Peter on the shore of Galilee, when Jesus asked Peter three times if he loved him (assuming they heard it)? Do you think this might have caused them to examine their own level of love and commitment toward Christ?

17. There are two appearances of Christ that we know very little about, just that they are mentioned in the writings of Paul. One was to James, Jesus' half-brother, and the other to five hundred believers. Do you think the disciples were there, at least for the appearance to the five hundred? How do you think they felt about that appearance, and what impact might it have had on their lives?

18. Describe how Jesus Christ's resurrection has impacted your own life, past, present, and future.

19

THE ASCENSION

Receiving a New Direction

There are times when you are more able to fully know an individual by studying and understanding the external events that helped to shape his or her personality and the choice of values that person holds dear. These events in our lives are often more foundational to our development than we may realize. No person is an island and none of us can avoid events that will affect the direction of our life. Our reaction to such events will change us, and our transformation will affect the people around us. Are we always aware of the full impact that our lives have on others, and that others' lives have on us?

We disciples were deeply changed by three key events: the resurrection of Christ, his ascension, and the day of Pentecost when the Holy Spirit came upon us. What we became individually and as a group can be explained by our having lived through those events. I am going to talk about the second event, the ascension of Christ into Heaven.

I already explained how the first of those three events, the resurrection of Christ from the dead, changed us from a band of discouraged, frightened, and defeated men into men with a renewed purpose. The resurrection infused us with new hope and restored our reason for living. However, the resurrection did not give us all that we needed, for we still lacked vision, direction, and the power to be effective in what we did. Yes, we were filled with joy and excitement, our spirits set ablaze by seeing and talking with the risen Christ during the forty days following his resurrection when he appeared to us a few times, but afterwards, we were left with our thoughts and many unanswered questions about our future.

Jesus' brief appearances gave us convincing proof that he was alive, instilling within us a firm belief in the resurrected Christ that was so deeply rooted that nothing could convince us otherwise. No, not even persecution, the threat of death, or the stories circulated by our religious leaders trying to prove that the resurrection had not happened. But the question remained: what were we going to do with our lives? Just knowing that he was alive did not by itself give us any sense of direction about what we should do next. How, we wondered, would Christ want us to live and what would he want us to do?

We had time to reflect on the three years we had spent with Christ. We now understood so many things that he had told us that we had failed to comprehend when we first heard them. He had often talked about the Kingdom of God or the coming rule of God on earth, but our minds did not grasp the real intent and import of his words. Maybe we thought we understood what he meant, but looking back, our level of understanding was not nearly deep enough. It was enough for us just to try to discover who he was.

Our newfound excitement about Jesus Christ's return from the dead led to talk about what we were going to do with our lives. We floated ideas, but to be honest, we just could not find a sense of common agreement about what our future life should look like. Jesus often talked about the Kingdom of God, and this theme kept surfacing in our discussions. We wondered if this would be the time when God would set up his Kingdom on Earth and searched anew some of the Messianic prophecies from the great prophet Isaiah as well as others that spoke about this future rule of God on earth. That Jesus was that Messiah, we had no doubt. Peter had affirmed that way back at Caesarea Philippi when he became the first of us to say that we believed in Jesus Christ as God's chosen One. But all of that, as important as it was now to us as a group, failed to give us any sense of clear direction or singular purpose.

Jesus appeared to us when we returned to Galilee. Later, we went back to Judea in preparation for the Festival of Weeks and to observe our Jewish festival of Pentecost. Pentecost is the time that we bring our "tribute of a free-will offering" to the Lord fifty days after the Passover. It was established as a Jewish festival during the time of

Moses to be a completion of the grain harvest, a time of rejoicing and giving of thanks for God's abundant provision for us.

After the celebration of Pentecost, we would normally have returned to Galilee, but during one of Jesus Christ's appearances, he had given us clear instruction to stay in Jerusalem and wait for the gift that the Father had promised to give us. We were reminded of the words of John the Baptist when he said that one was coming who would "baptize with the Holy Spirit." As we talked about this, its full meaning was still veiled. It is one thing to speak of an event after it has occurred; it was quite different when we were living before the ascension of Christ and the coming of the Holy Spirit on the first Pentecost after his resurrection. We tried to understand the meaning of what he was telling us, but we were never able to agree about its implications for us.

Forty days after the Passover, as Pentecost drew near, the second life-changing event took place. Back in Galilee, we had met the risen Christ on the shores of the lake, but now we were in Judea again, and Jesus appeared to us once more. Not only were we excited about another post-resurrection visit but we were looking for answers to our questions. Some, if not all of us, were wondering if Jesus was going to begin his earthly rule, and if we would once again follow him, maybe as we had done during the former "glory days" in Galilee and Judea. We were ready to receive our new marching orders!

On this occasion, Jesus took us with him. We left the city of Jerusalem, taking the short walk to Mount Olivet. Walking with Jesus again made us hope that a new chapter of ministry with him was beginning, but even more glorious than the first three years. Truth be told, none of us had any notion about the nature of the events that were about to unfold. One of us asked what we had all been wondering: *"Lord are you at this time going to restore the kingdom to Israel?"* We thought that his answer might give us a clue to understanding our future. If someone had asked us what we thought he was going to say, I expect that most of us would have affirmed our belief, or I should say more accurately, our hope that he would affirm that he was ready to establish his rule on earth.

As Jews, we had been taught from childhood about the coming Messiah and how he would rule from David's throne as King over all the world, a righteous King who would exalt the Jewish people to a place of predominance and through whom he would rule the nations of the world. Now, it felt as if we might be on the cusp of seeing those ancient prophecies fulfilled.

We waited with anxious anticipation for the answer to our inquiry and were surprised when Jesus said, *"It is not for you to know the times or dates the Father has set by his own authority."* What a letdown! Jesus' words completely failed to meet our expectations or give us the clear direction for our lives that was so central in our thoughts. It took a moment to take in his response. I must confess, it was discouraging. Having imagined how this moment was going to look, we now found ourselves left with the same unanswered questions that had been preoccupying us before, and the same uncertain future. What were we to do now?

Jesus, however, was not done. Everything was about to change. For the first time since His death, he told us of our new mission and gave us insight into what our futures held. He began with a promise, telling us that we were going to receive power when the Holy Spirit came upon us. We recalled the last night we shared with him before he was crucified. During that evening he had talked about the "Comforter" that he was going to send to be with us and work among and through us. He now spoke more directly about an empowering that we would receive. I grabbed onto his words, because they conveyed renewed hope for a meaningful and fruitful future ministry.

"You will be my witnesses," he said, *"in Jerusalem, and in all Judea and Samaria, and to the ends of the earth."* Those words from the Master would become the blueprint for our entire future. He was, in that moment, giving us the commission for which our hearts were searching. Instead of our dark, unseen, and unknown future, Jesus was showing us what the rest of our lives were going to be like. Of course, and as usual, none of us completely understood all that he told us. It would take time to sink in and take shape, but it was enough to ignite a fire of anticipation and expectancy.

Before we could respond to his commission, or even say anything, quite remarkably his feet lifted from the ground, and he began floating upwards towards the heavens. Our eyes wide in wonder, we fell to our knees, the glory of it all so overwhelming that we could not even speak. Our gaze followed him, barely blinking, as he rose ever higher into the sky... until we lost sight of him as he entered the clouds. Wonderstruck, we continued to search for a last glimpse of the Master, but he was already out of sight.

Suddenly and inexplicably, two beings appeared beside us dressed in sparkling white. Even though they had the form of men, I am convinced they were not mortals, but angelic beings sent from heaven. "*Men of Galilee,*" they said, *"why do you stand here looking into the sky? This same Jesus, who has been taken from you into heaven, will come back in the same way you have seen him go into heaven."* At first, we were so overwhelmed that we remained speechless. The two heavenly visitors vanished before we could question them.

We went back to Jerusalem and gathered as a group in the place where we were staying. Jesus had told us to wait in this city until we received the promise of power through the coming of the Holy Spirit upon us. We realized that Jesus was unfolding a purpose so different from what we had ever imagined before and after he was crucified, and that it was being revealed to us through three pivotal events. He had convinced us of the reality of His resurrection, given us a clear direction for our future work, the huge commission to be his witnesses to the whole world and he said that we would receive power to carry it out. I would like to share more about that at another time, but perhaps now you have a better understanding of the impact the ascension had on our individual lives and on us as a group.

DISCUSSION QUESTIONS

1. The opening paragraph of this study talks about the impact that others have on us and says that all of us are influenced by others in a formative way. Think of people that have had the most influence on your life. How did they help to make you the person that you have become?

2. Not only are our lives influenced by other people, but also by certain events that can help make us the people we become. Do any such events come to your mind? How have they been pivotal in making you the person you have become?

3. The Resurrection of Christ confirmed to the disciples that He was indeed alive and that he was the promised Messiah. When thinking about the impact that the resurrection had on them, what questions did it answer for them and what did it confirm for them? What questions were left unanswered even after they had seen the resurrected Christ?

4. This story mentions a period of confusion for the disciples after Christ was crucified and before Pentecost (when they were empowered for service). What questions do you think the disciples might have asked among themselves about their future, even after having seen the risen Christ?

5. Though it is not talked about much in this story, we do know that at least some of the disciples returned to Galilee and their former work of fishing. What does this tell us about their mental and emotional condition between the time they saw the resurrected Christ and the day he was taken from them into Heaven?

6. Just before Christ was taken to heaven, the disciples asked him when he was going to restore the Kingdom of God on earth. What does their question tell us about their expectations for the future? Do you think it suggests that they expected him to remain on earth with them and that they would work with Him on establishing his new kingdom?

7. What do you think went through the minds of the disciples when Jesus told them to remain in Jerusalem and wait until they received Power from the Holy Spirit?

8. What do you think the disciples thought and felt when Jesus told them they were to be his witnesses in Jerusalem and ultimately to the ends of the earth? Do you think this helped bring focus to their wondering about what they were going to do with their lives?

9. Describe how you think the disciples might have felt and thought when Jesus suddenly began to rise into the sky?

10. Describe how you think the disciples might have felt and thought when "two men dressed in white" appeared beside them. Do you think they promptly realized these were angels?

11. After the disciples returned from Mount Olivet, what do you think they talked about when they were alone once again in the place they were staying? What might have been the spirit of the group?

20

PENTECOST

The Empowering Presence

I now come to the third in the triad of events, previously unimagined encounters with the supernatural power of the living God, that were so transformational in our collective lives as Apostles. The following story is not just the account of a wonderful experience given to us Apostles, but to others too.

There were only twelve apostles, counting Matthias who was chosen by us to replace Judas Iscariot. We were, however, not the only ones who had believed in the resurrected Christ. Before Christ ascended to Heaven, he had appeared to about five hundred people, most of whom were believers. Just before that, about one hundred and twenty followers of Christ were gathered in one place. So, we were already many, but only our Heavenly Father knows how many exactly, because we had no organized way of counting everyone who had believed in Jesus.

To recap what went before, the first pivotal event in our lives was Jesus' resurrection proved by his appearances. During those times with us, he dealt with our doubts and shortcomings in our relationship with him. That gave us a new, firm relationship with the living Christ that nothing has been able to shake. The second pivotal event was the ascension of Christ when he entrusted us with a mission that gave direction and purpose to our lives because he told us that we were going to be his witnesses, first right here at home but ultimately to the ends of the earth. Yet something was still lacking for we felt inept, not knowing how to be his witnesses, and intimidated by our fear of the religious authorities after their unjust and cruel dealings with our Master and the terror they had put us through.

After witnessing Christ being taken back into Heaven, we returned to Jerusalem, just as he had told us to do. There was a ten-day gap between the ascension of Christ and the wonderful day when the Holy Spirit came to us. the third pivotal event. Still keeping a low profile, we were all together behind closed doors, praying and worshipping the living Christ. We talked about all the amazing and wonder-filled experiences we had had with Him and tried to understand more fully how we were going to be the kind of witnesses he wanted.

During that time, we made one of our first major decisions as a group. There were eleven of us disciples along with some women who were followers of Christ. Mary, Jesus' mother, and all his siblings who now regularly met with us. Throughout the day, others would come and join in our times of prayer and fellowship. I remember especially the day when about one-hundred and twenty of us had come together. Peter stood up and began talking. He had always been the natural, impromptu leader of our group, right back to the beginning of the three years we spent with Jesus. His customary role never changed, and we all continued to look to Peter to give us direction.

On that day Peter reminded us of the painful fact that after betraying Christ, Judas had hung himself in remorse for what he had done. Peter suggested that we needed to choose someone to replace Judas, and that seemed like a good idea to us. As we talked, we decided on two qualifications for a replacement: he had to be a follower of Christ who had been involved with us since the time of John the Baptist's ministry and he had to have seen the resurrected Christ.

Two names surfaced of men who met our criteria: Joseph called Barsabbas (also known as Justus) and Matthias. We asked God earnestly for His direction. By our casting lots to discern the will of God in this weighty decision, Matthias became Judas' successor. We all embraced him as one of us.

By the end of the ten days between Jesus' ascension and the day of Pentecost, Jerusalem had filled up with pilgrims from all the surrounding nations. At the Feast of the Harvest, the faithful come with thankful hearts for the harvest and for all God's good provisions for our lives, expressed by bringing tithes. During such times, an amalgam of the languages spoken throughout the world can be heard as people walk the crowded streets of the city or linger in the Temple court, fusing into a unique mosaic of cultures and ethnic groups.

On the day we call Pentecost, exactly fifty days after the Passover, a sound like a mighty wind suddenly surrounded us while we were seated together in a room – but there was no actual wind. The phenomenon filled us with surprise, awe, and many questions. What did this mean? Just as suddenly, a flame appeared in our midst and separated into smaller flames, each in the shape of a tongue, that settled on each of us. As well as the strange signs we could hear and see, each of us sensed something profound taking place in our soul. We glanced around at each other enquiringly, waiting, wondering, and wanting to understand the significance of that extraordinary moment. Suddenly it dawned on us, no doubt by illumination from the Holy Spirit opening the eyes of our spiritual understanding, that this was what Jesus Christ had told us about on the last day when we met with him on the Mount of Olives. He had instructed us to tarry until the Holy Spirit came upon us with power. Not only that, but we also recalled the ancient prophecy of Joel who had written about a day when the Spirit of God would be poured out on all mankind. The Holy Spirit's inner witness confirmed to us that this was the very day and hour he had prophesied about so long ago. Without delay, we got up and went out to the Temple to join the teeming crowds who were in a celebratory mood. I am sure that the Spirit of God, now dwelling in our hearts, prompted us to go there.

What happened next defies any human reason. Each of us was given a new language to speak, languages that none of us had studied or already knew. We all began speaking these foreign tongues. Later, we were told by native speakers of those languages who were present that we had spoken their mother tongue as well as their most eloquent speakers with fluency and grammatical correctness.

This, of course, was no normal occurrence! Our multilingual "performance" was creating a flurry of excitement among the people nearest to us, rippling out across the crowd gathered in the Temple Square. As people reacted in amazement to what was happening, others were becoming aware of the commotion and pressed into the ever-growing mass. Everyone wanted to see and hear this strange occurrence for themselves.

We were all speaking at the same time, each of us with newfound boldness, proclaiming the truths about the resurrected Christ in the new language we had suddenly found ourselves using. It was obvious that we were all Galileans so people kept asking one another,

"How can it be that these men from Galilee are speaking in our native language?" Some began saying we were drunk, but they could not have been more wrong. Having drunk too much wine might have had us all gabbling but would never have bestowed upon us the instant use of an unknown language. Witnessing such an unprecedented phenomenon, others were grasping at what is familiar to try to explain the impossible.

Thousands were now pressing around us, setting the stage for the next wonderful miracle God was going to do among us. The Spirit of God moved in Peter's heart. We were flanking him as he stood up to address the massive crowd. He declared that we were not drunk, as some of them were saying. After all, this was too early in the morning, not the time when people get intoxicated with wine. No, he said, this was the fulfillment of God's promise made through the prophet Joel so many years ago when he prophesied this outpouring of the Spirit of God upon all people.

God's second miracle again defied human understanding. At first, we had all spoken in languages we did not know, and native speakers of the languages had understood us. Now, the reverse happened. Peter spoke in his native tongue, and yet everyone still understood what he said *in their own language*! This time the Spirit was giving not the gift of speech but that of interpretation, allowing Peter's words to enter the mind and heart of the listeners in their own languages. Even just trying to tell you about it, so many years later, still stirs in my soul a reflective glow that never seems to die within me.

Peter preached a powerful sermon about Jesus. He talked about Jesus' life and death, his resurrection, and how he was now with God in Heaven, sitting at the Father's right hand. It was not just Peter's words that spoke; we all sensed a new power radiating from him. His words had a new commanding and heart-convicting authority about them, and a sense of God's presence. The crowd, who just moments before had been loudly accusing us of being drunk or had been caught up in animated conversations trying to understand and explain what was happening, now stood in hushed silence.

The Spirit of God moved in the hearts of those rapt listeners, and deep conviction came over them. The noise and commotion were replaced by a collective plea for help and direction. Someone voiced the question on everyone's mind: *"What should we do?"* Peter explained exactly what was required, telling them to *"repent and be baptized, every one of you, in the name of Jesus Christ for the forgiveness of your sins, and you will receive the gift of the Holy Spirit. The promise is for you and your children and for all who are far off – for all whom the Lord our God will call."* Peter continued to warn and plead with them, urging them to save themselves from the corruption of sin and wrongdoing. Not everyone did as Peter asked, but about three thousand souls responded to Peter's message by embracing as their own Lord and Savior the Christ he was telling them about. We invited them to follow us and led them just outside the temple walls to the pools of water used for purification before people entered the Temple Square. There we baptized this great crowd of people, adding to the growing number of believers in Jesus.

My reason for telling this exciting story is that it was the third powerful pivotal experience to transform our group. With the coming of the Holy Spirit, God gave us the divine power we needed to fulfill the huge, world-encompassing mission that Jesus Christ had given us ten days earlier before he ascended into the sky. Now I can tell you that everyone of us has been faithfully carrying out the task that Christ gave us to do. Some of us have even been martyred for bearing faithful testimony to Christ. Those who remain continue to press on, actively and powerfully being Jesus' witnesses to the whole world.

But there is one more thought that still lingers in my mind as I share this remarkable story with you. Remembering the sermon Peter preached, he included a prophetic statement of which I want to remind you. He said: *"Repent and be baptized, every one of you, in the name of Jesus Christ for the forgiveness of your sins. And you will receive the gift of the Holy Spirit. The promise is for you and your children and for all who are far off—for all whom the Lord our God will call."* This wonderful gift that was so graciously given to us that day is God's gift for all his children. That same Spirit that filled our hearts can fill your soul as well. That same power given to us to be his faithful witnesses is also available to you, all you who know and love our precious Savior.

DISCUSSION QUESTIONS

1. This is the third of three accounts of the events experienced by the disciples as a group: the resurrection of Christ, the Ascension, and the Day of Pentecost. Each of these events met a specific need of the whole group and was instrumental in preparing them to live righteous lives and serve effectively for the Kingdom of God. Share how you think these three events dovetailed together in preparing them to be faithful and effective followers of Christ. If any one of these events had been omitted, do you think that the apostles could still have been effective in their future ministries? And could we be effective in ours?

2. The opening paragraph talks about the experience of Pentecost being not only for the benefit of the disciples but for all believers ("The promise is for you and your children and for all who are far off—for all whom the Lord our God will call.") We often focus just on those who were present on the Day of Pentecost. Share how you believe Pentecost is a continual blessing to all believers and how we appropriate its benefits in our lives today.

3. Describe what you think it might have been like for the disciples during the ten days between the ascension of Christ and the Day of Pentecost.

4. It was during those ten days between the ascension of Christ and the Day of Pentecost that the group chose Matthias as the replacement for Judas. Bible scholars are divided as to whether Matthias was God's choice or, as some believe, that Paul was the apostle that God chose to be Judas' replacement. Share your opinion on this unsettled question.

5. Thinking about the previous question, what do you think motivated Peter to suggest that they needed to find a replacement for Judas? Do you think that God led them, by the casting of lots, to choose the right individual, or do you think this was something they did apart from God's direction?

6. There must have been a few people who met the qualifications set out by Peter for the replacement for Judas. There were 120 people in the room when they talked about Judas' replacement and yet only two names surfaced. Do you believe God had been preparing these two men for this very time and experience?

7. What might the group's initial reaction have been when suddenly and unexpectedly there was the "sound of a mighty wind" even though there was probably no actual wind blowing through the house?

8. Thinking about the previous question, what do you think they thought and felt, and how might they have reacted when the flame came among them and divided into smaller flames shaped like a tongue that settled on each of them?

9. How do you think they felt, thought, and responded when they all began speaking in different languages that they had never studied or already knew?

10. The crowd began to gather around them as people realized that something very unusual was happening. What were some possible things they might have been thinking as they tried to understand what they were hearing and seeing?

11. When Peter finished his sermon, what might have been some of the possible reactions of the other disciples and the crowd?

12. What do you think Peter (and the others) might have thought and felt about the response to Peter's sermon, with about 3,000 people embracing Christ?

13. We are not told what happened after the Day of Pentecost. How do you think Peter and the other Apostles ministered to the large number of people after the Day of Pentecost?

14. How do you think they managed to baptize the large number of people with a limited supply of water?

21

PAUL

The Man of Diverse Cultures

My travels have taken me into many countries of the known world, and I have preached the Gospel to people in many different countries. It seems that God had prepared me for this special assignment from the day of my birth. You see, I am a man of many cultures, and that has helped me understand and relate to both Jews and Gentiles. At least four cultures were predominant in shaping my life.

My mother named me Saul, a fitting Hebrew name that is the first culture that I would like to talk about. My name might suggest something of my divine destiny for the Hebrew name Saul means, "Asked of God." Perhaps my Gentile name, Paul, fits me best because it means "little one," and I am quite small physically. It is more important, however, to know whether a person's character could be considered as big or small.

When it comes to my religious culture, I can say without any reservation that I was as good a Jew as anyone, maybe too good. No one could question my zeal, and I could never be faulted for failing to live up to the expectations of my Jewish faith. I embodied everything right about the Hebrew way of life.

Once when writing to the Corinthians, I felt the need to defend myself and I took the time to remind them of how Hebrew I really was, circumcised on the eighth day, of the stock of Israel, of the tribe of Benjamin. And I bore the name of the great King who came from that same tribe. As I said, A Hebrew of the Hebrews.

My father was a Pharisee too. He was so careful to make sure that I was schooled in all the ways of the Jewish people. We celebrated every Jewish feast with meticulous care. My father was so concerned that I should be well educated. For the first years of my life, I attended the Jewish school for boys in my hometown. Then my father, afraid that I would be spoiled by the culture of my Gentile city, sent me to a boarding school in Jerusalem. He certainly did his best to ensure that I was being well educated, both mentally and spiritually. I sat at the feet of some of the best Jewish teachers of my time, including the great Gamaliel. As I told the Corinthians, I was taught according to the perfect manner of the law of the fathers, and not only in terms of formal education. My father knew that our Jewish ways required every young man to learn a trade, no matter how rich or influential his parents might have been. Living in Tarsus, it was not unexpected that I should become a tent maker because the city was famous for its tents – not just ordinary tents but prized and sought-after tents made of goat's skin. I became a good tent maker just as I was a good Jew. No one could fault me for being a good Hebrew. I was among the best of them all.

Old Gamaliel, as wise and gentle as he was, cautioned us students to be moderate but I was so full of zeal for my Jewish faith that I was willing to do anything for the cause, even commit murder. And that I did, with a holy vengeance. Even the mere mention of my name brought fear to Christians everywhere. I pursued them with holy hate, at least as I understood it. You could have called me a Jewish fanatic, but I didn't see it that way then.

But I was also a Roman. Not many Jews became Roman citizens, but my father did. How glad I am that he acquired this rare privilege and passed it on to me. I knew how to use my Roman citizenship when I needed it. I wasn't just a Jew who happened to have a Roman citizenship but was truly a man of mixed cultures. Religiously I was a Jew, as Jewish as they come, but part of me was Roman as well, and I too took pride in that. In fact, once I began working with the Gentile world, I preferred to use my Roman name, Paul, over my Jewish name, Saul. I understand well how Romans think. Maybe that is what helped me to relate to people so quickly when I went from place to place, preaching the good news to the Gentile world and ultimately in Rome. People talk about culture shock and cultural adaptation, which I never quite understood because, from my birth, I was a man of many cultures.

Hebrew, Roman, and of course, Greek. Anyone of my era knows that the Romans ruled the world, but the Greeks ruled the mind. Tarsus was a Greek city influenced by one of the greatest universities of my time. I never attended this university, but I still came under its influence. The Greco-Roman influence was felt in every corner and on every street of my city. Tarsus was a trading center. People from every part of the known world walked our streets and rubbed shoulders with us. I listened to their stories and was awed by their wisdom of the world. I learned the ways of the world from them too. It was like a personal university education. What a privilege to be born and raised in such a cosmopolitan center.

My fourth culture is much harder to define but is the one that characterizes me most. The other three I learned and absorbed from the time I was a little child. All three were everywhere and I became a part of them all even if my Hebrew background was the one of which I was most proud, at least until I was in my thirties. Something happened then that changed my whole life.

I never doubted that what I was doing was right. I had permission that I had sought, in my zeal for my Jewish culture and religion, to deal with the new so-called "followers of the way." Today they are called Christians but then, we just called them people that followed the way of the Galilean. I hated them and did everything in my power to destroy them. Like a destructive whirlwind, I was feared everywhere as I pursued these people and put them in prison. I was responsible for the death of more than I can remember. All the time, I believed that my persecution of them was justified.

During one of my trips to persecute the followers of "the way" something happened that would add the fourth culture to my life, the Christian culture. I was on my way to Damascus and was almost at the edge of the city when a brilliantly bright light suddenly surrounded me. It was noon, and the sun, already bright in the sky, was nothing compared to the light that enveloped me. My companions saw it too. All of us were thrust to the ground by its intensity. It just knocked me right off my horse. I was the only one to hear the voice. The others heard something but thought it was thunder. I, however, heard a voice so clear, distinct, and compelling that I shall never forget it, nor shall I ever forget what the voice said to me as I lay there on the ground.

He spoke to me in Hebrew, calling me by my Hebrew name, *"Saul, Saul,"* he said, *"why do persecute me?"* I asked him who he was and if I had ever had any doubts, they vanished, for he said, *"JESUS OF NAZARETH, THE ONE YOU ARE PERSECUTING."* Can you imagine what I felt like in that moment? A mixture of awe, fear, confusion, and realization. Everything was happening all at once. Jesus, the one I was persecuting, was talking to me in the bright light, and I heard His voice as clearly as I heard the voice of any man that has ever lived. *"Saul, you find it hard to kick against the pricks,"* he said. He was right. It was hard. I didn't understand what was happening to me, but I did know that I was at his mercy. If I was going to survive it at all, this was going to be a life-transforming moment.

Then I asked the most important question that I have ever asked in my life. I addressed him as LORD. LORD, the one who owned my life. Only a few minutes before, I had cursed him, hated him, and done everything in my power to destroy those who followed him. And now I was calling him Lord. *"LORD,"* I said, *"what do you want me to do?"* My act of surrender happened so quickly.

He told me to go to Damascus and wait. Someone would come and give me further instructions. That is exactly what I did. For the next three days I could not see anything. As far as I knew, I was going to be blind for the rest of my life but even that didn't seem so important at that moment. I could not forget what had happened and was trying so hard to understand the change that had come over me. I was different inside. I didn't hate him any longer and I wanted to be one of his followers. but I didn't know how. I waited for the messenger he had promised would come. I knew that I was now a Christian too. I had meant what I said when I cried out, *"LORD, WHAT DO YOU WANT ME TO DO?"*

Now I am a man with another cultural influence operating in my life, a culture from Heaven. That is the strongest of them all. I will recount later all that happened during the rest of my life. Suffice it to say here that I was obedient to Him, lived the rest of my life for him, and ultimately died for him. I never wavered in my commitment to this newfound Savior. He transformed my life that day, and I spent the rest of my years telling men and women everywhere about him!

I was eventually called the Apostle to the Gentiles. Maybe I was always supposed to be that. In his foresight and providence, by making me a man of many cultures, God was preparing me from the very beginning to have a cross-cultural ministry taking his message of salvation to the nations.

DISCUSSION QUESTIONS

1. In what ways do you see God preparing Paul, even in his youngest years, to ultimately become the "Apostle to the Gentiles"?

2. Can and does God use our cultural backgrounds and experiences to further our effectiveness for his Kingdom?

3. Do you believe that being a man of many cultures created cultural tensions in Paul, or caused personal conflicts?

4. Can you think of instances in the Bible narrative where Paul drew on his cultural backgrounds to establish rapport or to use that background to his advantage? Examples: When Paul arrives in a new place, he goes first to the Synagogue and reasons with the Jews. When arrested, he appeals his case to Caesar as a Roman citizen. When he is in Greece, he reasons with the intellectuals on Mars Hill about the unknown God.

5. Do you have examples from your own experience where your background, cultural identification, and training have been useful to you in dealing with other people?

6. To what degree did Paul's experience on the Damascus Road change his earlier behavioral patterns? Did he merely add another experience or did this encounter with Christ immediately override all the other experiences of life?

7. To what degree did your encounter with Christ change your behavior, ways of thinking, etc.?

8. To what degree should we draw upon our past experiences and culture after we find Christ and/or to what degree should we try to remove ourselves from them once we become believers?

9. What are some of the lessons we can learn from Paul about using who and what we are to reach others for Christ?

22

PAUL

The Early Years of my Life

You look surprised as you enter this deplorable cell. Is it the shock of seeing me chained in such a horrid place or is it my physical appearance?

I have been imprisoned many times because of my unwavering loyalty to Christ and my faithful witness to Him before all who were willing to listen. I suppose I have become accustomed to prison life, even if such surroundings are uncomfortable. I have been in prison for most of the past six years with some brief interludes: time spent in transit from Caesarea to Rome and a short period of freedom between my first imprisonment here in Rome and my recapture. The first time I was confined here was when I was held under house arrest for almost two years. That allowed me the joy of entertaining many people that my life had touched. During that time, I talked of Jesus with my guards, and the influence of my presence in Rome rippled throughout the entire city. As I do now, I spent my time profitably, writing to some of the churches that God has permitted me to establish.

This imprisonment is different, however. Yes, here I am in this holding cell, bound by chains, waiting to appear before Caesar... and for my almost certain death. I am not complaining. I have learned, as I wrote to the Church at Philippi, to be content in whatever circumstances I find myself. That does not mean that I don't become discouraged at times or have moments of depression when sitting here alone with my thoughts. No man relishes being forced to endure the discomfort of a Roman prison cell. Yet my contentment is not eroded by the outward circumstances in which I find myself.

Looking back over sixty years, I can say that I have lived a good life. Not many people of our times reach that age. I almost did not reach this milestone, my life having been threatened so many times in so many ways, including having been stoned and left for dead, shipwrecked, and violently assaulted. God spared me time and again.

As far as my physical appearance is concerned, what can I say? No one can choose the body they have. Sometimes people are a bit surprised, when they meet someone they have heard so much about, to see that I have small stature with bowed legs and balding head, close-set eyes, and a crooked nose. As people get to know me, I hope that they can overlook my physical features and sense my spirit, feeling my heart's passion for the Christ that I love and serve.

I was not always a believer in Christ, but I was a believer all right, in the Jewish laws and way of life. A Pharisee of Pharisees, my zeal for what I believed in was almost unequaled. I came from a family of Pharisees; my father also being a member of that select group. I was born in the city of Tarsus. Our family were Jewish, of course, but in many ways, we resembled Gentiles. I spoke Greek fluently, as well as Hebrew and Aramaic. My names reflected my dual identity; my Greek name was Paul and my Hebrew name Saul. I did not prefer one over the other. The choice depended on where I was and with whom I was speaking. When with Hebrews, I was usually addressed by my Jewish name. Even Jesus Christ, when he appeared to me on the road to Damascus, called me by my Hebrew name, "Saul". When I was living and working in the Gentile world, I was usually referred to by my Greek name, "Paul."

My early years and basic education were typical for a young boy in my community. It was expected that we would learn a trade that would provide for our needs. Even though I was the son of a Pharisee, I was still expected to have a marketable trade. You might remember that the Talmud says: "What is commanded of a father towards his son? To circumcise him, to teach him the law, to teach him a trade." Among the Jews it was thought that the failure to teach a son a trade was to teach him to steal. My father took this admonishment seriously. I was taught the art of tent making and I put the same zeal into learning my craft as I did into anything I undertook in life. I always wanted to do my best and to excel as a student and as a person.

Although we were influential, our family was not aristocratic, and was of modest means. Because my father was a Roman citizen, that privilege was bestowed on me. I always cherished my Roman citizenship, but ultimately, I was to embrace another citizenship that had even greater meaning to me, when I became a citizen of Heaven. While living on this earth, however, my Roman citizenship, coupled with my ability as a tradesman, gave me great freedom as I would later travel throughout the Roman Empire.

If I were to permit myself to brag in any way about the man I once was, my boasting would probably have found its roots in two very important aspects of my early life:

First, there was my zeal for my Jewish faith. I was indeed the son of very devout Jewish parents and raised in all the traditions of that lifestyle. I never rebelled in any way against the faith of my parents but rather embraced it with a personal fervor that was noticed by all who knew me. I once wrote that I was one of the best Jews and Pharisees of this generation. I was not trying to brag, nor was I inflating myself. Fervency characterized everything I did in life. This same zeal would result in my persecuting believers in Christ and, in later life, in my becoming an effective missionary for Jesus Christ himself! No matter what I did, I put all my heart and soul into it. When I described myself as the "greatest of sinners," it was not exaggeration. That is the way I felt about myself.

Secondly, there was my education. I might well have been justified in bragging about the unique and special schooling that was available to me. My hometown of Tarsus was one of the most influential cities at the time of my youth, a trading center that drew people from all over the world. We had an influential university in our city, although I did not attend there.

My earliest training began at the feet of my mother until I was about five years of age when my father took over. Under his watchful eye, I was immersed in the Scriptures of our Jewish faith, committing much of them to memory. I was also taught about the traditional writings of our faith and schooled in our Jewish history. All this was coupled with my training in the Greek language, history, and culture.

Probably the most significant part of my education was being sent to Jerusalem to attend the rabbinical school of Gamaliel, the most famous rabbi of that era. The religious school of Gamaliel was mainly oral and was biased against any book but the Scriptures. During a regular school session, learned men met with students to discuss the Scriptures. We were encouraged to think for ourselves, to question, doubt, and even contradict the teachers. When our schooling was complete, we were well versed not only in our Jewish Scriptures, but also in the tradition of rabbinical interpretation. These privileges would serve me well in the ministry that was to be placed upon me.

I once wrote to the believers at Philippi summarizing my view of myself: *"If someone else thinks they have reasons to put confidence in the flesh, I have more,"* I said, *"circumcised on the eighth day, of the people of Israel, of the tribe of Benjamin, a Hebrew of Hebrews; in regard to the law, a Pharisee; as for zeal, persecuting the church; as for righteousness based on the law, faultless."* Of course, that reflects the life I lived before I met Jesus Christ on the day when he appeared to me in person.

I am often referred to as the Apostle to the Gentiles. Having spent most of the second half of my life working with people from many different nations, it is true that I most closely identified with Gentiles. My early formative years gave me the skills that I would need to move comfortably between both the Jewish and Gentile communities. I was, as I said, a Pharisee of Pharisees who understood the Jewish mind and way of life, but my upbringing had been steeped in Greek culture. I speak Greek as a native language and understand and identify with the Gentile mindset.

Part of my extended family lived in Jerusalem. A sister and her son would be used by God to protect me when the Jews were plotting my death. My nephew came and told me, and then the Roman officer in charge of me, about the plot that some had to kill me. Two other members of my extended family, Andronicus and Junia, became believers in Christ before I did. None of this mattered, however, in those early years and did not in any way change my attitude toward the new sect of believers in Jesus Christ.

You will never really understand who I was during the first half of my life unless you grasp how intently I hated those "followers of Jesus." I viewed them as a scourge against Judaism. I believed they were blaspheming God and leading people astray from the true faith of our fathers. I was convinced that Jesus was nothing more than a man who was rightfully executed for falsely claiming to be God. I threw everything I was behind my desire to right this horrible wrong against our Jewish faith, relentlessly pursuing and persecuting this band of believers. Because of me many of them were put in prison, much like the one I am sitting in now. The blood of some of them is on my hands, and the level of pain and grief that I brought to those early believers haunts my conscience. Let me repeat my sincere evaluation of myself as the greatest of sinners. If anything can temper the severity of my violence against them, it is that I did it all in ignorance. I am convinced that God has forgiven me for my abominable acts against His children, but the consolation of forgiveness does not remove the remembrance of my atrocities against His people.

One day, I was going to Damascus with orders from the Jewish officials to find and imprison the believers who had fled there from my relentless pressure against them and their beliefs. That was the day that I encountered the very Christ whose followers I was persecuting. That is the subject of another amazing story.

My background shaped not only the man I was but was a preparation for the man I became. Before Christ met me, humbled, and reoriented me, my education, religious training, and zeal led me to the misguided conclusion that I should seek to eradicate any perceived threat. But after Christ confronted me, forgave me, and convinced me of his truth, my background was indeed the perfect foundation for my God-given ministry to the Gentiles. I am convinced that God gives each person a specific background to use for his glory. All our life, when placed under the control of the Holy Spirit, can become a tool that the Master uses for his purposes. My life is a testimony to that great truth.

DISCUSSION QUESTIONS

1. Paul was imprisoned many times, for as long as two years on at least two occasions. One of those times was under a form of house arrest and the other in a designated prison. How do you think Paul felt about and handled these different times of imprisonment? Do you think he ever questioned why God was permitting him to endure these long periods of confinement?

2. To the best of Bible scholars' understanding, Paul probably had a short time of freedom between his first and second imprisonment in Rome. The first was more of a house arrest with a large degree of personal privileges (visitors, supplies for writing, etc.). The second was probably a very short period as he awaited his appearance before Caesar and his execution. Do you think Paul handled these two different experiences differently? Try to describe what you think life might have been like for Paul in both.

3. The church has lifted Paul to the status of an almost superhero. We often fail to realize he was a man like all of us with the same feelings and emotions that we all experience. When reflecting on the many books he wrote in the New Testament, what might have been some of his strengths and weaknesses as a person?

4. Answering the previous question, which did you find easier to talk about, Paul's strengths or weaknesses? What does your answer to the previous question possibly tell us about the way we in the church have come to view Paul as a person?

5. When you think of Paul, what is your mental image of his possible appearance? The description contained in this story

was left to us by some of the early church writings [Acts of Paul and Thecla, written about A. D. 150 – "bald headed, crooked legs, eyes set close together and a somewhat crooked nose"]. Does that physical description of Paul surprise you, or is it different from the mental image of him you might have envisaged?

6. Having read the account above, we see how Paul was exposed and immersed in both the Hebrew [Jewish] and Greek cultures. He spoke Hebrew, Greek and Aramaic. How do you see God using this exposure to both cultures in the ministry of Paul? Do you think Paul might have been more at ease with one culture than with the other?

7. One of the characteristics of Paul that stands out above all the rest was his zeal in whatever he was pursuing. He was "zealous" in all his endeavors, extreme at times. What might have been some factors in his upbringing and schooling, etc., that might have developed this characteristic in Paul's life?

8. The city of Tarsus was a city of great note in the time of Paul, a center of commerce and trade with a famous university and social interaction. How do you think this might have influenced Paul? What traits might he have learned from this kind of social setting?

9. Do you think there is any significance in the fact that when Jesus Christ met Paul on the road to Damascus, Jesus chose to call him by his Jewish name, Saul, rather than by his Greek name, Paul? By which of these two names do you think he might have preferred to be called?

10. Do you think there is any significance in the fact that Paul was sent to Jerusalem to study under Gamaliel, one of the most noted teachers among the Jews of that time? He may have been only ten years of age when he was sent to study there. What might this tell us about Paul as a young man and about his parents and their attitude both toward Paul as a person and their Jewish faith?

11. From the historical record we have of the school of Gamaliel, the students were exposed to some of the greatest Jewish scholars of that time. They were also encouraged to question, argue points, to disagree and to think for themselves. Do you see any of this type of training coming out in the ministry and writings of Paul? Can you share any examples?

12. We know that Paul had family that lived in Jerusalem. Paul wrote in Romans 16:7 about two of his family members who became believers before he did. How do you think he felt about these individuals when he was persecuting the believers prior to his own conversion?

13. Paul was relentless in his persecution of the followers of Christ before his conversion. He broke up homes, put people in prison and was responsible for the death of some. Do you think any of this bothered Paul in his later life? Remembering that Paul said he was "the greatest of sinners," does that statement give us any insight into how he viewed his responsibility for the persecution of believers.

23

PAUL

Pursuing the Persecutor
Acts 9:1-19; Acts 22:6-21; Acts 26:12-18

When I hear people talk about a mid-life crisis, I think such an experience might be true of me. The catalyst for my radical transformation, however, did not come from some emotional or psychological need, but from a personal meeting with Jesus Christ who brought about a complete change of character, purpose, and direction in my life.

I must begin by telling you how greatly I hated Jesus and his followers. I saw them as a threat to everything in which I believed, and I vowed to do all I could to eliminate their new movement from the face of the earth. Totally convinced that I was doing the will of God, I was relentless in my pursuit of them, staining my hands with their blood, caring nothing for the human misery I was causing when I broke up homes. My hatred for the followers of Jesus Christ was profound, and my zeal to eliminate them ardent. So successful was I in my opposition and pursuit of them that after my spiritual transformation, the extreme cruelty of my actions toward them convinced me that I had to be the greatest of sinners.

One day, as some of my sympathizers stoned to death one of Christ's followers named Stephen, I stood by, guarding their cloaks. With every stone they hurled at his helpless body, I nodded in silent assent, taking sadistic pleasure in their brutal act. Stephen's death would serve as a solemn warning to any who dared to claim allegiance to Jesus Christ.

Exterminating Christ's followers became my sole ambition. I had sought the blessing of the appropriate Jewish officials to hunt down Christ's followers even beyond the borders of Israel. The Jewish leaders even furnished official documents granting me permission to do as I willed in neighboring countries, so my unchecked persecution of the believers knew no bounds. I had men and women alike beaten, imprisoned, and put to death. I can tell you that even to this very hour, as I sit here as an old man, I am unable to rid myself of the images of my savagery. Much later, when writing to the believers at Corinth, I said, *"For I am the least of the apostles and do not even deserve to be called an apostle, because I persecuted the church of God. But by the grace of God, I am what I am, and his grace to me was not without effect."* Only because of God's grace could a sinner such as I not only be transformed but also be used by God for his good purposes.

The 180-degree change in my life happened in one glorious moment when I was on my way to the city of Damascus with a band of men to rout the diaspora of believers. During the 140-mile journey, I was seething with hatred toward those believers. We were nearing the city when suddenly a blinding light flashed onto our path and engulfed us. My horse bolted, throwing me to the ground from where I struggled to get up to investigate the source of the dazzling white light. Before I had time to discover what was producing this strange phenomenon, I heard a voice speaking to me out of the bright light, light that I now describe as nothing less than a reflection of the glory of God, a celestial splendor befitting the speaker who, I would soon learn, was none other than Jesus Christ himself.

"Saul, Saul," said the voice, *"why do you continue to persecute me?"* I did not answer the question. In fact, the question of why would never be addressed. Rather, I requested the identity of the one who was speaking to me. *"Who are you, Lord?"* I asked. Though I would come to call him Lord for the rest of my life, the first time I used the title was as a term of respect for the powerful being clothed in blazing light, not an indication of any belief in him as the Lord God.

"I am Jesus, whom you are persecuting," he said. Those words cut to my soul, and deep, sickening fear gripped me. Was I about to die? Was the persecutor now being persecuted, the hunter now the prey of the one he had sought to kill? Such thoughts were short-lived, though fear gripped me tightly for several days.

Only God's wonderful grace, his undeserved favor, can explain what happened next. *"Now get up and stand on your feet. I have appeared to you to appoint you as a servant and as a witness of what you have seen and will see of me,"* he said, *"I will rescue you from your own people and from the Gentiles. I am sending you to them to open their eyes and turn them from darkness to light, and from the power of Satan to God, so that they may receive forgiveness of sins and a place among those who are sanctified by faith in me."*

The first thought that flashed across my mind was that this was not a death sentence after all. I was not to suffer the wrath of the one I hated and persecuted. At first, I could not comprehend all that he was telling me. How could it be that I, the persecutor, should become the ambassador of the one I despised? The deeply hardened hate in my soul began to melt, and I was faced with a dilemma. How does the hater respond to this kind of love, the persecutor to this kind of commission to proclaim the message he had sought to discredit? I would have to wait a few more days for the answer. The voice speaking from the dazzling light instructed me to go into Damascus where I would be told what to do next.

The brilliant light began to fade and was replaced with a darkness deeper than the blackest, moonless night. It took but a few moments to realize that I had become blind. I cried out in despair! Colliding thoughts tumbled into my mind... the words that I had just heard... the fear of physical affliction threatening my way of life... How, I asked myself, could a blind man do what Jesus had just commissioned me to do? I was confused.

My companions led me to a house in the city of Damascus. My official papers and my murderous purpose in coming here no longer mattered. Persecuting others could not have been farther from my mind. I was now captive to my thoughts and struggle, trying to bring reason out of the events of the past hours. For the next three days I shut myself away from the world, neither eating nor drinking anything. Sleep came sporadically, granting only brief interludes of relief from the spiritual battle waging within me. I barely knew the difference between day and night. No mortal or spirit brought repose to my troubled heart. As I poured out my restless spirit in prayer during that black midnight of despair, I had a vision of a man named Ananias coming to me and restoring my sight. That brought balm to my troubled soul and began to replace the fear of blindness with the hope of restoration. It was then that I began to ponder more fully the commission that I had received from the Lord on the road to Damascus.

I would learn later that the same Jesus who had appeared to me in the brilliant light was also speaking to one of his children, Ananias, the man that Jesus Christ had said was going to come to me. Ananias would later tell me how God had instructed him to *"go to the house of Judas on Straight Street and ask for a man from Tarsus named Saul, for he is praying."* He was told that *"In a vision he has seen a man named Ananias come and place his hands on him to restore his sight."*

Ananias shared with me the deep fear he had felt at being told to come and talk to me. My reputation had preceded me, and he knew about my deep hatred for the followers of Jesus and my desire to destroy them wherever they were to be found. He told me that he had said to Jesus that he had heard the many reports about me and all the harm I had done to his followers in Jerusalem. But Ananias said that Jesus had directed him to come to where I was. He told Ananias that I was his chosen instrument to proclaim his name to the Gentiles and their kings, as well as to the people of Israel. When Ananias was sharing all this with me, it brought such comfort to my heart, a reaffirmation of the same commission that Jesus had given me from the dazzling light. However, Ananias also said something distressing – that I would suffer much for the sake of Jesus. I had no way of knowing how prophetic those words were going to be. Now, with most of my life behind me, I know exactly what Jesus meant when he talked of the sufferings I would endure. There is much to say about them, but that's a story yet to be told.

When Ananias first came into the house, he used a word that described a whole new relationship. *"Brother,"* was what he called me with the first word he spoke. Yes, he called me a brother, not in a biological sense but, as I would soon come to understand, as the term used by the followers of Jesus toward each other. He was calling me a brother in Christ, a brother in the family of God.

"Brother Saul" he said, *"Jesus, who appeared to you on the road as you were coming here – he has sent me so that you may see again and be filled with the Holy Spirit."* He had barely finished

speaking when I felt a movement in my eyes. I reached up to wipe them and try to discern what it was that I was feeling. Something on my hands felt like scales. Then the darkness began to dissipate, and light began to appear. Blurred figures around me slowly came into focus. My eyes fixed on the face of Ananias, the one that God had sent to restore my sight. Not only did I feel the joy and relief of restored sight, but an inner peace flooded my soul, a depth of peace that I had never experienced before. I could not explain it.

    I arose, and Ananias took some water and baptized me. For the first time in three days, I ate. My strength returned and I began to live again. Not only was I recovering physically, but I was beginning to understand the spiritual transformation that was taking place. It would take time for me to grasp it all, but I would never be the same. The second half of my life has been lived in the reality of that transformation. I was changed and reoriented that day, but one thing remained the same: my zeal! The same zeal with which I had lived and defended my Jewish faith would now be equally strong in my witness to the living Christ who stopped me in my misguided tracks on the road to Damascus, then sent me there no longer to murder, but forgiven, changed, and with a new purpose in life, to tell the world of God's gracious pardon for "the greatest of sinners" and for all who will believe in Jesus Christ.

DISCUSSION QUESTIONS

1. Sometimes people think that Paul being knocked off a horse was a positive thing, a "special conversion experience." It is highly probable that Paul was so stubborn and set in his ways, so highly motivated to destroy Christians, that Christ had to take this extreme measure even to get his attention. How do you feel about the way that Paul was converted? Was it a special kind of glorious experience or a means of getting the attention of a stubborn and hardened spirit? Do you think the more ordinary ways in which the Holy Spirit speaks to men would ever have reached Saul, or did God need to use some extraordinary means to get his attention?

2. What do you think might have gone through the mind of Paul when he was standing guard over the coats of the men who were stoning Stephen? The Bible tells us that "he gave his approval" to their actions. What does this tell us about Paul?

3. There is an old saying that states, "Great sinners make great saints." What were some of the personal characteristics that were evident in Paul's earlier years of life that continued to surface after his conversion experience?

4. Thinking about the previous question, what were some of the personal characteristics and behavioral patterns that Paul needed to change after his conversion experience? Do you think these changed all at once, or did some of these behavioral changes take time?

5. What might have been Paul's initial reaction when Jesus identified himself and told Paul that the one he was persecuting was talking to him now?

6. Jesus asked Paul, "Why are you persecuting me?" Paul never did answer that question. Do you think there was any reason he did not give an answer? Instead. Paul asked, "Who are you?" Do you think Paul did not know who was speaking to him? Why do you think Paul said what he did?

7. Do you think Paul initially feared for his life, thinking that maybe Jesus was going to "eliminate" this threat against him and his followers by taking Paul's life?

8. What do you think might have been some of Paul's first thoughts and his emotional reaction when, instead of taking his life, Jesus told him that he was chosen to be one of Christ's messengers and that God was going to use him to further his cause and help make his name known throughout the [then known] world?

9. At what point did Paul's strong hatred toward Christ disappear? How hard do you think it was for Paul to let go of the deeply rooted feelings he had held for so many years?

10. How do you think Paul thought and reacted when the light faded, and he suddenly realized that he could not see, that he was blind?

11. We know that for some days Paul isolated himself, did not eat or drink, and was despondent. Try to enter Paul's life and describe how you think he was feeling. What might have been some of his patterns of thought?

12. At some point during those three days of despondency, Paul had a vision of a man coming to him and restoring his sight.

Describe how you think Paul might have thought and felt when God gave him this vision.

13. Knowing Saul's reputation as a persecutor of believers in Jesus Christ, how do you think Ananias felt, and what might have been some of his initial thoughts, when God appeared to him telling him to go and talk and minister to Paul?

14. What do you think Paul might have felt and thought when Ananias came and from the outset called him "brother"?

15. The Bible tells us that when God appeared to Ananias, He told him that Paul "was praying." Does this give us further insight into what might have been going on in Paul's mind and heart during the three dark days between his vision and the visit of Ananias?

16. How do you think Paul felt and thought when he realized he could see again?

17. What do you think Paul might have felt like and thought when Ananias revealed that God had told him to tell Paul that he "would suffer many things for the sake of Christ"?

18. Ananias immediately baptized Saul. How hard do you think it was for Paul to now embrace, love, and identify with the followers of Christ and become part of their new community and embrace their way of life.

24

PAUL

The Forgotten Years of Ministry

When people talk about my ministry, they mostly focus on my missionary journeys. They were certainly the most public parts of my life but were preceded by what I will call the "silent" years of ministry. The letters that I have written to the various churches contain glimpses into this part of my life, but I do not say much about my activities. Why? Perhaps because the intensity and success of the missionary journeys overshadowed the service of earlier years when I was beginning ministry for Jesus Christ.

The first years following my conversion on the road to Damascus were to some degree "set aside" in preparation for the more intense ministry God was going to give me. That does not mean that I was inactive or did not preach, but I took time to learn and grow in my new spiritual life. It is interesting to note how God sometimes uses many years of preparation prior to some condensed years of intense ministry. I think of Moses. God took eighty years to prepare him for his last forty years of leadership. It was true in my case too. I lived the first half of my life pursuing my Jewish faith and was over thirty when Christ met me on the Damascus Road. I am now in my early sixties, in prison, and awaiting my almost certain death.

Immediately after my conversion, I became involved in a completely new kind of ministry. Spending several days with the believers in Damascus was a time for me to sit at the feet of and learn from the very people I had set out to hunt, imprison, or worse. Now, like a dry sponge, I avidly soaked up everything I could learn about Jesus. Being so deeply versed in the Jewish faith gave me a good foundation of theological thinking. I knew a lot about Jehovah and his dealings with our ancestors. Nevertheless, I had so much more to learn about His Son.

In Damascus I did something that would set a pattern for the rest of my life. I went to the synagogue and began to preach boldly that Jesus is the Son of God. During the missionary journeys for which I would later become known, I always went to a town's synagogue first and reasoned with the Jews. It was only after they rejected me that I would begin preaching to the Gentiles. My first preaching began by proclaiming Jesus to the Jews in Damascus. People wanted to come and see this man who had been raising such havoc in Jerusalem and had come to Damascus with orders from Jerusalem in hand to persecute the followers of Christ. Hearing of my transformation incited a high level of curiosity.

My preaching was filled with newfound power. My audience was moved as they silently listened to every word. Except for the Jewish authorities, that is. My proclamation that Jesus is God's Son did not sit well with them at all. Soon a question was circulating: *"Isn't he the man who raised havoc in Jerusalem among those who call on this name? And hasn't he come here to take them as prisoners to the chief priests?"* The leaders of the synagogue tried to persuade me that what I was saying was not true, yet no matter how cleverly they talked, or how brilliantly they reasoned, I baffled them by giving an answer to whatever objection they made. My confidence as I preached Christ increased rapidly, and I felt comfortable in that ministry.

Within a matter of days, my popularity in the synagogue began to wane. I was no longer accepted there as I had been. Curiosity was turning to animosity. This too was setting a pattern that I would have to learn to live with for the rest of my life. Wherever I went, I generated a certain amount of suspicion, even hatred from the Jews. Little did I know how difficult my life was going to be! The haunting words of Ananias who delivered Christ's warning that I would suffer much for preaching about Him, were becoming my reality.

Before many days had passed, I began hearing rumors of a "conspiracy among the Jews" to kill me. My great fear made me realize what kind of terror I must have inflicted on the people I had persecuted. Is it ever possible to become conditioned to constant threats on one's life? Over the years I would learn to live with that ever-present possibility. Even today, I sit here waiting to hear when I will be executed. Never knowing, when I arise each morning, whether I will see the day's end, every day has become a precious gift of life. The first experience of hearing that people were plotting to kill me was the most difficult. Since then, I have looked death in the face many times and have learned, with God's help, to be content no matter what happens. The thought of death no longer holds the fear for me that it once did.

The followers of Jesus also heard the rumors of plots to kill me. They feared for my safety and decided it would be best if I left Damascus. By then the religious authorities had arranged to have people guard the city gates to prevent me from leaving the city. I was trapped! One of us, however, had the idea of lowering me over the city walls in a basket during the darkness of the night. I fled for my life!

I made a short trip to Jerusalem, thinking that perhaps I would meet with the Apostles. After all that I had done to them, you can imagine their level of fear. Barnabas came to my defense, and I stayed in Jerusalem for a short time. Peter and I spent fifteen wonderful days together in Jerusalem. I also had a brief visit with James the brother of Jesus. I did not meet with any of the others. My reputation was still creating doubt in the minds of some. But it was the Jews who became particularly uncomfortable with my presence in Jerusalem. I was moving about quite freely in the city, speaking boldly in the name of the Lord. I talked and debated with Hellenistic Jews whenever I could get an audience. Once again, however, it was just as it had been in Damascus. We learned that the Jews were planning to have me killed. Convinced that it was unsafe for me to remain in Jerusalem, the believers escorted me to Caesarea and from there sent me off to Tarsus.

For the next three years I moved from place to place. I continued to learn, my faith continued to grow, and my walk with Christ matured. There was time to read, study, and cultivate the discipline of prayer that would characterize the rest of my life. I did not adopt the seclusion of a hermit as I travelled, but gladly seized opportunities to share my testimony about meeting Christ, to preach to a crowd of people, or go into some synagogue on the Sabbath and reason with the congregation about the person of Jesus. When compared with my later ministry, however, these years appear to be a time of relative obscurity.

I regarded them as a time of special training with some unique experiences, one of which I have chosen not to talk about. In fact, I think Jesus made that choice for me. I have mentioned it on few occasions, and I did mention it in a letter I wrote to the Corinthians. To this day, I have found no explanation for how it happened, whether I went literally in my body into Heaven – or just in spirit – but the means do not really matter. What matters is that I was permitted to see "heavenly things" and learn things that I was later forbidden to even talk about. Had I chosen to, I could have bragged about this, but I found that silence was the best way to handle this unique God-given experience. On the one hand, it was a very special time of bonding between Jesus and me; on the other, it was also a crash course in discovering what God is like and a preparation for the high calling that God had placed on my life. Even sharing this much is more than I usually tell anyone.

Sometimes I have wondered what was going to happen to me. While my ministry brought me satisfaction, I always sensed that God had more for me to do. After all, he had told me on the very first day he met me, that I was going to be his witness to the Gentiles. Sometimes I wondered when this was going to happen.

Visiting me unexpectedly, Barnabas invited me to join him in Antioch. The irony of this invitation was that the church in Antioch had been birthed by the witness of faithful followers of Christ who had fled Jerusalem because of the stoning of Stephen and the persecution that I had brought upon the believers. Now they were inviting me, their former persecutor, to come and minister among them. I gladly accepted the invitation. Barnabas and I spent the next year in very fruitful ministry together in that city. Under our leadership, the church grew and prospered. It was here that people first started referring to us as "Christians." I enjoyed that good year.

During the year at Antioch a group of prophets came to our city, one of whom was named Agabus. He stood up one night and under clear direction of the Holy Spirit predicted that a severe famine would spread in parts of the Roman world. The economy around Antioch at that time was prosperous, and the leaders of our congregation decided they wanted to take an offering to help the brothers and sisters in Judea. We raised a substantial amount of money to help them get through the famine which occurred later, during the reign of Claudius. This offering at Antioch was the first of several that I would help raise for the hurting church in Judea. I also collected money for them from many of the Gentile congregations that I would establish in coming years.

The congregation decided to send Barnabas and me to Jerusalem to deliver the money on their behalf which was meaningful for me because it was an opportunity to give a little back to those from whom I had taken so much. From some, however, I had taken their lives. What did those whom I had had beaten and imprisoned think when we came with this love offering? I hoped that they saw in me the new man that I had become and were able to forgive me for the terrible things I had done to them.

After completing our compassionate mission, Barnabas and I returned once again to Antioch where I assumed we would continue our successful ministry, but God had a different plan. Soon after our arrival, the elders of the church met and decided to send Barnabas and me on a trip that would begin my missionary career.

As I said, everyone talks about my missionary journeys as the main events of my ministry, but the earlier years, following my conversion, were significant times of service and valuable on-the-job training. They were more tranquil than the later years which brought all manner of threats and persecution. Those years were so important for my personal growth, maturation, and preparation for the vast missionary task that God had planned for me. I could not have done the latter without the former.

DISCUSSION QUESTIONS

1. It appears that Paul was involved in early ministries. Only glimpses of this part of Paul's life appear in his writings and in the Book of Acts. Why do you think Paul in particular, and the Bible in general, say so little about these years in Paul's life?

2. When someone mentions Paul, what is the first thing that comes to your mind? Why do you think these items surface first in your thinking?

3. Preachers often say that Paul lived as a recluse in the desert, retooling and growing in his newfound faith in Christ. Yet the Bible does not seem to indicate that to be the case. He was involved in ministry, reasoning with the Jews in Damascus, for example, about the risen Christ. Before doing this study, what were your ideas about what Paul did between his conversion and the beginning of his ministry with Barnabas in Antioch?

4. Paul was well versed in the Old Testament and Jewish thinking. How do you think he learned the things he needed to know about Christ and the new Christian movement? There is no indication that he had any further formal training. What were some of the ways God may have used to prepare him for the new chapter in his life?

5. Moses was eighty years old before he began a ministry that would last for the remaining forty years of his life. Jesus was thirty when he began a three-year ministry. Paul was about halfway through his life before beginning his Christian ministry. What does this tell us about God's timetable for us? What might this tell us about our wanting to put new Christians

to work in ministry immediately, and about the place and role of preparation for ministry and service for Christ in the church?

6. How hard do you think it was for the believers in Damascus to begin to trust Paul, having heard about his persecution of believers in Judea, and having been on a mission to persecute them as well?

7. After Paul's conversion, he first went to the synagogue in Damascus and "reasoned mightily with the Jews." This would become a pattern in his ministry. In the Book of Acts, when Paul would go into a new area, he always sought out the Jews first and tried to "convert" them before preaching to the Gentiles. Why do you think Paul did this?

8. How do you think Paul felt and thought when the Jews in Damascus began to turn on him and were soon plotting his death? Remember, Paul had originally come to Damascus to imprison and kill Christians. Now it was he who was the object of a death plot. Do you think this suddenly made what he had been doing to others more real and personal?

9. What do you think Paul might have been feeling and thinking when the believers in Damascus feared for his life and let him down the side of the city wall in a basket so that he could escape probable death at the hands of the Jews?

10. The believers in Jerusalem had been persecuted very severely at the hand of Paul. When Paul came back to Jerusalem for the first time after his conversion: 1) How do you think Paul felt about facing this group for the first time? 2) How do you think the believers in Jerusalem felt about seeing Paul again for the first time following his conversion?

11. Thinking about the previous question, how do you think the believers in Jerusalem felt and thought when Barnabas and Saul (Paul) presented to them the significant offering to help them in their time of need?

12. Why do you think Barnabas was so willing to accept Paul and become the meditator between Paul and the believers in Jerusalem?

13. We know that Paul spent at least fifteen days in Jerusalem and met only with Peter and James. Why do you think he did not meet with the other disciples, or the other disciples with him?

14. We know that the Jews in Jerusalem soon turned against Saul after his appearance there following his conversion. These were the men who had worked so closely with Paul before his conversion to Christ. How do you think Paul might have felt about their turning their back on him and wanting to have him killed?

15. Many of the believers in Antioch were there because they had fled from Jerusalem because of the fierce persecution of them by Paul before his conversion. Now he has been brought back by Barnabas, and he and Barnabas served as their leaders for the next year. How do you think both Paul and the believers in Antioch felt about now having Paul as their leader when he had been responsible for imprisoning some of them and perhaps even having had some of their family members put to death?

16. We know about Paul's experience when he was taken to Heaven, as he shared a little about that in the Book of II Corinthians. This is something almost beyond our ability to

comprehend. As far as we know, Paul didn't talk about it. Why do you think Paul might have been so quiet about such a wonderful experience?

17. Thinking about the story today and the discussion these questions have produced, how do you see God using this entire chapter in Paul's life to prepare him for the missionary career that was to follow?

25

PAUL

Counting the Cost

Seeing only the fame of some of our lives, some people think that our service as Christ's Apostles was filled with joy and continual excitement. It is true that we all found great satisfaction in our faithfulness to Christ and in our service to Him and His Kingdom. I do not believe, however, that any of us would say that fulfilling our call as an Apostle meant that we lived glorious lives free from difficulties, trials, problems, and pain. Even in this prison cell, I am aware of the cruel deaths already suffered by some of our group that will likely befall me as well.

What I have had to endure during my years of ministry is representative of us all, for we have all had to endure persecution for following Christ. In a letter I just wrote to Timothy, I said, "...*all that will live godly lives in Christ Jesus will suffer persecution.*" And that has been our experience. At times I feel as if I deserve what I have received, my just deserts for my horrendous hounding of Christ's followers before he stopped me on the road to Damascus. But what have the other Apostles done to provoke the kind of hatred and cruelty that they have had to endure? Nothing but witness faithfully to the life, death, and resurrection of the Master.

From the moment I met Christ, I knew that my life was destined to be productive, but also beset with trials and difficulties. When Ananias came to me, he shared a message from God. I was, he said, a chosen instrument to proclaim Christ to the Gentiles and their kings, and he added that I was to suffer much for the name of Christ. It was good that I could not envisage what that would entail, or I might well have been reluctant to face my future. Looking back now, I see that my life has been full and productive, and I would not change that for anything. However, memories of the pain and suffering I endured for my service to Christ are still with me, and I bear on my body the scars of ill treatment, but by God's grace, I see them as symbols of faithful submission to the whole will of God, which includes the "bad" along with the "good".

Persecution began almost as soon as I started following the Master. Immediately after meeting him on the road to Damascus, I took up proclaiming enthusiastically that He had risen from the dead. I began telling the Jews in the Synagogue in Damascus about my newfound faith. At first, they listened with curiosity, wondering how this persecutor of the Nazarene had now become his loyal follower. But it did not take long, just a matter of days, before I was no longer an object of their curiosity but a target of their hate. After learning about their plot to kill me and knowing that the gates of the city were guarded, I escaped in a basket lowered over the city wall at the dead of night. From then on, a death sentence hung over my life and ministry.

I went to Jerusalem with Barnabas and again I talked about my encounter with Christ, reasoning with the Hellenistic Jews and any others who would listen. Once again after a short time, they too talked of killing me. I was taken down to Caesarea and from there sent to Tarsus where I spent some time in relative safety, a short reprieve from the troubles that would mark most of my life.

I soon experienced the searing pain of whip and rod being applied forcefully across my back. The Jewish authorities had me whipped on five separate occasions. At least those were more merciful floggings than I would have received from the Roman authorities, for the Jews were forced to limit the number of blows delivered to 39 at any one time. So, I received 195 lashes across my back from the Jewish authorities over a period of years. But the worst came with the beatings at the hands of the Romans. They had no restrictions to the number of blows a victim might receive at their hands. The intense pain of these thrashings renders a man almost unconscious, while he wishes that it would wipe out consciousness altogether. Without control or restraints, the wielder of the rod strikes mercilessly the lacerated and bleeding back of his victim. It was not uncommon for some to die during this act of violent cruelty. I suffered under the Roman rod on three occasions – and survived.

One time I was beaten in the city of Philippi. After the beating, I was cast into a dark dungeon of the inner prison along with Silas, our feet secured in stocks. The open wounds on our backs smarted and bled, yet we rejoiced in God and thanked him for the privilege of suffering for His sake. Amazingly, God graciously freed us by orchestrating an earthquake that shook the prison, freeing us from our restraints. Seeing that wonderful divine intervention, our jailor and his family decided to trust Christ! While I would prefer to talk about the good that came out of that dark episode of pain and suffering, I want to focus here on the cost of following Jesus and how that looked for me.

At Iconium we saw a great number of Jews and Gentiles believe in Jesus Christ. There too we had to contend with a Jewish element that always tried to undo any good we brought to a community. This time a strange alliance of Jews and Gentiles strove to destroy our ministry and to bring harm to us, even talking of stoning us. Having learned about their plot, we decided to leave that city, going to minister at the Lycaonian cities of Lystra and Derbe.

At first the response to our message was tremendous. After we healed a lame man, the locals wanted to make Barnabas and me into gods. That was an intense moment that showed to what extent they accepted us and were open to our message, until the Jews, who always followed us around, arrived and set about poisoning the minds of those people. I almost lost my life at Lystra. They took up stones and began throwing them at me. Can you imagine what it is like to be pelted with heavy rocks? The fear and horror of that moment, the instinct to run, but to where? As fast, hard projectiles broke my skin and bruised my bones until my whole body became a swelling mass of pain. I fell, unconscious. Thinking I was dead, they dragged my body outside the city where I eventually regained consciousness, finding myself surrounded by faithful men and women who had responded to the message I had brought to them. Although I hurt all over and my bruises and wounds were swollen and vivid, I arose, went back into the city, and spent another day there before leaving for Derbe. How grateful I was to God that I was able to walk without aid.

As I look at what it cost me to follow Christ, I must include three separate occasions when I was shipwrecked. Being on a sinking ship brings a whole different kind of terror. One imagines death by drowning or drifting on a piece of wreckage in a limitless body of water, not knowing if rescue will come, a slow death from thirst and hunger. On one of those occasions, I floated on a piece of the wreck for a day and a half before I was rescued. Many thoughts pass through the mind of a man during such a time.

I seldom felt free from the ever-lurking possibility of calamity. Often, a group of radical Jews who followed me everywhere trying to do whatever they could to undo the good that came through our ministry were my greatest trial. They would stir up a mob, often resulting in action against us. Sometimes we had to flee certain areas in fear for our lives. Other times we were beaten or imprisoned by these wicked opponents of our message and Savior. At other times, they incited Gentiles to turn against us.

I do not complain about all this but am merely giving examples of what it cost me to be a follower of Christ and a missionary to the nations around us. No, I do not complain because by God's grace I have learned to be content in whatever state I find myself.

There were times when the demands of ministry coupled with working to earn my living made me very weary. When I was too exhausted at the end of a long and trying day, sleep would often elude me. At times when I did not have enough to eat, I learned to live with hunger and still rejoice in the goodness of God. When my garments were well worn and threadbare or when I lacked warm clothing to ward off the cool winter chill, I found an inner peace in any circumstances. Of the thirty-five years I have served Christ, almost six were spent in prison and at this very moment, I expect my execution to be imminent, but that is not what consumes my thoughts for I am at peace about any outcome. Even though I may have suffered much for Christ, my soul rejoices in hope. As I wrote in one of my letters, *"For me to live is Christ, to die is gain!"*

There are many more examples I could share about hard and difficult times, but these suffice to illustrate the cost of being a follower and witness of the risen Christ in terms of loss of personal comfort and having to endure physical pain as an ambassador to the nations. The words of Ananias were indeed prophetic, but I have come to see my suffering as nothing compared with the privilege of serving Jesus.

None of us Apostles have escaped persecution, and several have already paid the price of discipleship with their lives. I do not think that any one of us would have had it any other way. We all believe that the reward awaiting us is far greater than anything men could do to us. Not one of us has desired or sought to be hated or persecuted. As all people, we prefer to be liked and accepted, and we long for our message to be embraced by all. We know, however, that that will not be the case.

In times when we fear what may happen or are asked to endure a time of deprivation of some comfort or are forced to endure physical pain, all we must do is remember the death of our Lord Jesus Christ on the cross. He experienced unimaginable terror and agony, both physical and spiritual, as He took upon himself the horror of my sins and yours, indeed the sins of all humanity, bringing unprecedented, unfathomable, unbearable separation from His Father, the costliest price he could possibly pay. In the blackness, pain, and desolation of that loss of his closest and dearest relationship, he cried out, *"My God, My God, why have you forsaken me?"* In the light of that greatest of sacrifices, I count it a small thing that I should suffer for Him. Indeed, I am ready to offer my life as a token of my gratitude and love for the One who gave His all for me.

DISCUSSION QUESTIONS

1. This study has focused on the difficulties Paul faced in his life. The opening paragraph stated that many people only focus on the blessings that come through serving Christ. When you thought about the life and ministry of Paul before reading this story, on what did your thoughts focus? Did this story help you understand more clearly the price that Paul had to pay for his loyalty to Christ and his Kingdom?

2. Writing to Timothy near the end of his life Paul said, "… all that will live godly lives in Christ Jesus will suffer persecution." To what degree do you believe this reflected his own personal experiences as well as his knowledge of what was happening to some of the other Apostles? How do you reconcile that statement with our lives in America today? How do we currently suffer persecution? How do you think believers in America might suffer persecution in the future?

3. How do you think Paul might have felt and thought during some of his trials, beatings, imprisonments, etc., when he remembered that in his earlier years, he had been responsible for doing these same things to followers of Christ?

4. When Ananias came to Paul, after Paul met Christ on the road to Damascus, he told Paul that he would be a source of great blessings to the Gentiles but also warned him that he would suffer much for his service to Christ. Do you think the words of Ananias helped Paul to put his sufferings into perspective?

5. It is highly probable that Paul bore scars from the many beatings he had received. How do you think Paul viewed these physical reminders of his suffering? Do you think they recalled

traumatic memories of what had happened to him, or were they more of a "trophy" in his service to Christ?

6. A group of Jews appear to have followed Paul around, causing people to turn against him and often inciting persecution, beatings, stoning, etc. What do you think might have been going through Paul's mind as he was being taken to be lashed with whips and beaten with rods? What might he have thought during the beatings? Do you think he harbored any resentment toward the men who were inflicting pain on him? He uses harsh words and comments about them in his letters, yet he shows such compassion and care for the Philippian jailor who had participated in his severe beating and put him in stocks. What made the difference in Paul's attitude between the Jewish agitators and the Philippian jailor?

7. What does the fact that Paul and Silas were singing hymns in the middle of the night, in stocks in the jail and having just been severely beaten, undoubtedly with open wounds on their back and in intense pain, tell us about these two men?

8. Out of all the things Paul experienced during his years of ministry, perhaps one of the most traumatic might have been the time he was stoned and left for dead. What do you think Paul might have felt and thought when they were hurling the stones at him? He must have been unconscious for those stoning him to think he was dead. What do you think Paul might have felt and thought when he regained consciousness?

9. Paul was shipwrecked on three different occasions. At least during one of those times, he floated on a piece of the wrecked vessel for a day and a half before being rescued. What do you

think Paul might have thought and felt during that day and a half?

10. It appears that Paul spent a total of somewhere between 5 ½ to 6 years in prison. Describe how you think Paul might have felt during his imprisonments?

11. Out of all the things Paul endured for Christ (beatings, stoning, shipwrecks, imprisonments, etc.), which to you think might have been the most difficult or the most unnerving?

12. Thinking about the discussion of the previous questions and the general flow of this story, what can we learn about Paul, his life, and his reactions when nearing the end of his life from what he writes, for example, "I have learned in whatever state I am in to be content?" or "for me to live is Christ, to die is gain"? How difficult do you think it might have been for Paul to come to the place where those two statements accurately reflected his spiritual and mental state?

13. We often look at Paul as a great spiritual giant. Yet, he was as human as any of us. Do you think he often became discouraged with all that he had to face? Do you think he ever just longed to be free from the persecution and suffering he had to endure? How do we become content in all circumstances?

26

PAUL

Important Women in my Ministry

Some of my statements in the letters I wrote have caused some people to believe that I was against women being directly involved in ministry. Some even go around saying that I have deep-rooted negative feelings toward women in general. So, I would like to clarify my position regarding women. Believe me, I do not hold negative feelings about them at all. What people have said about me has led me to reflect on some of the remarkable women that have entered my life and ministry. They have been very special people to me.

I believe that God helped me to write the many letters I sent to some of the churches. At times, it seems that some of my words might appear to be harsh. I hope those to whom I have written letters over the years will understand my purpose in sending them. You must understand that I feel constrained to write the thoughts that occupy my mind, thoughts that I trust are being placed there by God himself. They are thoughts that swell up within me, compelling me to write what burns in my heart.

Sometimes the ideas just flow, as if placed there by an unseen force, one I always believe to be the Spirit of God himself. Yet I am still human enough to wonder how the letters that I write will be received. Still human enough to want to be accepted, loved, and respected. I sometimes fear that I might offend or alienate some people by the things I say, write and do. Mind you, those human feelings, as real as they are, do not prevent me from stating what I believe God has put in my mind and heart, but I still sometimes wonder if those to whom I write will feel they are being blessed by my words – or perhaps feel offended.

That was a long introduction to answer the question about my attitude toward women. But I wanted to help you understand that I believe what I have written about women in ministry and life in general was given to me by God.

I once wrote these words to the churches in Galatia: *"There is neither Jew nor Greek, there is neither slave nor free, there is no male and female, for you are all one in Christ Jesus."*

I know some Jews will be deeply offended when they read this, feeling that I have set down an equality between them and non-Jews. For centuries they have believed that they alone have special access to Jehovah. But, as I just wrote, *in Christ* all of that has changed. It really doesn't matter anymore whether you are a Jew or not. All that matters is your belief in the risen Christ.

"Jew" or "slave" are the terms that will create a response among the Romans who always fear uprisings from the large segment of our society that serves Roman lords as slaves. I think it fair to say that more than a third of the population in the empire are slaves. So, I would assume, that after reading the words I just penned, some will fear that they might become the seeds of a slave rebellion, promoting equality between slaves and their owners. I am not addressing social equality, however, for I am writing about a *spiritual* equality, but some will undoubtedly criticize me for what I have just said.

As I reflect on this, these words grip me the most: *"there is no male nor female."* Of course, you understand the social climate in which we are living when male chauvinism seems to be evident in all the cultural practices of current society. I am often accused of being a chauvinist myself because of things that I have preached and the positions I have taken about women and their leadership role in the church. I have taken this position because of the abuse of some, but I can assure you that I am not a chauvinist.

When I ponder the question, my mind can't help reflecting on my years of ministry and remember some of the most remarkable women that have had, in their own ways, an influence and at times a direct impact on my own life and ministry. There were far more than I probably can even remember and certainly more than I would have time to think about today. But even now in this time of reflection, some of those godly saints come to the forefront of my mind.

There was Lydia of Thyatira. Most of my converts came from what we might call the salt of the earth. It always seemed harder for those in the upper echelons of society to respond to the message of Christ, but that was not the case with Lydia. Originally from Thyatira in Asia Minor, Lydia was an agent of the lucrative dye and fabric industry based in that city. Their purple cloth is known throughout all the empire and sought after by kings, emperors, and others of high social rank. I am not sure why she moved from Thyatira to Philippi in Macedonia, but once there, her business continued successfully. Philippi was a Roman colony which attracted many retired politicians and military leaders.

I remember how, after receiving a vision to go into Macedonia, I wondered how I would be received, and if the Europeans would be receptive to the message that I was bringing. I never imagined that a woman would be the first convert in Europe.

When I arrived in Philippi, I found a group of believers in our God according to the traditions of the Jews. There were many Gentiles who looked toward the Jewish faith with some hope of finding the true God. I took the opportunity to preach to a group of women who were studying the Scriptures. My words found a fertile heart in the person of Lydia who quickly responded to the message I had brought to them. Yes, she was my first convert in Europe and immediately she and all her household were baptized.

Lydia insisted that I come and stay in their house while we were in her city. It didn't take a lot of persuasion on her part, and I enjoyed the comfort of her home, her hospitality, and the interaction with her family. For as long as I was in Philippi, this was truly my home away from home. Yes, what fond memories I have of Lydia. Even after a horrid ordeal in the Philippian jail and the terrible beating we received there, she still cared for us until we left Philippi. We continue to get positive reports about the continuing faith of this precious woman and the good she still does for the Kingdom of God.

Then I think of Damaris. I doubt that most believers would even know to whom I am referring, but I have fond memories of this outstanding woman. After I arrived in Athens, I began reasoning with the Jews in the synagogue. When they rejected my message, I turned to open air preaching in the city streets.

Before long, I was invited to reason with the Greek scholars in the Areopagus, the place where the intellectuals of the city gathered to debate whatever current issue seemed worthy of their attention. They listened attentively to what I had to say. You will remember that this was a place for men, although some women were to be found among them. These women were not seen as equals of men but were essentially escorts or mistresses of these great minds, well-educated women providing company and intellectual conversation for prominent men. Damaris was one such woman, moving in the rarefied air of Greek academia and high culture.

I remember how few of those intellectuals ever embraced the message I shared with them, but a few did. What I especially remember about Damaris was her enthusiastic embrace of my message and of the Jesus I shared with her. I didn't stay in Athens long, but I always held on to the hope that this woman would use her influence among those that would be largely untouched by most of our believers.

It seems to me that women are often more ready to embrace Christ than are their male counterparts. When they do become believers, they seem so dedicated and willing to be of use to Christ, and often to me as well.

How could I let these thoughts flow through my mind and not remember the beloved Priscilla and her faithful husband? Unlike Lydia and Damaris, this couple didn't come from the upper, more influential echelons of society. No, they were just typical middle-class businesspeople, making a living with their tent making skills.

I met this couple after I left Athens and went to the Greek city of Corinth where I would spend the next year and a half in a productive evangelistic effort. I needed some way to support myself during those months of ministry. I was a tent maker by trade, so there was a natural affinity with this couple who shared the same vocational skills.

There were other things that helped me feel at ease with them. They were a cross cultural couple and could identify with some of my experiences. Aquila was a Jew from Pontus and his wife, Priscilla, was originally a non-Jewish woman from Rome. They had lived and worked in Rome as tentmakers. When Caesar decreed that all Jews had to leave the capital city, Priscilla and her husband moved to Corinth and set up their business there. It didn't take long for the three of us to develop a deep bond of friendship, and I was so glad when both became followers of Christ. I poured myself into this wonderful couple for a year and a half. As we worked side by side, we enjoyed such rich times of fellowship.

When the time came for me to leave Corinth, Priscilla and Aquila decided it was time for them to leave as well, so we traveled together. How wonderful it was to have this dedicated couple as my traveling companions. They truly refreshed my soul. They stayed with me until we reached Ephesus. On that occasion, I didn't stay long but promised to come back. I wanted to return to Ephesus and fully expected to see this precious couple again. So, my good-byes were softened with the expectation of a future reunion. But that would never happen. Instead, I would go to Jerusalem, be arrested, and ultimately be taken as a prisoner to Rome.

These have been good thoughts today. I am glad I took the time to remember some of the fine women who graced my life. And yet, thoughts of other faithful women, those with a place in history, start to invade my mind. Names flood in: Sarah and Rebecca, Rachel and Leah… I remember hearing their stories and learning about what dear mothers they were to their children. How could I not think of the mother of Moses, or Deborah and her role as a judge of Israel? If I permitted my mind to wander further, I would find myself developing a list of so many great and faithful women of God. How precious they all are, faithful to their families and to the God they served! How could I forget? There was Ruth and Naomi, Bathsheba and a host of others.

My heart is warmed as I think about these women. And I do not want to forget my own mother. What cherished memories I have of her! Her love has followed me all the days of my life.

No, I am not a chauvinist as some claim that I am. In fact, I believe with all my heart that women are as equal in the eyes of God as any man that has ever lived. I would agree that there are sometimes different roles given to them, but whatever God asks of either male or female, it is with an equal status in his eyes, as part of a cooperative effort to further the Kingdom of God.

As I sit here pondering this, it just seems to me that maybe being a mother might be one of the greatest callings that God has given to any person. I wonder what the church would have been like if it hadn't been for those many faithful women who embraced the message of Christ.

DISCUSSION QUESTIONS

1. There is diversity of thought on Paul's teaching about women and their involvement in ministry. What is your understanding of Paul's position when it comes to women's roles in ministry? What do you think Paul permits and what do you think he prohibits in relation to women in ministry?

2. What exactly do you think Paul meant when he said that "in Christ there is neither male nor female" when he was writing his letter to the Galatians?

3. In one sweeping sentence, Paul spoke to long-standing cultural perceptions. He said there was "neither Jew nor Gentile," "neither slave nor free," "neither male nor female." Thinking about that statement, how do you think:
    a. The Jews might have thought about his statement of equality between Jew and Gentile?
    b. The Romans, who were slave owners, might have thought about his statement of equality between "free and slave"? Do you think they might have feared this statement would encourage slaves to rebel?
    c. People in general might have thought at a time when males were dominant in almost every way over women about equality between "male and female"?

4. Do you think Paul might have been surprised when his first convert in Europe was a woman?

5. What can we learn about Paul as a person and his attitude toward some of the social norms of his times when he begins teaching and preaching to a group of Jewish women when he first arrived at Philippi?

6. Do you think we can discern anything about Paul in his accepting Lydia's invitation to stay in her home while he was preaching in Philippi?

7. After Paul was released from prison and had been beaten at Philippi, Lydia took him back into her home until he left the city. Do you think Lydia feared what might happen to her because of her care for Paul from the leaders of the city? Do you think this action on her part tells us anything about the personality and the faith of Lydia?

8. Damaris was probably a woman of some questionable behavior. We know little about her, either before Paul visited Athens or after he left. All we know is that Damaris embraced the message of Paul in Athens when few others did and that she tried to use her influence to support Paul and his message. How do you think Paul felt about her? How do you think men in Athens might have felt about her embracing Paul's teaching?

9. Thinking of the previous question, we know nothing more about Damaris than a brief statement. Paul did not leave a church behind in Athens. What do you think might have happened to Damaris and her newfound faith?

10. An obvious close relationship developed between Paul and Priscilla and Aquila. What do you think this deep and long-standing relationship might have meant to Paul? What were some of the ways this couple may have ministered to Paul?

11. As you think back over your life, can you remember some significant women that influenced your spiritual pilgrimage? In what ways did they make a difference in your life.

27

PAUL

A Rookie Missionary

I trust that what I have already shared about my early life, conversion, and beginnings in ministry has helped lay the foundation for what I am about to cover. Having talked about "the cost of discipleship," it would be easy to dwell on the difficult times, but what would be gained? I prefer to see my scars as a means of identifying with my Savior who suffered and bled for me. By God's grace, I have come to the place where I can say that all I have gone through is nothing compared with what lies before me. I would rather talk about the good life that I have lived and focus on the missionary journeys in which I participated. Almost half of my life was spent traveling to tell all who would listen the good news that I had to share.

I do not fear that I might try to generate self-pity when describing the hardships that I have endured, but rather that in some subtle, carnal way I might try to bring glory to myself because of the wonderful things that God has done through me. Pride is such an invasive sin that all too often motivates human speech and behavior. Humanly speaking, I have no reason to boast about my many accomplishments. In fact, my spiritual pilgrimage has brought me to the place where I can look you in the face and say, *"But God forbid that I should boast except in the cross of our Lord Jesus Christ, by whom the world has been crucified to me, and I to the world,"* just as I wrote to the churches in Galatia.

As I sit here in this prison awaiting my death, I do not focus on what I have done, but on the crown that awaits me and the expectation of hearing my master affirm that I have been a loyal and faithful servant. Standing near death, the past becomes distant and less significant as I look eagerly toward a different world, even though I am indeed grateful for the wonderful opportunities I have had to serve

Christ and His Kingdom and for the way God worked through me for His glory.

I took three missionary journeys, the first lasting about a year and a half. When I was persecuting the believers in Christ, I had no idea how my life would later intersect with theirs again in a very different way. My intense persecution resulted in many of them scattering from Judea to places such as Antioch in Syria, and Cyprus. How could I have dreamt that God planned for me to minister to these very believers who had once fled my wrath? Or that they would become the people that would sponsor me and send me out on my first journey?

Barnabas was sent by the elders in Jerusalem to investigate what they had been hearing about the growing congregation of spiritual refugees in Antioch, and to provide leadership for that fledgling church. Not long after he arrived in Antioch, Barnabas came to Troas looking for me. We had spent some time together on a previous occasion when I had gone to Jerusalem shortly after my meeting Christ on the road to Damascus. Barnabas asked me to go with him back to Antioch, which I did, and we spent approximately a year ministering to the believers together. That was a time of growth for me as I learned much from Barnabas, my elder both in years and in ministerial experience. During that year, the church in Antioch raised an offering for the saints in Judea who were suffering because of a drought as well as spiritual persecution. Barnabas and I took the offering to Jerusalem. After giving it to the saints, we returned, bringing back with us John Mark, the younger cousin of Barnabas. I had no idea that my life was about to change in a way that would affect everything I did from then on.

During a time of intense fasting and prayer, the congregation sensed that God was telling them to send Barnabas and me on a special assignment to spread the good news about Jesus to those who did not know Him. I did not know at the time that this would birth a missionary movement, the beginning of taking the gospel to the Gentiles. As we continued to fast and pray, the Holy Spirit confirmed to the congregation and to Barnabas and me that this was God's plan. The congregation came together, placed their hands on us, and sent us off on our first missionary journey. We took young John Mark with us.

After walking to the port near Antioch, we crossed the Mediterranean Sea to the seaport of Salamis on the Island of Cyprus.

We hardly knew what we were doing. Why did we choose Cyprus for this first trip? Firstly, because there were believers who had fled there because I had persecuted them in Jerusalem. Secondly, Barnabas had been raised there and was familiar with the island. Cyprus seemed, therefore, like a natural starting place.

We crossed most of the island, sharing about Christ, but we had very little success as few accepted our message. It would have been easy to become discouraged and question whether this was the most effective way of spreading the good news about Jesus until something happened that put new vision and energy into that first missionary venture. We had reached the city of Paphos in the southwest part of the island. Here we had one of our earliest and most significant converts. The Roman proconsul, Sergius Paulus, had heard about our visit and summoned us to come and share with him what we were proclaiming to others. We did that, but we were quickly to learn how Satan was going to do all he could to destroy the effectiveness of our preaching. In this case, he stirred up the proconsul's associate, Elymas, who was a Jewish magician and false prophet. Elymas did all he could to discredit our message and prevent Sergius Paulus from believing. Feeling the Holy Spirit stirring in my soul, I looked into the eyes of Elymas and pronounced these God-inspired words, *"O full of all deceit and all fraud, you son of the devil, you enemy of all righteousness, will you not cease perverting the straight ways of the Lord? And now, indeed, the hand of the Lord is upon you, and you shall be blind, not seeing the sun for a time."* I should not have been surprised but was nonetheless awestruck when Elymas reached up to his eyes and cried out woefully that he could not see. His blindness was temporary but served its purpose. Sergius Paulus was amazed to see this, and became a believer in Christ, embracing the message we had been preaching to him and the people under his rule. What a wonderful beginning to this trip!

We boarded another ship and sailed to Perga in South Central Asia Minor. This stop was a sad one that would result in some heart searching for me in the years to come. Young John Mark, for his own reasons, decided to give up, abandon us, and return to his home in

Jerusalem. I was sorry to see him go, and I must confess, I felt bitter toward him. It would take me many years to resolve the matter in my soul. As the years passed, my hard feelings waned. I came to realize how valuable he was to God's Kingdom and made peace with him and with myself.

Barnabas and I continued our journey to another city called Antioch where our ministry was fruitful as many people responded to our message not only in the city, but throughout the surrounding countryside. Another good beginning for our first missionary endeavor! The Jews in this area, however, began stirring up opposition to us, inciting a group of people that wanted to force us out of the area. They were successful in their efforts. We would soon learn that this behavior was an almost predictable pattern that would repeat itself so many times as I travelled to share the good news. We left Antioch and walked to Iconium in Galatia.

In Iconium God enabled us to preach boldly, and we performed many miracles under the Spirit's leadership. All of this resulted in many Jews and Greeks believing in Christ. Again, we saw that everywhere we went, our success would also draw opposition. We eventually learned that some of the unbelieving Jews and Gentiles had the blessing of the city leaders to stone us! We thought it prudent to leave and walked to the nearby cities of Lystra and Derbe.

In Lystra, the people reacted in an unusual and bizarre way. While preaching at the gates of Lystra, I noticed a lame man listening intently to what we had to say. God enabled me to heal the man which, while personally satisfying, was of even greater significance because he became a brother in Christ. The crowd went wild when they saw the lame man walking. They decided that we were the Greek gods Zeus and Hermes who had come to visit them. They immediately began to prepare to offer sacrifices to us. This caused us a bit of panic, and only with the greatest of persuasion did we manage to prevent them from doing such a terrible thing, convincing them that we were only men just like them.

We did not have long to rejoice in the good things that happened at Lystra. Soon, some of the unbelieving Jews from Antioch and Iconium arrived there and stirred up the crowds against us and the message we were preaching. Until now, they had limited themselves to threats, and we had not experienced any physical harm. This time, however, they seized me and dragged me outside the city where they threw stones at me. What a terrible experience that was! I raised my arms and tried to cover my face and head, but the stones just kept coming, pelting me painfully until I lost consciousness. I was left for dead laying there in the dirt. The believers began to gather around my limp body. I think God did a miracle that day, for I stood up, very much alive, and was able to walk back into the city.

We crossed the mountains to the city of Derbe where we were able to leave behind many converts to the Christ we were preaching. This became a highlight of this first journey. I cannot talk about our time in Derbe without special mention of a young man that we met there called Timothy. Our lives would become so interwoven in the years to come as Timothy would become like a son in the Gospel to me – a wonderful, rewarding relationship.

After time spent in Derbe, the furthest point on our first trip, we felt it was time to return to Antioch in Syria, so we began backtracking the route we had taken, revisiting the believers we had made during this journey. It was such an encouraging experience to see the growth already beginning to occur in the lives of these new believers.

When we finally returned to Antioch, where we had been commissioned and sent out as ambassadors of Christ, we were able to give a glowing report about the almost two years of travel and ministry to people, both Jews and Gentiles, whom we sensed were hungry to hear the message about Jesus. Looking back now, I realize how many things were established during this first trip that would set a pattern for the other two journeys to follow. It was the beginning of a rich and rewarding chapter of life, one that was often, as I shared before, also laden with many problems and difficulties.

I can tell you with the greatest certainty that this first missionary trip was planned by God and that He called me and Barnabas to undertake it. How wonderful it is to know that God chose us to start a new missionary enterprise to spread the good news about his Son Jesus to a hungry and waiting world.

DISCUSSION QUESTIONS

1. In the opening paragraph of this story, the question is asked about what would be gained by dwelling on the negative things that have happened in our lives. Why do you think some people want to talk about or dwell on the negative rather than the positive aspects of life? What do you think they gain, if anything, by doing this? What might be some of the negative effects of dwelling on the negative rather than the positive aspects of one's life?

2. Paul saw the scars he bore as a reminder of his identity with Christ. What are some of the things we can do to turn our negative experiences into something positive and constructive in our lives?

3. The opposite of dwelling on the negatives of life is to have an unwholesome fixation on the accomplishments of one's life. In what way are we in danger of turning the positive parts of our lives into something that becomes destructive and harmful to us as a person?

4. How does our focus on Heaven and what lies ahead affect our attitudes to both the positive and negative experiences of our life now?

5. It is interesting that the church at Antioch in Syria was made up of people who had fled from Judea because of the persecution directed by Saul [Paul]. Later he would become a co-pastor with Barnabas of these very people for a year, and it was these same people who commissioned him and Barnabas to go on their first missionary journey. Describe how you think the relationship between Paul and those he had persecuted was when he came to

help pastor their church? Do you think they had a hard time forgiving and forgetting the deeds of their former persecutor? Do you think Paul had any emotional struggles in pastoring them when he remembered his part in persecuting them?

6. Reflecting on your discussion related to the previous question, what do you think Paul might have thought and felt when Barnabas first came to Troas and asked him to come back to Antioch to work alongside him with this group of people that he had once persecuted?

7. There was no precedent for Barnabas and Paul in terms of what a "missionary" should look like or do. What might have been some of their initial expectations, hopes, or ideas about what this first trip might look like and should accomplish?

8. It appears that there was very little success during the first part of their journey on the island of Cyprus. Do you think Barnabas and Paul were discouraged during these early weeks of preaching and wondered if what they were doing was profitable? John Mark abandoned them shortly after they left Cyprus. Do you think the fruitless beginnings of their missionary journey contributed to John Mark's decision?

9. Barnabas and Paul went to Cyprus first because Barnabas was from there. We can assume there were people there that he knew, perhaps even extended family. Do you think that the familiarity of Barnabas with that area was a help or a hindrance to their early missionary activities and was related to the lack of initial response during those first weeks of ministry?

10. What do you think might have been some of the initial responses of the proconsul and those who were there when Elymas was struck blind at Paul's command?

11. The Bible tells us that the blindness of Elymas was not permanent, and in time he got his sight back. What changes do you think came to Elymas because of what happened to him? Do you think he became a believer?

12. How do you think both Barnabas and Paul felt when John Mark left them and returned to Jerusalem?

13. Paul would experience something during this first missionary journey that would become a pattern for his life: being persecuted by those who opposed his preaching. Ultimately, he probably came to expect this. How do you think Paul might have felt and thought when he first began to experience persecution on his first missionary trip, including being stoned and left for dead?

14. Paul began performing miracles during this first missionary journey. There is no indication that he had been able to do this prior to this trip. What do you think Paul might have felt and thought the first time a miracle occurred in his ministry?

15. What do you think both Barnabas and Paul might have felt and thought when, after they healed the lame man, the people in Lystra began gathering, wanting to make a sacrifice to them, believing they were two of the Greek Gods who had come to visit them?

16. We can assume physical damage was done to Paul when he was stoned. He was left for dead, which suggests he was

unconscious. Yet not long afterwards he stood up, and there was no indication that he had any physical damage from the stoning. He immediately walked back into the city of Lystra. It appears that God healed him completely and immediately restored him to health. What do you think the people of Lystra thought and felt when they saw Paul alive and unharmed?

17. Perhaps the most significant thing that happened in Derbe (and one of the most significant things that happened on this whole trip) was Paul meeting Timothy and Timothy's conversion. We know how Timothy became a "son in the Gospel" to Paul and the role he had in the ministry of the early church. Are there any people in your life that you can think of that have either touched your life or that you have touched in a way that made a profound difference in both their (or your) life and perhaps made a difference for the Kingdom of God?

18. As noted in one of the previous questions, there was no precedent for Barnabas and Paul for what a missionary experience ought to be like. What lessons, both positive and negative, do you think they learned on this first trip? What were some of the things they took from the experiences of this trip which showed up in some of the other two trips Paul would make?

28

PAUL

A Man with a Restless Heart

Some of life's events transform us. Such was my first missionary journey that changed my life forever. After returning to Antioch, we spent the next year and a half ministering to the congregation that had commissioned us and sent us out on that first missionary journey.

I did not realize that Barnabas and I had created waves among the Jewish believers. One day a delegation of Jewish believers arrived in Antioch, teaching that our Gentile converts needed to be circumcised according to Jewish law and tradition. Barnabas' and my attempts to reason with them were to no avail. Perhaps I should not have been surprised, having experienced opposition from various Jewish troublemakers in some of the places we had visited on our first trip. This, however, was different. These Jews were not trying to protect their religious beliefs, for they were believers who had embraced Christ as the Messiah and yet they maintained their loyalty to Jewish traditions and teachings. To the two of us it seemed to be an attempt to syncretize their Jewish ways with their new understanding of what it means to follow Christ.

To make a long story shorter, the church at Antioch thought it would be wise for us to take this matter to the disciples who were in Jerusalem. So once again, Barnabas and I started out on another journey together, sharing with passersby along the way the story of God's gracious work among the Gentiles. We were amazed that people we met on our route became excited about what we were saying and embraced our teaching, rejoicing with us about what God had done through us. When we arrived in Jerusalem, we were given the same warm reception by the disciples and leaders of the new Christian movement there. What we needed was a formal endorsement of our ministry among the Gentiles, as well as settling the question of circumcision once and for all. Some of the key leaders gathered to debate the issue. In the end, with a couple of minor concessions to appease the stricter group of Jewish believers, they agreed that keeping Jewish laws and traditions was not necessary to living out our faith in Jesus Christ. Barnabas and I were so glad not to have to place that burdensome requirement on our Gentile converts.

We returned to Antioch and continued to have a good ministry among the growing congregation, yet I sensed a stirring in my soul. My thoughts often turned to the precious people we had worked with on our first journey. I was aware that we had not spent much time with them to help them become established in their new faith. As weeks became months, my desire to return to them increased until I could not continue without knowing how they were faring. When I approached Barnabas with the idea of a return trip, he was very open to the idea, perhaps as excited as I to revisit the fledging congregations.

Something then happened that I wish could have been different. Now that I am old, I realize that I was wrong, and I have been able, to a large degree, to resolve in my soul what I felt so strongly about at the time. Barnabas suggested that we take John Mark with us, but I firmly refused to even consider that. Barnabas was as emphatic about bringing John with us as I was in opposing the idea. We were deadlocked over this issue, and even making the trip hang in the balance. Finally, we agreed that each would pursue our own idea. Barnabas took John Mark with him on their own trip. I chose a new partner for the trip that so deeply burned in my mind and heart. Silas became my travel partner for my next two trips. Silas was already known as a prophet among us and recognized as one of the early leaders of our new movement. We enjoyed a good working relationship.

Nothing about this second trip came anywhere near to what I had envisioned. I wanted to go back to the churches we had established but God had other ideas. We were in fact able to revisit some of the churches we had established on my first journey and rejoiced to see how the believers had fared, standing strong in their newfound faith, and some already being persecuted for their faith. While on this second trip, I wrote two letters to the believers in Thessalonica to encourage them to remain strong during their struggles and suffering.

We returned to Lystra where we had met Timothy, a young man who impressed us greatly with his zeal, demeanor, and ready willingness to embrace Christ as his Redeemer and Savior. I decided that I wanted Timothy, who had so much to offer, to join us for the remainder of our trip, seeing this as an opportunity to mentor his nascent leadership abilities.

Timothy's mother and grandmother were Jewish women who had also embraced Christ as their Savior. They had set a godly example for Timothy to follow that was very different from that of his Greek father. I cannot say I was a seasoned missionary with comprehensive knowledge and experience, for I still had much to learn, even as I do today as I sit here in jail.

As we attempted to minister to both Jews and Gentiles, I wondered what effect Timothy's lack of circumcision would have. I also knew that orthodox Judaism maintained that Jewishness came by way of the maternal line and Timothy's mother was Jewish. I thought about this dilemma, remembering how a few months earlier we had debated in Jerusalem whether circumcision was necessary for Gentile believers. Finally, I decided that because of his mother, Timothy was more a Jew than a Gentile. I believed that having him circumcised would ensure that he would be received with respect as a Jewish believer, thus eliminating one barrier to our ministry. This illustrates what I wrote than, "*I have learned to become all things to all men that by that all means I might win some.*" There are times when deference, yielding to what may be technically right in order not to offend those to whom we minister, may open the way. While I was sorry that Timothy had to suffer that painful ordeal, it seemed most expedient for the effectiveness of our overall ministry.

Timothy joined Silas and me and we set out from Lystra, ministering in some of the other areas I had previously visited. It was my desire to go into Asia Minor to preach the good news of Jesus Christ, but as I said, this trip did not proceed as planned. We came to my old stomping grounds in Troas where I experienced another transforming moment in my life.

In Troas I had a vision of a man asking us to come to preach in Macedonia. The idea of going into Europe to preach among the Greek people had never entered my mind! This whole idea, coming so unexpectedly, was about to turn my world upside down. As I look back on it now, however, God had prepared me for this moment from the time of my birth. I had been raised among Greek-speaking people, was fluent in the Greek language, and understood Greek culture and way of life. Why should I have been so surprised when this guidance was given to me in such a vivid way? From that moment, I knew that we would spend the remainder of our trip not in Asia but in the land that lay across the limpid waters of the Aegean Sea.

Without going into all the details of our time in Greece, I will mention what stands out most. It was here that we added Luke the physician to our team. Like Timothy, he became loyally involved in the remainder of my missionary life, both men proving to be a great blessing to me.

We boarded a ship and sailed from Troas to the Roman colony of Philippi where we began our European ministry. On our first Sabbath, we went down to the river where we expected Jews to be gathering and found a group of Jewish women. One of them, Lydia, quickly accepted our message and became our first convert on European soil. After she was baptized, she invited us to stay in her home while we were in Philippi. This gracious hostess was an encouragement to us all. Her whole household soon believed in Jesus, and her home became the meeting place for those who were being added to our group.

Our ministry in Philippi was rich and productive, though not free from difficulties. One day we cast demons out of a slave girl, because of which her owner brought Silas and me before the city magistrates. We were cruelly beaten and thrown into prison. Although suffering physical pain, we sang hymns and rejoiced in God's goodness. Then God did a miracle! He caused an earthquake that destroyed the prison, releasing all the prisoners. We huddled together in a dark corner of the prison, wondering what would happen next. This was a frightening moment, filled with uncertainty and confusion. The Philippian jailer, fearing his life would be taken for having let the prisoners escape, was about to commit suicide, thinking that death by his own hand was better than enduring shame, ridicule, and ultimate execution at the hands of his harsh superiors.

Having assured him that we were all still there, he fell at my knees and asked how he could be saved. He had witnessed our singing and rejoicing before the earthquake and now saw in us what he lacked in his own life and earnestly desired. He and his whole household became believers and were baptized! In the morning, the magistrates were more than glad to release the two of us, beseeching us to leave town. We refused to do so, however, unless I received a public apology for the way I, a Roman citizen, had been violated and mistreated. I can still see the fear on the face of the magistrate when he learned that I was a Roman citizen and realized that he had been responsible for my beating and mistreatment. When it was time for us to leave Philippi, the new congregation collected a gracious offering to help us on our journey. With a tearful farewell, we left and headed for Thessalonica.

On our arrival, we went to the synagogue and preached the good news. Before long, we had converts among both the Jews and Greeks, including some of the influential women of the city. I am amazed at how quickly the Spirit of God raised up a dedicated and strong group of believers in such a short period of time. We had not been there long, however, before a group of Jews rose in opposition against us, forcing Silas and me to flee by night to the city of Berea.

Out of concern for the new group of believers in Philippi, we left Timothy behind for a period to encourage and give them further instructions on how to live as Christ's followers. I strove in prayer for these new believers, knowing how much opposition they would face from the people that had run us out of town. I was troubled on their account until Timothy joined us again and gave a glowing report that the new believers were standing firm in their new faith. I wrote letters to this generous group that gained a special place in my heart to encourage them on their pilgrimage in Christ.

As soon as we arrived in Berea, according to our custom we began teaching in the Jewish Synagogue. Unlike in so many other places, this group of Jews received us and our message with great eagerness. They would open the ancient Scriptures, seeking to discern how what we were saying matched their holy script. Many of these Jews believed, as did a few prominent Greek men and women. News of our successful ministry filtered back to the Jews in Thessalonica. Before long, a delegation of Jews from Thessalonica came and agitated people in this city as well. I was admonished to leave for my own safety. This time I went alone, leaving Silas and Timothy to continue serving the new group.

I continued to the city of Athens where I reasoned with the intellectual elite of the nation. Even though the interaction was good, little was accomplished while I was there. Some individuals were touched, and a few lives changed, but it seemed that spiritual blindness prevented these great minds that thought they knew so much about life from seeing the truth of God in Christ. My heart was growing restless, and I asked that Silas and Timothy join me as quickly as possible.

I left Athens and went to the city of Corinth, a particularly wicked place. I came to this city trembling with fear as I remembered the persecution that I had endured in some of the previous cities and the nature of the perpetrators behind it. Corinth was a city where God moved, however, and many people responded to the message of Christ and formed a band of new believers. Among them were Priscilla and Aquila, fellow tent makers who would join my inner circle of friends and partners in ministry.

I stayed in Corinth for a year and a half, working alongside Priscilla and Aquila and making my living as a tentmaker so that I never needed to take compensation for my work among the group of believers. Soon Silas and Timothy would join me in Corinth. It was not long, however, before the Jewish people rejected our message, so we turned our attention to the Gentiles who were far more receptive than I had anticipated. Before long there was a thriving group of believers in this city too.

One night the Lord spoke to me in a vision, *"Do not be afraid; keep on speaking, do not be silent. For I am with you, and no one is going to attack and harm you, because I have many people in this city."* These comforting words helped calm my fearful, troubled heart. Yes, I had come with fear and trembling, but also with a deep assurance of protection and success for which I thanked God.

Again, despite the rich, productive ministry in Corinth, the familiar, restless feeling returned to me. I believe it was the voice of God's Spirit. He had other things for me to do, and other people were able to lead this growing congregation of believers. I concluded that God did not want to use me as a pastor, but rather as an itinerant missionary evangelist. My conviction grew that I did not want to preach where others had already preached or spend my time with one group of people when the rest of the world needed to know about Jesus Christ. Once again, I bid farewell to another group of converts. Taking leave is never easy, for hearts are bound together by the Spirit of God in friendships as deep as familial ties.

We left Corinth and went to Ephesus for a very brief time. As usual, I reasoned with the Jews in the Synagogue. They asked me to stay with them, but I refused, for I felt that it was time that I should return to Antioch, and I wanted to go to Jerusalem as well. It was time for yet more goodbyes, none more painful that leaving Priscilla and Aquila, who had accompanied me to Ephesus. They decided to remain in Ephesus, making it their new home. I shared my intention to return to them, but explained that for now, I had to follow God's leading.

Several years had passed since I had left Antioch, so I was excited to return to the saints there who had played such a significant part in my earlier life and ministry. Having sailed from Ephesus, I arrived in the coastal city of Caesarea from where I traveled to Jerusalem. I gave a report to the leaders about all the wonderful work of God in the Gentile world. From Jerusalem, I returned to the warm, welcoming embrace of the believers in Antioch who had accepted, affirmed, and supported me from the early years of my ministry. What joy we shared as I reported on all the wonderful happenings during my remarkable journeys. While the commission and ministry God had given me belonged to the world, as shown by how he led me to new places by stirring my spirit and giving me clear direction, my heart and spiritual home were among the precious saints at Antioch who recognized and shared God's great missionary vision.

DISCUSSION QUESTIONS

1. What do you think Paul might have felt and thought when he first encountered the Jewish Christians from Jerusalem who said the Gentile converts needed to be circumcised and follow Jewish laws and customs?

2. Paul's ministry among the believers at Antioch was thriving, but he proposed to Barnabas that they make this second missionary journey. What do you think caused Paul to want to make the second journey?

3. Do you think that as the years passed, Paul regretted his decision not to take John Mark with him on this second journey?

4. How do you think the confrontation between Barnabas and Paul over taking John Mark with them on this journey affected their relationship? How do you think the other believers felt about the conflict between Barnabas and Paul?

5. Why do you think Paul wanted to take Timothy with him on this journey? What do you think Timothy felt and thought when he was invited to join Paul and Silas?

6. Paul decided to have Timothy circumcised before he could join them. Remembering that at the Jerusalem council Paul had defended the Gentiles over not needing to be circumcised, what do you think motivated Paul to have Timothy circumcised? Do you think others might have felt that this decision showed inconsistency in Paul?

7. The comment Paul made in I Thessalonians that, "I have become all things to all men that by that all means I may win some" was mentioned in this story. What exactly do you think Paul meant by that statement? What freedom and/or responsibility does that give us to enter the culture and lifestyles of some even when their values may be different from ours? What freedoms does this adaptation give to the believer?

8. Paul had intended to go into Asia Minor and revisit places where he had been before and probably take the Gospel to others in that area. However, his plans were changed by the vision he had to take the Gospel to Greece. What do you think some of Paul's initial feelings and thoughts might have been when he realized that God did not want him to go where he had intended to go? What do you think he felt and thought when he realized he was being asked to go into Europe?

9. It appears that Luke probably joined the other three at this point in the story and traveled with them for the rest of this journey. What do you think might have motivated Luke to join the other three and why do you think Paul might have wanted to have Luke travel with them?

10. Do you think Paul might have been surprised when Lydia so quickly embraced Christ? How do you think Paul might have felt about having a woman become his first convert in Europe? How do you think Paul and the others traveling with him might have felt and thought when she opened her home to them, and they stayed there for the rest of their time in Philippi?

11. Paul had a very fruitful ministry in Philippi with many converts and a new church being established in the city. Yet it was here that he was severely beaten and put in stocks. It was here that he

saw the miraculous deliverance from the jail by an earthquake, and the conversion of the Philippian jailor and his family. As the years passed, how do you think Paul viewed and thought about his time in Philippi?

12. What do you think motivated Paul to ask for a public apology from the magistrate at Philippi for the way that he, a Roman citizen, had been treated? What do you think he wanted to achieve by forcing this kind of public apology?

13. Paul had good success in his work at Philippi and then went to Thessalonica. He did not stay there long because of threats against him yet he left behind a strong, growing group of believers. Do you think Paul was surprised at how quickly people in Europe were willing to accept what he was preaching?

14. In Berea Paul had an exceptionally good reception and response among not only the Gentiles but also the Jews in the Synagogue. Do you think Paul might have been surprised by the reception he received there among the Jews?

15. In direct contrast to what happened in Philippi, Thessalonica and Berea, Paul had very little success in the city of Athens. There were a few converts but by and large, they did not embrace his message. How do you think Paul felt and thought about the difference in this city from the other three? What might have been some of the factors that resulted in the Athenians' lack of response to Paul and his message?

16. Paul left Athens and went to Corinth, a city known as particularly wicked. He wrote that he had gone to Corinth with "much fear and trembling." He had by this time been persecuted (beaten, put in jail, etc.) in three of the four cities where he had

preached. He had had unfruitful ministry in Athens, yet he also had great success in three of the four cities through the response to his ministry and the establishment of congregations in these areas. Why do you think Paul said that he was full of fear and trembling when he came to Corinth? Of what do you think he was afraid?

17. Paul stayed in Corinth for a year and a half, longer than in most places [he did later stay in Ephesus for two years]. Why do you think he stayed here for a prolonged period?

18. Do you think Paul ever thought about staying in one of the cities and becoming a pastor of the congregation there rather than continuing as an itinerant missionary?

19. What can we learn about God's guidance from examples in Paul's life?

29

PAUL

Establishing the Believers

A bit of soul-searching helps a person recognize his or her motivations. You might wonder what lay behind my desire to make my third missionary journey after all the persecution and misery I had endured on the two previous trips. If I had cared only for my own life and welfare, it would have been easy to dwell only on the negative events of my life. I have, however, a deep sense that my life is not my own. First, my life belongs to Jesus whom I serve faithfully every day. When thinking about what motivated me to make a third trip, I have to say that my life also belongs to the new believers in the many places I visited during my two previous trips. To summarize, my third trip was a systematic revisitation of the places to which I had already been as I longed to return and build up the faith of new believers who had responded to my preaching.

I am a man of my word. During my second missionary journey, on a brief stop at Ephesus, I promised that I would soon return to spend time with them. I did not say that flippantly but had every intention of fulfilling my promise. The believers in Ephesus were not my only concern, however; I pray every day for all the new churches established during my previous trips. I eagerly long to know how each is doing. As a father cares for his biological son, I feel like a spiritual father to them. While ministering at Antioch between my second and third trips, I lived with my yearnings to see the other churches.

Soon, my desire to set out became overwhelming. Traveling overland, I crossed Galatia and Phrygia in Asia Minor, visiting the churches in Derbe, Lystra, Iconium, the other Antioch – all places I had visited on my first journey. It was good to see everyone again and to know that most were standing firm in their faith. While my stays in each place were relatively short, I stayed long enough to see that the Holy Spirit was bearing much fruit in these communities. What words can describe the joy of seeing good results of my labors in the souls of men? How grateful I am to know that the Kingdom of God has expanded because of my willingness and obedience in serving Christ.

The Holy Spirit had been working behind the scenes. A believer named Apollos, an eloquent speaker, had arrived in Ephesus and impressed the believers with his character and abilities for ministry. My friends Priscilla and Aquilla, however, realized that his understanding of Christ and the truths of the Gospel was limited so they took him under their wing and helped fill in his lack of knowledge. He had a desire to go into Greece, and the saints at Ephesus wrote a glowing letter of recommendation and sent him on his way. He went on to have an effective ministry in Corinth.

After spending some time with the churches in Asia Minor, I came to Ephesus, such a special place for me. On my arrival, I encountered twelve men who were converts and disciples of Apollos. As with Apollos, their understanding of the Gospel was incomplete. I helped them grow in understanding and baptized them in the name of Jesus. The Holy Spirit came upon this small band of men, and they began talking in tongues and prophesying.

As I ministered in the synagogue for the first three months, some people believed the message, but others hardened their hearts, opposing me and my message. I decided it was best to stop working in the synagogue and preach elsewhere. During my two years in Ephesus, God did extraordinary miracles, healing people and expelling evil spirits. The power of Satan was broken, and former magicians burned their books of magic arts in a great bonfire. Many new believers were added to the church. My soul rejoiced at all that God was accomplishing through our ministry. So mighty was the working of the Holy Spirit that amazingly, even handkerchiefs and aprons that had touched me were taken to the sick, bringing cures for their illnesses and causing evil spirits to flee. The power of God's Spirit swept through the hearts of so many, vanquishing the power of Satan.

I was not called to pastor congregations of believers, however, and God's Spirit spoke to me in my restlessness, showing it was time to leave this wonderful band of believers. After painful farewells, I sailed across the Aegean Sea to Macedonia and continued by foot to Philippi, Thessalonica, and Berea. I spent some time encouraging the believers in their growing congregations. Once more my soul rejoiced to see the believers standing true to Christ and growing spiritually. This was a source of deep joy, worth more to me than all the gold this world could offer. Though at times I am hungry and persecuted, I consider myself a rich man, and my riches can never be stolen by the evil designs of men.

 I went on to Greece where I stayed for three more months before feeling strongly impelled to return to Jerusalem and then, God willing, make another trip to Rome. That conviction became firm. I had no idea, of course, what the future held, or that I would go to Jerusalem only to be arrested and imprisoned for several years before ultimately coming to Rome as a prisoner.

 I had planned to sail from Corinth and on to Jerusalem but discovered that some Jews were plotting to waylay me on the voyage, so I returned to Macedonia by land, giving me another opportunity to visit the precious believers in Berea, Thessalonica, and Philippi. Here I caught up with Luke again, and we stayed to observe Passover with the believers. Luke and I set sail for Troas, arriving after five days of travel. I had sent Timothy and some other traveling companions ahead of me. They helped to raise a monetary gift for the church at Jerusalem. We all had a wonderful reunion at Troas and spent a week together in a personal retreat.

 One night in Troas was different, however, out of the ordinary even for me. When I met with the believers on the Sunday of that week, I preached long into the night. There was so much that I wanted to share with the believers, and the congregation did not seem to notice the hours slipping by. A young man named Eutychus was present, perched on a windowsill on the third floor of the building where we were meeting. At about midnight, the weary young man dozed off and fell backward through the open window to his death. In his great kindness, God permitted me to bring Eutychus back to life. What excitement, awe, and wonder swept through the crowd! We went back upstairs where I preached, taught, and fellowshipped with this group of believers until dawn. Such an extraordinary night stands out among the acts of God that I experienced.

The conviction that I was to go to Jerusalem continued to burn in my soul. I purposed to be in that special city by Pentecost, so I needed to hasten and not linger anywhere for long. For that reason, I decided to bypass Ephesus on my return voyage because I knew I would be tempted to stay longer than I should. I sent word ahead, asking the Ephesian elders to meet me in Miletus, which they did. It seemed as if God was giving me a glimpse into the hardships that I was about to face, beginning with my time in Jerusalem. As I shared with the elders about the dark cloud that was beginning to descend, they seemed not only to understand but to confirm to me that they too sensed that very difficult times lay ahead. Our good-byes were tearful. I believe each of us realized that this would be our last time together on this side of Heaven.

We continued our journey toward Jerusalem, stopping at several places along the way, meeting with God's precious people, and sensing yet again that this was another final good-bye as the premonition grew that something unpleasant was about to happen. The Spirit of God was speaking to others too. While I was spending about a week with the believers in Tyre, in Syria, the believers begged me, for my own safety, not to go to Jerusalem, confirming my thoughts about my dark and uncertain future. Thanking them for their concern, I also confirmed my need and desire to go to Jerusalem, despite what we all sensed lay before me if I did make Jerusalem my next destination.

I finally arrived in Caesarea and stayed with Philip the evangelist. While I was there, the prophet Agabus came and told me that I would be imprisoned if I went to Jerusalem. So, there was another voice of confirmation about the difficult path that lay ahead, but I was resolute about completing God's mission as planned. After several days, a group escorted me to Jerusalem and to the home of Mnason, an old saint who hosted me and my companions.

If the purpose of our discussion today is just to talk about the third missionary journey that I made, I would have to say that my arriving in Jerusalem was the end of that journey. In a broader sense, it was not only the end of a journey, but it was also the end of my freedom and way of life. The rest of my story is about imprisonment and suffering. I did, however, fulfill my desire to visit Rome and here I sit in Rome… in this dingy prison cell. I do not think I will be in Rome much longer. I believe I am about to exchange this cell for a glorious place in Heaven. I know that my days on earth are numbered, but my soul is full, rejoicing in both the promise of what lies before me for eternity, but also in the glow of satisfaction over all that God permitted me to do with and for Him during the last half of my life.

DISCUSSION QUESTIONS

1. What do you think motivated Paul to make this third missionary journey? To what degree do you think both the successes and the difficulties (persecutions, etc.) played on his mind and soul as he pondered whether to make this trip?

2. Can you in any way identify with Paul in his desire to return to visit the churches he established? Have you ever sensed that you should do something even though it might go against what others would think or expect you to do?

3. Paul found great joy as he visited some of the churches that he had established on his previous missionary journeys and found people standing firm in their faith. Share some of your own experiences that later brought to you great joy.

4. During his second missionary journey Paul had promised that he would return to Ephesus and minister there. He stayed for about two years, longer than in any other place he had visited during his three missionary journeys. What might some of the reasons have been that motivated Paul to stay with this church for what was, for him, an extended time of ministry?

5. As this trip continued, a strong desire was growing in Paul's heart to return to Jerusalem. We know that he was warned by several people that he should not go there, or he would be arrested. Yet Paul seemed compelled. Why do you think he was so determined to return to Jerusalem?

6. Thinking about the previous question, we know that Paul was collecting an offering from all the churches he was visiting to take to the church at Jerusalem which had come upon some very

difficult times. What does the receiving of this offering and his desire to go to Jerusalem tell us about his feelings toward the Jewish Christians and possibly about his own identity as a Jew?

7. What do you think was the effect on the believers at Troas, and their response to the raising of Eutychus, the young man who fell asleep at midnight and fell from the third-floor window? How do you think Paul might have felt about what happened and how God used him to bring this young man back to life?

8. It appears that Paul and the elders of Ephesus both understood when Paul met them briefly on his returning to Jerusalem, that this would be their last time together. How do you think they felt about this final good-bye? Have you ever had an experience where you had to say a final good-bye to someone, knowing you probably would not see them again? Can you describe what that experience was like!

9. How do you think Paul felt and thought when the believers at Tyre in Syria begged him not to go to Jerusalem, warning him about what they believed would happen to him? How do you think the believers there felt and responded when Paul would not listen to their admonition?

10. Thinking about all you know from your studies of Paul and his life and having read these stories about the man, try to summarize your feelings about the type of person Paul was.

11. As you reflect on Paul's life, what do you think were some of his strengths and weaknesses as a person. In what ways can you identify with Paul?

30

PAUL

The last trip

    The many wonderful experiences of my life are accompanied by regrets as well. No man's life is perfect, and I am certainly not without guilt. In fact, I refer to myself as the chief of sinners for what I did against the believers before Christ met me on the road to Damascus. Thinking of the sad chapter of my life preceding that encounter only serves to remind me of God's great graciousness even to me as a persecutor of believers who loved his son, Jesus. Remembering those shameful acts, I have to say that I have experienced "grace upon grace," a breadth of mercy and depth of forgiveness so undeserved yet so abundantly showered on a wrongdoer such as I.

    Do not think of me as a super saint or exalted person who is above the feelings that are common to humans. Sitting here in this dreary prison is not easy. My spirit is sometimes downcast. I know that my life could end any day. Perhaps I have borne enough physical pain and suffered at the hands of men often enough to know that I can endure whatever is inflicted on me, yet the idea of any human action severe enough to end my life looms over my soul. There is comfort in knowing that when that happens, it will free my spirit to go straight into the presence of God, but that does not cancel in my mind the discomforting thought of the painful process that will claim my physical life.

    Do I ever fight depression during the long days and lonely nights in this prison cell? Of course, I do. It is here, however, that I find solace that lifts my soul from emotional despair, for the abiding presence of God's Spirit is a deep well of comfort, as are the memories of all the goodness of God throughout the latter half of my life.

So, I come to what I am going to call my fourth missionary journey, though it was not exactly a journey, for I was a prisoner for much of the time, having spent four of the last five years of my life in some form of captivity. During the other year when I was free, I traveled between Jerusalem and Rome. I still choose to call it a "missionary" venture because of the ministry God gave me during those difficult years.

I had returned to Jerusalem from my third missionary journey in time to celebrate the Passover, with the conviction that my coming to this city was going to result in some trouble. That had been confirmed by a vision that others had seen as well. I had not been in Jerusalem long before the warnings that I had been given became my reality. At first, I was welcomed warmly by the believers and church leaders to whom I gave a wonderful report of all that God had done through us in so many places in Asia Minor and Greece. What a time of rejoicing we shared together, a glorious moment of praising God for his goodness not just to the Jews, but to all who had believed in His son, Jesus! That joy and excitement would not last for long, however.

I had heard about many Jews who, even though believers, still clung to their Jewish ways. I was a threat to them, apparently, for many of them believed that I was teaching disobedience to the laws of Moses and Jewish tradition, especially by not requiring Gentile believers to be circumcised. Even though I tried to convince them otherwise, assuring them that I was not an enemy of the laws of God, it was to no avail.

Shortly after arriving in Jerusalem, I went to the temple to make a Jewish vow. Part of my motivation for that was to appease the Jews who were so suspicious of me, for I wanted to assure them that I had not abandoned my Jewish identity. A week passed, then all the predictions began to play out. Some of the Jewish agitators that I had had to deal with during my previous missionary journeys had also come to Jerusalem to celebrate the Passover. When they saw me, they lost no time in stirring up the crowd milling about in the temple square. *"Fellow Israelites,"* they shouted, *"help us! This is the man who teaches everyone everywhere against our people and our law and this place. And besides, he has brought Greeks into the temple and defiled this holy place."*

I had not brought anyone into the temple with me whether Jew or Gentile; it did not matter. A violent and chaotic riot ensued. The unruly crowd pushed me around and beat me. Word reached the Roman authorities who always feared any kind of uprising in the city. Soldiers were sent who arrested me and carried me off in chains, supposedly for my own safety. So began the five years of imprisonment that have brought me to this point.

While being taken from the temple area, I was given an opportunity to address the crowd. I shared about my meeting the risen Christ. They listened to me until I mentioned my involvement with the Gentiles which incited them to clamor for my death. I was taken to the Roman barracks where a lower ranking officer ordered that I be flogged and interrogated to try to find out what it was about me that had caused such an uproar among the people. Having been flogged too many times before, I had no desire to endure this needless torture again, so I told them that I was a Roman citizen. I saw a wave of fear pass over the faces of those responsible for my situation. Even the commanding officer of the barracks seemed frightened when he realized he had put a Roman citizen in chains without just cause.

I was released and taken before the Jewish leaders, including the high priest, and given an opportunity to defend myself. When I said that I was just defending the reality of the resurrection of the dead when talking about the risen Christ, I caused a division among them leading to a debate between the Sadducees and the Pharisees over their strongly held positions concerning resurrection. It caused quite a stir! The Pharisees defended me, stating that I was innocent. So chaotic was the reaction that Roman soldiers were again sent to take me away for my own safety. Once again, I found myself housed in the barracks where I could safely spend the night. The Lord appeared to me in a most unique way there and told me to take courage. He said that even as I had testified about him in Jerusalem, so I would also testify in Rome.

I did not know that it would be several years before that would happen, and that those years would be spent in confinement. After it was discovered that some radical Jews were plotting to take my life, I was escorted out of Jerusalem to Caesarea by a large group of Roman soldiers under the cover of night. I was placed under the jurisdiction of the governor Felix and guarded in Herod's palace.

Yet again, I had to face the Jewish authorities who had been brought to Caesarea to present their case. The governor did not announce any decision at that time, but placed me under guard, allowing me some freedom. My friends were able to take care of my needs. While I did not enjoy confinement, it could have been far worse. I thank God for His goodness in allowing interaction with many people and a continuation of my ministry during that time.

I had no idea that my confinement in Caesarea would last for two years, and that the reason for that was the rife corruption in that society. Although I had tried to move things forward with Felix, he was waiting for me to offer him a bribe before making a favorable judgment on my behalf. I was unwilling to resort to that, and so I lingered in Herod's jail, making the best of my situation with God's help.

Eventually something happened that finally broke the deadlock. The governor Felix was replaced by Porcius Festus, who immediately made a trip to Jerusalem where he met with the Jewish authorities. They asked for me to be brought back to Jerusalem to stand trial in their courts. Festus, however, returned to Caesarea saying that they needed to go back with him and hold the trial there. The Jewish leaders brought many charges against me. Festus then wanted to know if I was willing to go to Jerusalem to stand trial before the Jewish authorities. I knew that if I did, it would be my death sentence, so intense was their hatred against me. I told Festus that as a Roman citizen, I was going to appeal to Caesar. While that kept me from the control of the Jewish authorities, it also resulted in more years of imprisonment. I had the opportunity to tell my story to King Agrippa who would have freed me if I had not already made my appeal to the emperor. His hands were tied, and I was ordered to be taken to Rome to stand trial before Caesar.

We left Caesarea in the fall. During the voyage we were caught in a terrible storm that wrecked our ship, forcing us to spend the winter on the isle of Malta. God had shown me that none of us on the ship would be lost, and I had some great opportunities to share about Christ during the voyage and the time spent on the island. Apart from being a prisoner, I had little to complain about as we spent the next three months being graciously cared for by the residents of Malta before we could once again safely set sail for Rome. My good time of ministry among the citizens of Malta included the performing of many miracles as people were healed and their lives were changed.

The rest of the voyage was short, and I was soon on land again, a prisoner being taken to Rome to stand trial before Caesar. Many would have considered this to be more of a curse than a blessing, but I saw it as an opportunity to talk about Jesus to the highest levels of Roman society. Even if I came in chains, I was still coming as an ambassador of God's Kingdom, representing the King of all Kings. Even the lofty Caesar seemed but a mere man in comparison with the One I was representing and serving. In my spirit, these chains were not an inhibition to my work, but my means of access, permitting me to go where I could otherwise not have ministered.

Once again, I had to wait for another two years. This time, I did not live in a prison cell as in Caesarea, but under house arrest. While I was not permitted to come and go as I pleased, I was given a high level of freedom, being able to entertain visitors and write long letters. Yes, I wrote to several groups of beloved believers that I had served on my three previous missionary journeys. Some of my letters were more personal in nature, such as those to Timothy and Titus whom I wanted to encourage in their ministries. I made the best of these two years and the limitations placed upon me, doing all I could to further the expansion of the Kingdom of God.

Again, I do not want anyone to think of me as a super saint. I knew good times but also bouts of depression, moments when my spirit soared as I rejoiced in great happenings, and periods when my heart and soul sank heavy and low.

Finally, I was transferred to this place, what I consider to be a waiting room until I am summoned to make one more trip – out of this world to be with Christ in person. I know that my earthly days are numbered, but how can I not rejoice with the living hope that burns so brightly within me? As I said in one of the letters I wrote from this very prison, **"for me to live is Christ, and to die is gain."**

DISCUSSION QUESTIONS

1. Paul must at times have thought about being executed. Even though he knew he would be in Heaven, he must still have dreaded having to go through the act of execution. How do you think Paul might have felt when these thoughts came to him?

2. What do you think were some of the thoughts and emotional experiences Paul may have had during the closing months of his life spent in a Roman jail?

3. Paul had been warned not to go to Jerusalem or he would be arrested. He also sensed this reality in his own soul, undoubtedly thoughts put there by God himself. Even though he had this "head knowledge" of what would probably happen, how do you think he felt and what might have been his thoughts when, after just over a week in Jerusalem, he was arrested and imprisoned? Do you think that Paul, after he was arrested, questioned the wisdom of his decision to come to Jerusalem, given the prior warnings? Or do you think Paul saw all of this as part of a larger plan that God had for him?

4. How do you think the Roman soldiers, who were about to flog Paul, felt when they learned that he was a Roman citizen?

5. Paul said that "he was all things to all men that by that means he might reach some." When he came to Jerusalem, he went into the temple and made a Jewish vow to show that he was not against the Jewish laws or way of life. When arrested, he used his Roman citizenship to prevent himself from being flogged. When with the Gentiles, he defended them against Jewish attempts to make them go through Jewish rituals to be "true

believers" in the minds of some Jews. These are examples of how he became "all things to all men." What can we learn from Paul's example that might help us to be more available to people today who hold different viewpoints and convictions on various points? What is the difference between "being all things to all men" and compromising the convictions that we hold?

6. While in prison, the Lord appeared to Paul and told him that just as he had been able to give testimony about Him in Jerusalem, so he should have the same opportunity to share about Him in Rome as well. How do you think Paul felt and thought when he had this unique experience with Christ? Do you think Paul realized that this meant he would continue to be a prisoner to enable this to happen? If so, do you think Paul had any idea that he would spend the next five years in prison or under arrest while in transit between Jerusalem and Rome?

7. Paul was confined in Herod's prison in Caesarea for two years, though he was given some level of freedom in at least being able to have visitors and carry on some level of ministry. He was held there for this long period because Governor Felix wanted him to make a bribe to secure his freedom. How do you think Paul felt and thought about being held for such a long time just because he would not bribe the governor?

8. After Porcius Festus replaced Felix as governor of the region, he immediately acted regarding Paul. He had some Jews come to Caesarea to make their charges and then asked Paul if he was willing to go to Jerusalem to appear before a Jewish court. It was then that Paul said he, as a Roman citizen, was making an appeal to Caesar. Why do you think Paul made this request? What do you think the Jewish authorities felt when they realized that they would not be able to try Paul themselves?

9. King Agrippa would have freed Paul if he had not appealed to Caesar. Do you think Paul had any regrets for having made this appeal when he realized that he could have been a free man had he not done so?

10. We know that, even before his arrest, Paul had had a desire to visit Rome. Now he was going to have that desire fulfilled, but as a prisoner defending himself before the emperor. Do you think the way he eventually got to Rome dampened his enthusiasm about finally being able to witness in Rome?

11. Paul was under house arrest in Rome for two years. About the only restriction was that he could not leave his house, but he remained free to entertain people, to write and minister to his visitors. How do you think he might have felt about his situation for those two years? What emotions might he have experienced during that period?

12. What do you think Paul might have felt and thought on the day when the soldiers appeared to take him to his execution?

31

BARNABAS

Reflections by Paul

All that I have been able to accomplish in my ministry has been in part because of godly people who came alongside me as partners in my missionary endeavors. One of the most influential men at a very critical period of my life was Barnabas, a fellow Apostle. Why do I refer to him as a "fellow apostle"? You might remember that Luke, when writing his memoirs of our missionary journeys, referred to both "Barnabas and Paul" as Apostles. He realized how the two of us were equals in ministry and position among the churches. Yes, I considered Barnabas to be a fellow Apostle along with all the other loyal disciples of Jesus. Not everyone would agree with that. Some do not even consider me to be an Apostle, much less Barnabas. They regard only those men who were the close disciples of Jesus Christ to be worthy of that designation. But I believe that we too received a divine commission and that I was called to be an "Apostle to the Gentiles." Both Barnabas and I were commissioned by the church at Antioch and sent out with the authority and blessing of the church. Barnabas, at least on that first missionary journey, was equal in every way to me and was as much an Apostle as I.

So many things happened that can only reaffirm the working of the Holy Spirit in weaving together people and life-changing events. No man is an island; we are all influenced by others and live in the hope that our lives have a positive effect on those around us. That dynamic is illustrated by the way that Barnabas helped to mold me into the man that I became.

I believe that God brought us together. We were raised in different parts of the world; I, as you know, in Tarsus in Asia Minor, and Barnabas on the island of Cyprus. One thing we had in common was that both of us were raised by devout and strict Jewish parents. My heritage tied me to the tribe of Benjamin and his to the tribe of Levi. Beyond that, we had little in common at the beginning of our friendship. I, as you so well know, was the persecutor of the early believers. He was a most true and loyal leader in that early movement. It might surprise you that his real name was not even Barnabas, for that was a nickname given to him because of his outstanding service to the early church. His given name was Joses, but his nickname more appropriately reflects his character. Barnabas means "son of encouragement" or sometimes, "son of exhortation." Barnabas was just that kind of man, always encouraging and serving others tirelessly for the Kingdom of God, always willing to do whatever the leaders asked of him. No one questioned his faith or loyalty to Christ or His church.

Perhaps nothing reflects more completely a person's commitment to a cause than his or her willingness to give generously toward fulfilling its mission and purpose. It seems that what our heart cares about is tied to our purse strings. Barnabas was an excellent example of such financial stewardship. When money was needed by the church in Jerusalem to care for the growing body of new believers, many began selling their land and property, giving the money to the leaders in Jerusalem to help meet that need. Barnabas was among the first to willingly give up what he owned and bring the money from the sale of his property to Peter and John to be used to help meet the needs of people who were becoming believers in Christ. I have heard the testimony of so many who came to the Lord through the life and witness of this godly man of great faith, whose character showed that he was obviously full of the Holy Spirit.

On a more personal note, I would like to tell you how God used Barnabas to help me to become an established believer and servant of Christ. While I was persecuting the early believers, several of them fled from Jerusalem to Antioch, an important city where they established a church. Their faithful witness to Jesus drew Gentiles into their fellowship, and the church was thriving. It was here that Christ's followers were first called "Christians."

News about what was happening in Antioch soon reached the believers in the mother church in Jerusalem. Wanting to find out for themselves exactly what was happening, they sent Barnabas to oversee this new, budding church. Barnabas was surprised, even overwhelmed, by what he found in Antioch. This was no handful of people but a new church that was bursting at the seams, growing not only in number but in spiritual depth. No man was more qualified and spiritually gifted to begin mentoring this group of believers than Barnabas. He had a natural gift of knowing how to come alongside, not dictating or lording it over people, but able to stand with and help grow those that God brought along his path.

While all this was happening in Barnabas' life, Christ met me on the road to Damascus, and I began my fledging ministry in the area around Tarsus. The news of my conversion had spread among all the believers. Many wondered about the validity of my conversion and had every reason still to fear me, knowing of the cruel treatment I had infamously inflicted upon the followers of Jesus Christ.

Amazingly, God brought Barnabas and me together; an unlikely partnership of two people from such different backgrounds. Barnabas began his work at Antioch and before long found his labor there to be so extensive and weighty that he needed help. I came to his mind, no doubt by the prompting of the Holy Spirit. Barnabas came to look for me in Tarsus and convinced me to return with him to Antioch where we spent the next year in ministry together. I learned so much during that time, and could have had no better mentor than Barnabas, not only to learn about ministry, but also to observe his deep love for people. As I recall those years together, the older I have grown, the greater has become my respect for Barnabas as an authentic man of God.

The believers in Jerusalem still had a critical need for financial help. The believers in Antioch responded by taking a gracious offering to bring relief to the poorer Christians in Judea, sending Barnabas and me to deliver the offering to the church leaders in Jerusalem. Barnabas tore down the wall of distrust that was an obstacle to those who wondered about my reported change of heart and helped them to embrace me as a brother in Christ. Barnabas dispelled the fear in the wary hearts of many that I had previously persecuted, as he vouched for my character and my true allegiance to Christ.

I could not have asked for a more faithful companion during our first missionary journey. We worked well together, sharing joys, hardships, and persecutions – all part of that wonderful venture. On returning home, we gave a glorious report of all that God had done among the Gentiles, how so many had become believers, and churches had been started in various places in Asia Minor and into Greece. Some considered us to be a perfectly matched team. Maybe we were, at least for that chapter of our lives.

We continued working as a team in the church at Antioch, but my restless heart longed to return to see how the new believers were doing and to encourage them in their newfound faith. I started to plan a second missionary journey. Naturally, I approached Barnabas and asked him to go with me again. What happened next saddens my soul. Now, an old man nearing the end of his earthly life, I see things a little differently than I did then. I was at fault as much as he. Barnabas was excited about going with me but wanted to take his cousin, John Mark, along too. That was the same John Mark that had deserted us on our first missionary journey. My strong feelings about what I saw as a failure pushed me to insist adamantly that I was unwilling to take another chance with John Mark. Was that a good decision on my part? As an old man I must admit that perhaps I was less gracious than I could have been. I certainly did not have the "spirit of encouragement" that Barnabas possessed, nor the willingness to forgive and overlook what seemed to me such a disqualifier of John Mark. In time I would not only forgive John Mark for what he did but also come to realize his usefulness to the Kingdom of God. In fact, I later asked for him to be brought to help me in my ministry that was restricted by my physical confinement. Two ingredients, the Spirit of God and time, brought healing of the wrongs and hurts that lingered in my heart and mind.

My reservations about taking John Mark took the form of my dogmatic insistence that he was in no way going to be part of our team. While Barnabas did not respond in anger, neither did he submit to my stubborn spirit. He said that if John Mark could not come, neither would he! I was stunned. I felt as if he had thrust a dagger into my soul, but I was not going to back down on my stance. So it was that our deep and meaningful working relationship came to an abrupt and less than gracious ending. Was God pleased with my stance? Thinking about it now, maybe I could have handled it differently. Whether or not God was pleased is a moot point now. What really matters is that God, as He so often does, used our human failures to work out His purposes for each of us. I chose Silas to become my new partner in ministry, and Barnabas took John Mark with him on their own ministry pursuits. Sadly, this disagreement ended the working relationship between Barnabas and me. We still respected each other and rejoiced in each other's successes, but the close friendship and rich working relationship that we once enjoyed would never return in the same way.

To be totally honest, I must confess that there was another time that Barnabas deeply disappointed me. This time I have to say that I believe the blame rested with him. I am convinced that I was justified in my action, even though it meant confronting both Peter and Barnabas along with many others.

Peter had come to Antioch for a while so there were the three of us: Peter, Barnabas, and me enjoying wonderful fellowship and ministering together to both Jews and Gentiles. Peter had already come to understand that God's grace was for all men, both Jews and Gentiles. God taught him a powerful lesson on the subject by giving him a vision of unclean animals descending from Heaven that God told him to eat. This led Peter to go to the house of Cornelius where he was a part of the outpouring of the Holy Spirit upon a band of Gentile believers.

Sadly, when some men came up to Antioch from James' church in Jerusalem who still held strictly to Jewish customs and ways of doing things, both Peter and Barnabas drew back from eating and interacting with the Gentile believers in Antioch while the group from Jerusalem were visiting. I saw this as nothing but hypocrisy on the part of Peter and Barnabas as well as the other Jewish believers now residing in Antioch. I became so angry about their behavior, publicly rebuking them for their hypocrisy and inconsistency.

I am so glad that the Holy Spirit is in control of our lives, and that He refines and changes us. He had a lot of work to do in my case! He places models and mentors around us from whom we learn, and whose example we can imitate. As I look back, in some ways I stood in the shadow of Barnabas. Our differences were complementary and necessary to our great and synergistic partnership in God's work. He had the outstanding gift of being able to relate to people in kindness and love that melted stubborn, hard hearts. He deserved the sobriquet, Barnabas, "the one who encourages." I would not be what I have become without him, my fellow Apostle.

DISCUSSION QUESTIONS

1. We often think of the Apostles being only the original disciples of Jesus. We also know that Paul is often called "the Apostle to the Gentiles." Luke, in writing the book of Acts, referred to both "Paul and Barnabas" as Apostles. Have you ever thought about Barnabas as being "an Apostle"? What is your understanding of what was required to be an Apostle? Do you think Barnabas fits your understanding of those qualifications?

2. This story is written from the perspective that people have influenced us and that we have had a significant influence on others. Share about some of the people that have had an impact on your life and about some people you believe you have influenced.

3. What does it say about Barnabas' character that the world only knows Barnabas by his nickname, "one who encourages," and not by his given name?

4. The statement was made in this story that one of the ways we often prove our loyalty to a cause is by our willingness to support it financially. Do you agree with that statement?

5. Barnabas undoubtedly knew all about Paul and his past (persecuting the church, etc.). Why do you think Barnabas went to find Paul, took him, and introduced him to the church leaders in Jerusalem, becoming the bridge between him and the Jewish believers who still feared and questioned the authenticity of Paul and his profession of faith? What do you think might have helped Barnabas to believe in Paul and want to help him get established in his faith and ministry?

6. The church at Jerusalem sent Barnabas to Antioch to see what was happening and oversee the development of the new church. When he arrived, he would learn that there were not only Jewish believers, but many Gentiles that had been converted and were part of this new church. Do you think Barnabas at first had any problem on a personal level with the Gentile believers?

7. Paul came back to Antioch with Barnabas, and they spent a year working together with the believers at Antioch. We know a lot about Paul and his personality. He was a natural leader and could be strong-willed. We can assume that Barnabas was at first the more dominant of the two in their leadership at Antioch, Barnabas being the "head pastor" so to speak and Paul the "assistant pastor." Do you think Paul had any problem adapting to this role? Do you think Paul was open to and readily accepted learning from Barnabas during this year together?

8. Thinking about the previous question, we know that once they embarked on their missionary journey, Paul comes to the fore and is shown as the leader and more dominant team partner. How do you think this change of position occurred? How do you think Barnabas might have felt about the more dominant role that Paul assumed?

9. Up to the time of the second missionary journey, there is no hint in Scripture of any division or major difference of opinion between Barnabas and Paul. Then comes the sudden break in their relationship over taking John Mark with them on the second missionary journey. What can we learn about Paul's spirit and personality from the way he reacted to Barnabas wanting to bring John Mark with them? What can we learn about the temperament and spirit of Barnabas in his refusal to go if he had to leave John Mark behind?

10. How do you think the other believers in Antioch felt about and viewed the split in the relationship between Paul and Barnabas?

11. We know that Paul ultimately changed his attitude toward John Mark. Perhaps he felt the young John had matured or perhaps he saw a change in his own attitude as a person. In either case, he later asked that John Mark be brought to him to help him while he was in prison. What does this tell us about Paul as he aged? What might have happened in John Mark's development in the meantime? Do you think that Barnabas had discipled him? If Barnabas was still alive when this happened, how do you think he felt about the change in Paul's attitude?

12. We know that Paul changed his attitude toward John Mark as Paul aged. Do you think he changed any of his thoughts about and attitudes toward Barnabas as he aged? Do you think Paul ever felt that the split between him and Barnabas was at least in part his fault?

13. Paul was obviously very upset and disappointed with both Peter and Barnabas when they quit eating with Gentile believers when some of the stricter Jewish believers came to Antioch from Jerusalem. He confronted them publicly and gave them a verbal rebuke for their actions. How do you think Peter and/or Barnabas felt when Paul openly confronted them for their behavior? Do you think that they then began fellowshipping with the Gentiles even though the Jews from Jerusalem were still there, or do you think they continued to remain separated until the Jews had left? When it came to this issue, Paul undoubtedly felt he was right and that the position he took was a spiritually correct one. Do you think Peter and Barnabas thought Paul was correct in his admonishment and rebuke or do

you think they felt Paul had acted harshly and perhaps not in a manner that was bathed in Christian love and kindness? Do you think they may have felt Paul should have talked to them privately rather than calling them out publicly? How do you feel, did Paul act in the best manner or should he have confronted them privately and personally? Give a reason for your answer.

14. Thinking about the discussion in the previous question, this incident occurred between the first and second missionary journeys. The relationship between Barnabas and Paul was still a strong one. Do you think this incident had any effect on Paul's attitude toward Barnabas when he refused to back down on the question of taking John Mark with them on the second missionary trip?

32

APOLLOS

The Eloquent Preacher

I do not feel that I have any claim to be called a disciple or an apostle, but my life and ministry have in many ways dovetailed with those of the Apostle Paul. So perhaps it is fitting that my story be told in close association with the work that Paul so nobly accomplished.

The first parallel between Paul and me is our ethnic and religious identification, though we are totally opposite in both. It is true that we both claim to be Jewish by faith but Paul's association with Judaism stems from his Jewish parents. He was born a Jew and, as you so well know, could claim to be a Jew in every sense of the word. As a pharisee, the first half of Paul's life was dedicated and loyal to all that Judaism entailed. By his own confession, there were few men that equaled his zeal and devotion to his Jewish faith.

I, on the other hand, am a Jew by choice, not by birth. My very name, Apollos, tells you that I am not from a Jewish background, but a Greek one. I was not raised in the land of the prophets but in the influential Greek city of Alexandria. This city was founded by Alexander the Great and became the largest city on the Mediterranean Sea with a population of over five million. It was the center of Hellenistic civilization and boasted, among other establishments, a well-known university and one of the largest libraries in the world. Pharos, our famous lighthouse, is recognized as one of the seven wonders of our world. I have always been proud of my Greek heritage, but I refused to embrace Greek mythology. I had a sharp mind, and it did not take me long to realize that the gods of Greece were nothing more than idols conceived in the minds of men. In my quest for truth, I found the clearest and most reasonable concept of a living God in the teachings of the Jewish faith. Soon I enthusiastically embraced Judaism as my own and became what people call a Hellenistic Jew.

I threw myself into my new faith with a remarkable zeal and spirit. Such spirit would come to characterize all my life's endeavors. Everything I ever did was done with my whole heart and soul. In that, Paul and I were very much alike. The drive to excel and to do our best propelled us both to become high achievers in the proclamation of our faith and in our life's work.

Yes, Paul and I had much in common: Paul was a Jew who happened to be raised in a Greek cultural setting, thus being able to embrace both the Jewish and the Greek worlds. I was a Greek who chose to enter the Jewish way of life, so likewise able to relate to both the Jewish and Greek worlds.

I never did anything halfheartedly. When I chose to embrace the Jewish faith, I immersed myself in the study of Jewish law and the Jewish way of life. I was intent on being as much a Jew in heart as any who were born and raised in that faith. I became competent in the Scriptures, an expert in Jewish law.

In the pursuit of my new Jewish faith, I encountered the teachings of John the Baptist and soon found myself adhering to the truths he had taught and preached. The teachings of John the Baptist brought me to a place where I was able to embrace Jesus of Nazareth as the Messiah promised by the prophets of old. This, however, did not happen overnight but evolved as a process. First, I embraced and mastered the teachings of traditional Jewish thought. Further insights were gained through the teachings of John the Baptist. His ideas influenced me so much that when I started preaching, they became the core of my messages, that my listeners must repent of their sin and embrace Jesus Christ as the promised Messiah. Now I realize that in my first years of preaching, I presented a shallow and incomplete message, but I did not know more at the time. I can honestly say that I preached with my whole heart all that I knew and understood. The polished excellence of my delivery caught the attention of others; at least that is what I have been told. I do not want to brag or try to portray myself as something that I am not. I merely relate to you the opinion of those who listened to my preaching and witnessed my life and ministry. I prefer to say that I believe that God gifted me, enabling me to preach with a power and fluency that seemed to captivate my audiences. I am grateful but also humbled by the way God chose to use my life.

If asked what my greatest strengths of ministry were, I would say that I was first and foremost an apologist, always ready to explain to any who might question, the reason for the faith that I and others held as truth. Defending that faith on an intellectual level, I enjoyed opening the Scriptures to show how Christ fulfills all the messianic prophecies. God had gifted me in such a way that I could effectively answer the critics and present the faith in a way that convinced others to embrace Christ as the Messiah as well.

Soon I became an itinerant preacher proclaiming Christ as the Messiah. My travels brought me to the city of Ephesus where I experienced a transforming moment.

God has a way of bringing people into our lives at key moments and using them to bring us into a more complete understanding of who He is. That is exactly what happened to me. I was preaching and effectively defending the truth of Christ as the Messiah against attacks by Jewish leaders who wanted to argue otherwise. Two very precious children of God, Priscilla and Aquilla, heard what I was doing and recognized the fluency and power with which I spoke. But they also quickly realized that my depth of understanding of Jesus was incomplete. It was not that I was preaching something that was not true but that I did not fully grasp the extent of the ministry that Jesus had when he lived among us. So, they took me under their wings, explaining to me the life that Jesus lived and all the wonderful things that he did. I could not learn enough about Jesus Christ, and my understanding of who Jesus was and what he did for us grew exponentially. My preaching took on a new level of intensity. I gladly preached Christ crucified and resurrected from the dead.

Like Paul, I too had a restless heart and could not happily remain in one place content to pastor a congregation for a prolonged time. I felt I needed to move on and leave Ephesus, now equipped with a greater understanding of both Christ and my mission to proclaim Him to others. I, like Paul before me, crossed the Aegean Sea and stepped onto the soil of Europe. I was armed not only with a greater concept of

Christ but also with letters of recommendation from the Asian brothers in Christ who encouraged the brothers and sisters in Europe to welcome me and open their arms and hearts to my ministry.

I soon found the dear believers that had been touched by Paul on some of his earlier missionary endeavors, and God used my teaching to greatly help these young congregations. I often refuted the Jews in public, showing by the Scriptures that Jesus Christ was the promised Messiah. I had the joy of building on the foundation that Paul had laid in Greece and helping bring to maturity many of the disciples that had trusted in Christ under his ministry.

My travels brought me to the city of Corinth where I found a thriving church. Its members spoke well of their founder, the Apostle Paul. Of course, there were among them many Jews who had converted from their Jewish faith to trust Christ as their Messiah. This group of believers often chose to identify with Peter rather than Paul as their spiritual father. I would soon discover that I was ministering to a group of people immature in their faith and carnal in their behavior.

I realize that we all have our own personality and that we attract certain people to us more than others. At Corinth, this had become a greater problem than it seemed to be in other places. I preached and taught the truths as I understood them about Christ and His church. I realized that a group of people was claiming that I in some ways stood above Paul and others who had had input into the lives of this congregation. It soon became evident that a specific spiritual problem existed in this congregation. In fact, many such problems would surface over a short span of time. This congregation was separated into factions over personalities. Some claimed to be loyal to their founding father, Paul. Others said they identified with their Jewish roots, claiming Peter as their spiritual hero. Then there were those who claimed that I was the gifted one and identified themselves as my followers. Both Paul and I recognized that this very unhealthy spiritual climate needed to be addressed. My feeling was that I needed to move on, that a prolonged time of ministering to this congregation would only add to the problem. Paul felt he needed to write to this congregation to address this problem, and several others of which he was aware in the life of this church.

Both Paul and I were saddened by the spirit of the Corinthian believers. Neither of us ever felt superior to or better than the other. It is true that we were opposites in so many ways. By his own confession, Paul came preaching a simple message in a spirit of fear and uncertainty, yet he left behind a thriving group of believers. I came using all my intellectual abilities and eloquence and defended the faith against any who attacked it. I also reasoned and taught the believers with the skill and professional excellence that others noted and talked about. Each of us was merely being who we were and using the skills God had given us to reach and teach others for Christ. We did not consider one of us to be better than the other and wished that others would not either. Unfortunately, however, they chose to identify with one or the other and to exalt us in a way with which we were uncomfortable.

Paul has preceded me to Heaven, and I have grown old. When I reflect on our two lives, I am still amazed at how God used us both to become probably the best-known leaders of the Gentile churches. Paul, the Jew who became the Apostle to the Gentiles and I, the Greek who became a Jew. Both of us found the living Christ and served Him with all our heart and soul. Others may have followed one of us more than the other but we both knew whom we followed – and in that we were one in spirit and purpose.

DISCUSSION QUESTIONS

1. Apollos, along with Paul, was probably one of the most influential leaders among the early Gentile church movement, yet we hardly hear about him in sermons today. When you hear the name Apollos, what image do you have of this individual?

2. Discuss the interesting parallel yet significant differences between Paul and Apollos, one who was a Jew turned Gentile preacher and the other who was a Gentile turned Jew. Discuss the way you see God having prepared each of these men to become the two key leaders in the early movement among the Gentile churches.

3. Apollos was from the very important Greek city of Alexandria in Egypt which was noted for its significant university and one of the largest libraries in the known world at that time. We know he was a polished and eloquent preacher and apologist and, like Paul, an intellectual. Paul seemed to be more down to earth while Apollos is portrayed in Scripture as one who openly used his intellectual abilities in defense of the Gospel. Both men were highly educated. What effect do you think having been raised in the intellectual center of Alexandra had on forming the personality and way of preaching that Apollos had? Discuss the way that God can use both approaches that we see in Paul and Apollos to reach people. Can you give examples of preachers or church leaders that were more like Paul or more like Apollos and to which did you relate most in terms of style of ministry?

4. Whatever differences in culture or style Paul and Apollos might have had, they shared one thing in common – doing everything with all their heart and soul. How much do you think attitude and effort play in a person's success? Can you give an example

of a person who was gifted but not motivated, or of one who maybe was not noted for exceptional talent but had great zeal for what they did?

5. We do not have the whole story, but at some point, Apollos met either John the Baptist or some of his followers and embraced the teachings of John relating to repentance and Jesus Christ being the Messiah. We know that Apollos had an incomplete understanding of Christ, yet he preached with zeal all that he did know. How do you think Apollos thought and felt when he met Priscilla and Aquilla and realized that what he had been preaching was only part of the whole? Do you think he might have felt in any way "threatened" when they first confronted him with his lack of knowledge about all that Christ did and about his death and resurrection, etc.?

6. Apollos' strength seems to be as an apologist, defending the faith and the truth of Christ before the Jewish critics who wanted to destroy the message of the early believers. How important do you feel this kind of ministry was to the early church? How important are apologists to the church today?

7. The Bible tells us that when Apollos left Ephesus, the elders had sent letters of recommendation to the churches in Greece, encouraging them to accept Apollos and his ministry. How important were these letters for both Apollos and for the work he wanted to do? What does it tell us about Apollos as a man that these key leaders were willing to write these letters of recommendation?

8. Scripture does not tell us much about the ministry of Apollos, other than some broad statements about his eloquence and power as a preacher and apologist. We know he had a very

successful ministry. The one place we do know about was his preaching at Corinth, "watering what Paul had planted." Yet in the end, his success as a preacher also became the source of division among the believers. The church divided over who was the better preacher, Paul or Apollos, and factions formed in the congregation over personalities. It is obvious that both men had good ministries at Corinth, and both had a strong following. How do you think this problem at Corinth might have been avoided? Can you think of examples where a church became divided over personalities? What caused that division and how was it resolved?

9. How do you think Paul and Apollos felt about each other?

10. How do you think both Paul and Apollos felt when they realized what was happening among the believers at Corinth, partly due to divisions related to their respective ministries among them?

11. Any discussion of the ministries of Paul and Apollos can lead to discussions about the way that congregations relate to different styles of preachers. How can a congregation make the transition from one pastor to another as smoothly as possible?

INDEX

Aegean Sea, 256, 267, 293
Agabus, 268
Alexandria, 291, 296
Alphaeus, 149
Ananias, 212, 213, 214, 217, 228, 231, 233
Andrew, 5, 9, 13, 14, 19, 20, 21, 23, 25, 33, 40, 62, 63, 67, 68, 82, 87, 101, 110, 112, 113, 117
Andronicus, 205
Antioch, 253, 254, 259, 260, 265, 281, 282, 283, 284, 285, 288, 289
Apollos, 266, 291, 296, 297, 298
Aquila, 239, 240, 243, 258, 259
Asia Minor, 238, 255, 261, 265, 266, 274, 281, 283
Athens, 238, 239, 243, 258, 262
Barnabas, v, 229, 230, 253, 254, 260, 281, 282, 283, 284, 285, 287, 288, 289, 290
Barsabbas, 186

Bartholomew, 112, 141
Bathsheba, 240
Berea, 257, 262, 267
Bethany, 121
Bethsaida, 2, 13, 14, 110
Caesar, 150, 199, 202, 207, 239, 276, 277, 279
Caesarea, 14, 36, 63, 202, 229, 259, 268, 275, 276, 277, 279
Caesarea Philippi, 36, 63
Capernaum, 2, 3, 25, 47, 64, 80, 90, 101, 141
Casearia Philippi, 24
Corinth, 211, 239, 240, 258, 259, 262, 263, 266, 267, 294, 298
Cornelius, 26, 52, 285
Cyprus, 281
Damaris, 238, 239, 243
Damascus, 196, 197, 199, 203, 206, 208, 211, 212, 214, 228, 229, 233, 273, 283
Damascus Road, 199
Dead Sea, 111

Deborah, 240
Derbe, 230, 265
Domitian, 104
Dorcas, 56, 60
Egypt, 14, 62, 296
Elijah, vi, 48, 53, 55, 57, 58, 63, 65, 82, 83, 85, 103, 104
Emmaus, 123
Ephesus, 158, 240, 259, 263, 265, 266, 268, 270, 271, 293, 297
Eutychus, 267, 271
Felix, 275, 276, 279
Field of Blood, 158
Galacia, 237
Galatia, 265
Galilee, 2, 13, 14, 16, 19, 26, 33, 68, 90, 111, 113, 131, 141, 159, 165, 187
Gamaliel, 195, 204, 208, 209
Garden of Gethsemane, 17, 82, 103
Greece, 199, 256, 261, 266, 267, 274, 283, 291, 294, 297
Hebron, 159
Herod, 14, 57, 60, 82, 87, 275, 276, 279
High Priest, 24, 28, 39
Iconium, 230, 265

Jairus, 52, 56, 58, 82, 103
James, 1, 2, 5, 8, 9, 11, 16, 17, 19, 21, 23, 24, 26, 35, 52, 53, 57, 60, 64, 66, 67, 80, 81, 82, 83, 84, 85, 86, 87, 88, 89, 100, 102, 104, 120, 134, 144, 146, 148, 149, 151, 153, 159, 285
James the Less, 149, 153
Jerusalem, 37, 39, 46, 63, 84, 103, 107, 141, 148, 158, 185, 186, 195, 204, 205, 208, 209, 213, 229, 240, 253, 255, 259, 260, 267, 268, 270, 271, 274, 275, 276, 278, 279, 282, 283, 285, 287, 288, 289
Jesus, v, 1, 2, 3, 4, 5, 6, 7, 8, 9, 10, 11, 13, 15, 16, 17, 18, 19, 20, 21, 22, 23, 24, 25, 27, 28, 29, 30, 33, 34, 35, 36, 37, 38, 39, 40, 41, 42, 44, 45, 46, 47, 48, 50, 52, 53, 54, 55, 56, 57, 58, 59, 62, 63, 64, 65, 66, 67, 68, 69, 70, 71, 72, 78, 80, 81, 82, 83, 84, 85, 86, 87, 88, 90, 92, 93, 94, 95, 97,

98, 100, 101, 102, 103, 104, 106, 107, 111, 112, 113, 114, 115, 116, 117, 118, 120, 121, 122, 123, 125, 126, 127, 130, 132, 133, 134, 135, 137, 138, 139, 140, 141, 142, 143, 144, 146, 148, 149, 150, 151, 152, 153, 156, 158, 159, 160, 161, 162, 163, 164, 165, 166, 185, 186, 187, 188, 189, 197, 202, 203, 204, 205, 208, 210, 211, 212, 213, 214, 215, 216, 217, 228, 230, 232, 233, 237, 239, 254, 255, 256, 259, 265, 266, 273, 274, 277, 281, 282, 283, 287, 292, 293, 294, 297

Joanna, 120
Joel, 187, 188
John, 2, 5, 8, 9, 11, 13, 15, 16, 17, 19, 20, 21, 23, 24, 26, 33, 35, 37, 38, 46, 48, 52, 53, 62, 64, 66, 67, 72, 80, 86, 87, 88, 101, 102, 104, 106, 107, 108, 110, 111, 112, 121, 130, 134, 140, 145, 146, 148, 153, 155, 158, 186, 254, 260, 282, 284, 288, 289, 290, 292, 297
John Mark, 254, 260, 284, 288, 289, 290
John the Baptist, 20, 88, 106, 111, 186, 292, 297
Jonah,, 13
Jordan, 15, 20, 101, 111, 141
Jordan river, 15, 20
Jordan River, 101, 111, 141
Joseph, 112, 141, 186
Joses, 281
Judas, 13, 35, 41, 54, 67, 68, 70, 81, 84, 90, 120, 130, 137, 142, 143, 144, 145, 146, 149, 153, 158, 159, 160, 161, 162, 163, 164, 165, 166, 185, 186, 190, 191, 213
Judas Iscariot, 13, 35, 41, 81, 90, 158, 159, 160, 185
Judas Thaddaeus, 142
Judas the Less, 142, 144, 145, 146
Judea, 13, 15, 16, 81, 90, 101, 121, 122, 126, 159, 165, 283
Junia, 205
Justus, 186

Kerioth, 159
King Agrippa, 276, 279
Lazarus, 53, 56, 65, 88, 114, 121, 122, 126, 131, 137
Leah, 240
Levi, 281
Lydia, 238, 239, 243, 256, 261
Lystra, 230, 255, 265
Macedonia, 238, 256, 267
Magdala, 81
Malchus, 46
Malta, 276
Martha, 56
Mary, 56, 80, 103, 107, 120, 123, 133, 135, 161, 185
Mary Magdalene, 120
Matthew, 2, 8, 64, 67, 81, 90, 96, 97, 98, 144, 150, 154, 155, 156
Matthias, 185, 186, 190
Mediterranean Sea, 291
Miletus, 268
Moses, 48, 53, 55, 57, 58, 63, 65, 82, 83, 85, 103, 104, 112, 141, 240, 274

Mount of Olives, 17, 187
Mount of Transfiguration, 48, 69
Mount Tabor, 53, 57
Naomi, 240
Nathaniel, 15, 141, 142, 144, 145, 146, 149, 153, 159
Nazareth, 14, 15, 93, 101, 112, 116, 141, 146, 292
Passover, 15, 62, 63, 67, 69, 114, 117, 142, 186, 267, 274
Patmos, 104, 108, 148, 151
Paul, v, vi, 24, 25, 35, 36, 40, 46, 104, 108, 151, 190, 194, 195, 199, 200, 203, 207, 208, 209, 215, 216, 217, 233, 234, 235, 242, 243, 260, 261, 262, 263, 270, 271, 277, 278, 279, 280, 281, 287, 288, 289, 290, 291, 292, 293, 294, 295, 296, 298
Pentecost, 5, 18, 27, 39, 47, 52, 55, 59, 69, 83, 84, 87, 88, 102, 148, 186, 190, 192, 268
Perpetua, 44

Peter, 5, 6, 8, 9, 16, 19, 20, 21, 28, 29, 30, 31, 32, 33, 34, 35, 36, 37, 38, 39, 40, 41, 42, 44, 45, 46, 47, 48, 49, 50, 58, 59, 60, 61, 62, 64, 65, 67, 68, 69, 70, 72, 78, 81, 82, 84, 87, 88, 102, 103, 104, 107, 110, 121, 130, 131, 133, 144, 146, 148, 159, 160, 186, 188, 189, 191, 192, 282, 285, 289, 294
Pharisee, 194, 203, 205
Pharisees, 67, 203, 204, 205, 275
Pharos, 291
Philip, 17, 111, 114, 116, 117, 118, 141, 159, 268
Philippi, 202, 205, 229, 238, 242, 243, 256, 257, 261, 262, 267
Phrygia, 265
Pontus, 239
Porcius Festus, 276, 279
Potter's Field, 158
Priscilla, 239, 240, 243, 258, 259, 266, 293, 297
Rachel, 240
Rebecca, 240
Rome, 2, 14, 24, 91, 92, 104, 108, 150, 154, 195, 202, 207, 239, 240, 267, 269, 274, 275, 276, 277, 279, 280
Ruth, 240
Sadducees, 275
Salome, 80, 100
Salome,, 80, 100
Sarah, 240
Saul, 194, 195, 197, 203, 208, 211, 213, 215, 217
Silas, 229, 234, 254, 255, 256, 257, 258, 260, 284
Simon, 1, 2, 8, 9, 14, 16, 17, 19, 20, 21, 28, 29, 30, 31, 32, 33, 35, 37, 38, 39, 40, 41, 42, 44, 45, 46, 47, 48, 49, 50, 69, 70, 82, 148, 149, 150, 151, 152, 153, 154, 155, 156
Simon the Zealot, 149, 150, 154, 156
Stephen, 82, 210, 215
Syria, 268, 271
Tabitha, 56, 60
Tarsus, 195, 203, 204, 208, 213, 229, 281, 283
Thaddaeus, 142
the Sea of Galilee, 1, 14, 34, 36, 46, 48

Thessalonica, 255, 257, 258, 262, 267
Thomas, 26, 54, 67, 114, 120, 125, 126, 127, 131, 133, 135, 137, 138, 139
Thyatira, 238
Tiberias, 14
Timothy, 228, 233, 255, 256, 257, 258, 260, 267, 277
Troas, 255, 256, 267, 271
Tyre, 268, 271
Zebedee, 80, 100

Made in the USA
Columbia, SC
09 June 2024